'Tis the good reader that makes the good book.

Ralph Waldo Emerson

DEEPER *Reading*

Comprehending Challenging Texts, 4–12

Kelly Gallagher

Stenhouse Publishers
Portland, Maine

Stenhouse Publishers
www.stenhouse.com

Library of Congress Cataloging-in-Publication Data
Gallagher, Kelly, 1958–
    Deeper reading : comprehending challenging texts, 4–12 / Kelly Gallagher.
       p. cm.
    Includes bibliographical references and index.
    ISBN 1-57110-384-8 (alk. paper)
    1. Reading comprehension. 2. Reading (Middle school). 3. Reading (Secondary). I. Title.
LB1050.45.G34 2004
372.47—dc22   2004052469

Cover photograph by Photodisc, Getty Images

Manufactured in the United States of America on acid-free paper
10 09 08 07 06 05 04 9 8 7 6 5 4 3 2 1

For Phil Paxton,
who took me out to the ball game

CONTENTS

ACKNOWLEDGMENTS

I'd like to express my appreciation to Bill Varner, my editor at Stenhouse, for his guidance and expertise in the shaping of this book. Bill, it is a genuine pleasure working with you. Additional thanks at Stenhouse to Brenda Power for her suggestions in the early stages and to Martha Drury for her production design. Thank-yous also go to Philippa Stratton, Tom Seavey, and the staff at Stenhouse for their continued support in making me feel part of the Stenhouse family.

I am grateful to John Powers, whose influence in these pages cannot be overstated.

Many thanks to Jane Davis for thirty-eight years of teaching inspiration.

Thank you to my students at Magnolia High School—all of you contributed to the writing of this book.

Thanks also to my English-teaching colleagues at Magnolia High School for their role in shaping my teaching: Melissa Cook, John Greenwald, Amie Howell, Virginia Kim, Sheri Krumins, Margaret Macchia, Esther Noh, Robin Turner, Michelle Waxman-Marks, and Dana White.

Thank you to my principal, Ken Fox, for his continued support.

Kudos to Ron Strahl, Jan Strahl, Nina Woolridge, Julie Lecesne-Switzer, Mike Switzer, Joanna Exacoustos, Ellen Lafler, Norelynn Pion-Goureau, Stephanie Sullivan, and all my comrades at the South Basin Writing Project, who continually inspire me with their dedication to the profession.

My heartfelt appreciation goes to my mom and dad for raising me as a reader.

Thank you to my beautiful daughters, Caitlin and Devin, who lost a lot of "daddy time" during the writing of this book. Caitlin, now that the book is finished, I promise to watch more episodes of *Jeopardy* with you. Devin, I'll attend more of your lacrosse matches.

Special thanks to my wife, Kristin, who holds the family together when her husband is lost in writing. At this very moment she is outside stringing Christmas lights on the house. If there were a Spouse Hall of Fame, she would be inducted unanimously on the first ballot.

And last, I'd like to publicly apologize to my dog, Beezus, who didn't get walked much while I wrote this book. I pledge to change that.

CHAPTER ONE

Why Reading Is Like Baseball

Here is a sentence I'd thought I'd never write: My beloved Anaheim Angels ended forty-one years of pain and futility by winning the World Series. To this day, two years later, I wake up expecting it all to be a perverse dream. But it's true; it happened. I attended game seven, and I saw it with my own eyes. Divine intervention occurred in Anaheim. On one magnificent fall evening, all those years of ineptness, all those years of painful pennant collapses, all those years of broken promises were washed away. (Readers in Boston and Chicago, take heart—jinxes can be broken. Anything is possible.)

My loyalty to the Angels began one summer day in 1968 when my Uncle Phil took me to my first professional game. It was a beautiful day, not a cloud in the sky, a slight breeze blowing in from center field. As we walked into the stadium, the grass was so green it hurt my eyes. The sharp crack of the fungo bat, swung by Jimmy Reese (a former roommate of Babe Ruth's), echoed through the air. To top it off, the Angels' opponents that day were Reggie Jackson, Blue Moon Odom, Catfish Hunter, Joe Rudi, and the rest of the hated Oakland Athletics.

In the third inning, Jim Spencer, first baseman for the Angels, hit a foul ball that ricocheted off a seat straight into my eager hands. My first game ever, and I caught a foul ball (a feat that I have been unable to repeat in the thirty-five years since). The Angels won the game on a line drive single by Jim Fregosi. All in all, a perfect introduction to baseball. I was never the same.

Now, a generation later, both my daughters are baseball fans. My older daughter, Caitlin, has developed into a baseball snob, refusing even to acknowledge the existence of any team that plays in the shadow of "her" Los Angeles Dodgers. My younger daughter, Devin, roots for the Angels—and thank goodness the Angels did not collapse because she was beginning to exhibit symptoms of permanent psychological damage. Another Angels meltdown and there's no telling what the long-term effects would have been on her sunny disposition.

About now you might be asking yourself: Why the baseball anecdote in a book about the teaching of reading to secondary students? The answer is simple: While I was sitting at game seven of the World Series I was struck with the realization that baseball is a metaphor for how adolescents read. Reading is like baseball. Allow me to explain.

Seeing the "Real" Game

Even when only five years old, my daughters had a rudimentary understanding of the game of baseball. A five-year-old's understanding of baseball goes something like this: Our guy is going to stand on a hill and throw a ball as hard as he can to our catcher. The batter, with a bat cocked over his shoulder, is going to try to hit the pitch. If the batter makes contact with the ball he will run like crazy to as many bases as safely possible. Our team will try to catch the ball and throw it to get the runner out. If the runner makes it all the way around the bases, his team will score a run (or a "point," as Devin used to say). If we get three outs, the good guys will get their chance to bat and score runs. Our opponents will do this nine times, we will do this nine times, and whoever scores the most runs will be declared the winner. If the Angels are the winners, we go home happy. If the bad guys are the winners, we go home sad.

Even at the age of five, my daughters had these basics of baseball down. (They also understood at all times the exact section and row of the roving cotton candy vendor, but that's another story.) It could be said that at a certain level they "understood" the game.

But did they? As they sat right next to me watching the game, I was seeing things on the field they were oblivious to. I saw the catcher peek into the dugout for a sign from the manager, which was then relayed to the pitcher. I saw the center fielder realize the catcher was setting up for an outside pitch, so he cheated a few steps to his left to get a jump on any ball hit to right field. I then noticed the base runner on first base look to the third-base coach for a secret sign to see if he had permission to try to steal second base. This made the shortstop and the second baseman nervous, because if that runner were to attempt a steal of second base, one of them would have to cover second base and catch the throw from the catcher. Yet they didn't want the hitter to know who would be covering the base, because he might try to hit the ball through the hole left by the covering fielder. Therefore players have devised a secret sign, which they flash (and change) just before every pitch. All this, and more, occurs prior to every pitch. In other words, there are many games within the game of baseball. My daughters, sitting right next to me, had no inkling of these other moves. They watched and "understood" the game on a surface level while I watched and understood the same game on a much deeper level. We watched, and yet did not watch, the same game.

It dawned on me sitting in the stadium that my high school students read text a lot like my daughters were "reading" baseball games. My daughters were able to read the game on a superficial, surface level, but they were unable to see the deeper, richer meaning of the game. They were unaware of the craft, the complexities, and the nuances of the game of baseball.

Isn't this how many secondary students read text? They rarely get below the surface to the richer, deeper meaning of the text. They think one reading is sufficient; they don't have the skills to uncover the craft, the complexities, and the nuances of the text. They can read and "comprehend," but they do so almost exclusively on a surface level. They miss much of the deeper beauty of the game.

I should note that my daughters, now both in their teens, have developed the ability to read baseball expertly. They are attentive to many of the nuances of the game—nuances often missed by the casual fan. They are able to anticipate managerial strategies. They now read the game at a fairly sophisticated level, but they were *taught* how to do so. They did not acquire their skill spontaneously or randomly. My daughters can now "read" baseball because over a number of years, through scores of games, they sat next to me. I taught them to recognize the difference between a screwball and a slider. I instructed them on the intricacies of the Infield Fly rule. I coached them to anticipate the squeeze play. In short, I taught them how to read the game, much like my Uncle Phil taught me, and much like my grandfather taught him.

Digging Deeper

This book is about teaching adolescent students to become good readers, not of baseball, but of the challenging works of fiction and nonfiction they will encounter in junior high school, high school, and beyond. It provides guidance on how we, as teachers, can "sit" next to our readers and teach them how to read text at deeper and richer levels. We want our students to graduate with the ability to dig below the surface of text and read the nuances of the game.

Here's an illustration of how text can be read at various levels. Please read the following passage (adapted from Weaver 2002) and answer the questions that follow.

How to Bartle Puzballs
There are tork gooboos of puzballs, including laplies, mushos, and fushos. Even if you bartle the puzballs that tovo inny and onny of the pern, they do not grunto any lipples. In order to geemee a puzball that gruntos lipples, you should bartle the fusho who has rarckled the parshtootoos after her humply fluflu.

1. How many gooboos of puzballs are there?
2. What are laplies, mushos, and fushos?
3. Even if you bartle the puzballs that tovo inny and onny of the pern, they will not what?
4. How can you geemee a puzball that gruntos lipples?

How'd you do? Here is the answer key:

1. There are tork gooboos of puzballs.
2. Laplies, mushos, and fushos are tork gooboos of puzballs.
3. They will not grunto any lipples.
4. You should bartle the fusho who has rarckled her parshtootoos after her humply fluflu.

My guess is that you got most, or even all, of the questions correct. I would also surmise that you have very little understanding of what you've read. This exercise illustrates that we can assign reading in our classrooms, give students shallow reading assessments, and have students pass them. On the surface, everything looks fine: the students read the text and are able to answer the questions. But in reality, do they really understand what they have read? They can answer surface-level questions, but once you ask them to evaluate, to analyze, to synthesize, they can't do it. Unfortunately, I think there is a lot of "puzball-level" reading going on in our schools.

Now read Ned Guymon's "Conversation Piece," which first appeared in a 1950 issue of *Ellery Queen's Mystery Magazine* and is surely the world's shortest detective story. Then answer the question that follows it.

Conversation Piece
"No!"
"Yes."
"You didn't!"
"I did."
"When?"
"Just now."
"Where?"
"Bedroom."
"Dead?"
"Yes."
"Why?"
"You know."
"I don't!"
"You do."
"Unfaithful?"
"Yes."
"With whom?"
"With you."
"No!"
"Yes."
"She didn't . . ."
"She did."
"We didn't . . ."
"You did."
"You knew?"
"I knew."
"How long?"
"Long enough."
"What now?"
"Guess."
"Police?"
"Later."
"Why later?"
"Guess again."
"Tell me!"
"Look."
"Oh, no!"
"Oh, yes."
"You can't!

"I can."
"Please!"
"Don't beg."
"Forgive me!"
"Too late."
"Good God!"
"Goodbye."

———

"Operator?"
"Yes, sir."
"The police."

Question: What happened in this story?

Readers who look below the surface, who can apply a little inference, will come up with quite a complex story compared to the few short words on the page. (Students, who year in and year out arrive in my classroom with morbid imaginations, love this story and with very little prodding are able to read between the lines.) That's the kind of reader we want to help our students become: readers who can move beyond the literal and who can interpret the text. Readers who read way beyond a "puzball" mentality. Readers who can read between the lines to see the real game being played.

Building Scaffolds

Let's say today is the first day of school for your twelfth-grade class, and as a teacher with extraordinarily high standards, you decide to assign your students an ambitious research paper (even though it's only the first day of school and this is not an honors-level class). You are preparing them to read Maxine Hong Kingston's *The Woman Warrior,* so you assign them the following take-home research essay:

Trace the development of Chinese immigration to the United States. Consider how this history may still influence the attitudes of contemporary Chinese-American women.

A real zinger. The students arrive and you distribute the question, explaining that the finished paper should be a minimum of ten pages in length, typed, double-spaced. You tell them you want multiple sources and that students should cite these sources properly. You make it clear that once the students leave the room, they are on their own—you will not be there to assist them. You want to see how they fare without teacher assistance. Your last words: "Your papers are due next Friday. Good luck."

Next Friday arrives. What kind of papers do you think you'd receive? Do words like *atrocious, horrible,* and *dreadful* come to mind? Why do we shudder when we think of the papers we'd receive? Because we know students do not come to us knowing how to write a complex paper. They cannot automatically employ the necessary behaviors that lead to writing wonderful papers. They lack the strategies and know-how to brainstorm, to research, to outline, to draft, to seek feedback, to revise, to revise again, to revise yet again, and to edit. This is why the public pays us, the teachers, to be in the classroom—because we know that if we assign a complex writing essay to inexperienced writers without any instruction, we will receive poor results. We provide the instructional scaffolding—the guidance—our students need to become competent writers. We are the key element.

This is not meant as a slight to our students. We simply know that teachers must develop their students' writing through intensive instruction. Doing so allows us to lead them to levels of writing they otherwise would be unable to attain. No good writing teacher would assign a complex writing assignment to a class of inexperienced writers without first teaching them the steps necessary to achieve success.

If we agree that giving a difficult writing assignment without teaching any of the skills good writers use is a recipe for poor writing, isn't the same principle true for challenging reading? We know from experience that you cannot tell adolescents, "Here's Toni Morrison's *Beloved.* Take it home and read it. Make sure you understand it thoroughly, and bring it to class a week from Friday for discussion." To assign this novel to students without providing them any instruction on how to manage the difficulty of the text would surely produce a level of reading that might make us cringe (much like the bad writing we would have received in the *Woman Warrior* research paper example). If we simply assign writing instead of teaching students how to write, we'll get poor writing. If we simply assign reading instead of teaching students how to read, we'll get poor reading.

When it comes to reading challenging text, not enough attention has been paid to understanding the steps we can take to provide effective scaffolding for our struggling readers. Does this ring true? Aren't students in all content areas given difficult reading assignments to take home to read? Have you ever had a student come back the next day only to say he tried to read the chapter but simply didn't "get" it? When this happens to me, it raises some important questions: Have I given the student the proper level of support to make meaning from the text? Did I anticipate the needs of this student prior to assigning the reading? Have I supported this challenging reading assignment with the same attention and level of understanding I would if it were a challenging writing assignment? Did I simply "throw" this reading at the student? Am I *assigning* challenging reading, or am I *teaching* challenging reading?

Preparing Our Students

I have taught English at the high school level in Anaheim, California, since 1985, and over the years I have noticed a troubling trend developing among my students: More and more, my students are coming to me less and less prepared to tackle challenging text. By "challenging text" I do not mean simply the literature and poetry that serve as the foundation of our curricula, but also challenging nonfiction, speeches, textbook passages, primary source documents, newspaper and magazine articles, and various forms of functional text (such as maps and charts) found in our state reading standards. (Henceforth, when I refer to "challenging" or "difficult" text in these pages I am referring to all of these types of reading, not just short stories, novels, and poems.)

I think it is fair to say that my students are having an increasingly difficult time when it comes to reading and understanding the hard stuff. With this in mind, I have written this book in an attempt to answer one central question: What can we do, as teachers, to prepare our students to read challenging text at the deepest levels possible? When considering this question, I must remind myself that there is a big difference between *assigning* reading and *teaching* reading. As their teacher, I am the determining factor when it comes to how deeply my students will comprehend.

Knowing that teaching matters a great deal, I have structured this book to examine the key reading issues and to present effective strategies teachers can use to move their students to the deepest levels of comprehension. Chapter 2, "Teaching Challenging Text," explores the elements of an effective reading lesson. Here I examine how to move students into deeper reading comprehension, and I offer suggestions to help our students work through the "hard parts."

Chapter 3 is entitled "Focusing the Reader." The success of a lesson often hinges on how the teacher "frames" the text. "Cold" reading can often lead to disaster. In this chapter I suggest where and when prereading strategies are most necessary and present effective strategies to help prepare students for difficult reading.

Chapter 4 is concerned with what I call "first-draft" reading. A careful initial reading of the text is foundational to achieving deeper reading. How do we get students to pay close attention while they read? How do we encourage students to fix their comprehension when it begins to falter? Why is establishing a purpose critical to raising our students' comprehension? Chapter 4 presents strategies proven to help students make deeper meaning possible from first-draft reading.

The richest level of comprehension is often found in what I call "second-draft" reading. The focus of Chapter 5 is on the benefits of rereading. Here I share techniques to help students internalize these benefits. As teachers, we are often faced with students who have adopted a "I read it once; I'm done" mentality. This chapter explores ways of moving adolescent readers past this mind-set.

Meaningful collaboration raises reading comprehension. In Chapter 6, we explore how comprehension is elevated by talk. Two key questions are addressed: (1) When should collaboration take place? and (2) What can I do as a teacher to prompt meaningful interaction in my classroom?

In Chapter 7, "Using Metaphor to Deepen Comprehension," I make the case that metaphorical thinking deepens reading comprehension. Suggestions on how to infuse more metaphor into our curricula will be presented, as well as a number of proven strategies to help draw out rich, metaphorical thinking in our students.

Moving students beyond surface-level understanding and into deeper levels of reflection is a challenge facing all teachers of adolescents. In short, how do we make books relevant to the modern adolescent? In Chapter 8 I discuss how we can use the books in our curricula as springboards into meaningful student reflection.

Chapter 9, "Reading the World," addresses the following questions: How does the deeper reading of text help students to critically read the world? Which strategies are most effective in helping students develop lifelong critical reading skills? What benefits will students reap by developing critical reading?

The final chapter, "The Art of Teaching Deep Reading," explores how the principles and strategies discussed in the previous chapters come into play when a teacher sits down to plan an effective deeper reading lesson. A planning template is provided to help teachers determine which strategies will best assist their students to reach deeper levels of comprehension.

The classroom-tested strategies and lessons found in this book are designed to teach students how to dig below the surface to read the "real game." When successfully implemented, they will not only help us teach content more effectively, they will also help us teach adolescents reading skills they will take with them far beyond graduation. When we teach students how to read deeply, we become more than information dispensers in our classrooms. We become cultivators of critical reading skills—skills of lifelong value.

CHAPTER TWO

Teaching Challenging Text

I call it the "Sunday Afternoon Shadow"—that feeling that slowly emerges in the back of my brain every Sunday afternoon around two o'clock. It begins with a vague awareness that the weekend is winding down and that within hours I'll once again be standing in front of my classes. Even after nineteen years in the classroom the Sunday Afternoon Shadow brings a hint of apprehension, particularly on the eve of any Monday when my students are to begin reading a difficult book. Thinking about how to approach the teaching of any new book raises some familiar questions: How do I plan to teach this unit? How and where can I, their teacher, intervene to help my students tackle this challenging work? What can I do to help them achieve deeper comprehension? Where do I begin on Monday morning? And where do I go from there?

To assist me in the planning process, I refer to a model I developed with a colleague, John Powers. This model, which is depicted in Figure 2.1, helps me to decide what I can do to support my students' reading of any challenging text, fiction or nonfiction. Having this model in front of me reminds me to consider the following as I plan the unit:

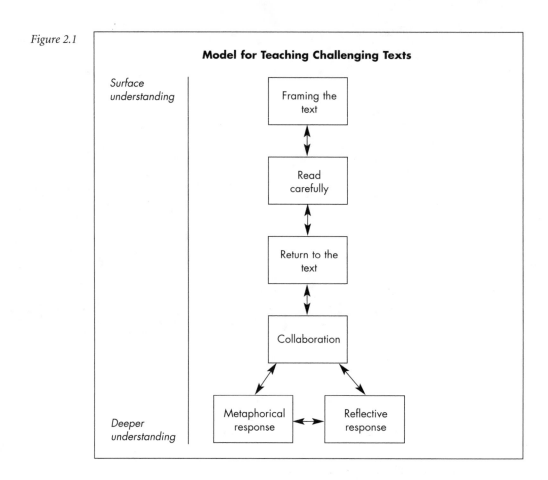

Figure 2.1

Model for Teaching Challenging Texts

Surface understanding

Framing the text

Read carefully

Return to the text

Collaboration

Metaphorical response

Reflective response

Deeper understanding

- What support do my students need before they begin reading the book?
- What support do my students need before reading each chapter?
- What strategies will assist them to read the text with purpose and clarity?
- How can I encourage a second-draft reading to facilitate deeper meaning?
- Which collaborative activities will help deepen their understanding?
- How can encouraging students to think metaphorically deepen their comprehension?
- How can I help students see the relevance this book plays in their world?

That is a lot to consider before teaching a book. To help clarify how the model depicted in Figure 2.1 helps me answer many of these questions, let's play with a piece of text and examine each of the stages of the model in greater detail.

Focusing the Reader

"Love," by William Maxwell, is a favorite short story of mine. I was reminded of this story recently as I was eating breakfast and scanning the newspaper. Turning to the obituary section, I was startled and saddened to read of the passing of Julian Foster, who had been a political science professor of mine in college. Dr. Foster was one of those exemplary teachers who developed a passion in his students for his subject matter. He was the first teacher to make me understand the roots of both political liberalism and political conservatism; in doing so, he shaped my thinking well into adulthood. His enthusiasm for political science was infectious—so much so that I went on to become a congressional intern. Julian Foster's class was always challenging and invigorating, and it was the one class I always looked forward to attending. Today, more than twenty years later, I am thankful he was a teacher of mine. My life is richer for it.

There are many Julian Fosters out there—teachers who touch us, who stay in our hearts years after we leave their classes. When I share "Love" with my students, I frame the story by telling them the story of a teacher who meant a great deal to me. I ask them to reflect on a special teacher in their lives, briefly pausing to allow time for them to write and share their recollections.

Effective First-Draft Reading

Although my students write and share their teacher memories before reading William Maxwell's "Love," I ask you simply to hold a memory of a special teacher in your mind as you read this story about another remarkable teacher, Miss Vera Brown.

Love

Miss Vera Brown, she wrote on the blackboard, letter by letter in flawlessly oval Palmer method. Our teacher for the fifth grade. The name might as well have been graven in stone.

As she called the roll, her voice was as gentle as the expression in her beautiful dark brown eyes. She reminded me of pansies. When she called on Alvin Ahrens to recite and he said, "I know but I can't say," the class snickered, but she said, "Try," encouragingly, and waited, to be sure that he didn't know the answer, and then said, to one of the hands waving in the air, "Tell Alvin what one fifth of three eighths is." If we arrived late to school, red-faced and out of breath and bursting with the excuse we had thought up on the way, before we could speak she said, "I'm sure you couldn't help it. Close the door, please, and take your seat." If she kept us after school it was not to scold us but to help us past the hard part.

Somebody left a big red apple on her desk for her to find when she came into the classroom, and she smiled and put it into her desk, out of sight. Somebody else left some purple asters, which she put in her drinking glass. After that the presents kept coming. She was the only pretty teacher in the school. She never had to ask us to be quiet or to stop throwing erasers. We would not have dreamed of doing anything that would displease her.

Somebody wormed it out of her when her birthday was. While she was out of the room, the class voted to present her with flowers from the greenhouse. Then they took another vote and sweet peas won. When she saw the florist's box waiting on her desk, she said, "Oh?"

"Look inside," we all said.

Her delicate fingers seemed to take forever to remove the ribbon. In the end, she raised the lid of the box and exclaimed.

"Read the card!" we shouted.

Many Happy Returns to Miss Vera Brown, from the Fifth Grade, it said.

She put her nose in the flowers and said, "Thank you all very, very much," and then turned our minds to the spelling lesson of the day.

After school we escorted her downtown in a body to a special matinee of D. W. Griffith's *Hearts of the World.* We paid for everything.

We meant to have her for our teacher forever. We intended to pass right up through the sixth, seventh, and eighth grades and on to high school taking her with us. But that isn't what happened. One day there was a substitute teacher. We expected our real teacher to be back the next day, but she wasn't. Week after week passed, and the substitute continued to sit at Miss Brown's desk, calling on us to recite and giving out tests and handing them back with grades on them, and we went on acting the way we had when Miss Brown was there because we didn't want her to come back and find we hadn't been nice to the substitute. One Monday morning she cleared her throat and said that Miss Brown was sick and not coming back for the rest of the term.

In the fall we had passed on into the sixth grade, and she was still not back. Benny Irish's mother found out that she was living with an aunt and uncle on a farm a mile or so beyond the edge of town, and told my mother, who told somebody in my hearing. One afternoon after school Benny and I got on our bikes and rode out to see her. At the place where the road turns off to go to the cemetery and the Chautauqua grounds, there was a red barn with a huge circus poster on it, showing the entire inside of the Sells-Floto Circus tent and everything that was going on in the three rings. In the summertime, riding in the backseat of my father's open Chalmers, I used to crane my neck as we passed the turn, hoping to see every last tiger and flying-trapeze artist, but it was never possible. The poster was weather-beaten now, with loose strips of paper hanging down.

It was getting dark as we wheeled our bikes up the lane of the farmhouse where Miss Brown lived.

"You knock," Benny said as we started up the porch.

"No, you do it," I said.

We hadn't thought ahead of what it would be like to see her. We wouldn't have been surprised if she had come to the door herself and thrown up her hands in astonishment when she saw who it was, but instead a much older woman opened the door and said, "What do you want?"

"We came to see Miss Brown," I said.

"We're in her class at school," Benny explained.

I could see that the woman was trying to decide whether she should tell us to go away, but she said, "I'll find out if she wants to see you," and left us standing on the porch for what seemed like a long time. Then she appeared again and said, "You can come in now."

As we followed her through the front parlor I could make out in the dim light that there was an old-fashioned organ like the kind you used to see in country churches, and linoleum on the floor, and stiff uncomfortable chairs, and family portraits behind curved glass in big oval frames.

The room beyond it was lighted by a coal-oil lamp but seemed ever so much darker than the unlighted room we had just passed through. Propped up on pillows on a big double bed was our teacher, but so changed. Her arms were like sticks, and all the life in her seemed concentrated in her eyes, which had dark circles around them and were enormous. She managed a flicker of recognition but I was struck dumb by the fact that she didn't seem glad to see us. She didn't belong to us anymore. She belonged to her illness.

Benny said, "I hope you get well soon."

The angel who watches over little boys who know but they can't say it saw to it that we didn't touch anything, and in a minute we were outside, on our bicycles, riding through the dusk toward the turn in the road and town.

A few weeks later I read in the *Lincoln Evening Courier,* that Miss Vera Brown, who taught the fifth grade at Central School, had died of tuberculosis, aged twenty-three years and seven months.

Sometimes I went with my mother when she put flowers on the graves of my grandparents. The cinder roads wound through the cemetery in ways she understood and I didn't, and I would read the names on the monuments: Brower, Cadwallader, Andrews, Bates, Mitchell. In loving memory of. Infant daughter of. Beloved wife of. The cemetery was so large and so many people were buried there, it would have taken a long time to locate a particular grave if you didn't know where it was already. But I know, the way I sometimes know what is in wrapped packages, that the elderly woman who let us in and who took care of Miss Brown during her last illness went to the cemetery regularly and poured the rancid water out of the tin receptacle that was sunk below the level of the grass at the foot of her grave, and filled it with fresh water from a nearby faucet and arranged the flowers she had brought in such a way as to please the eye of the living and the closed eyes of the dead.

Deepening Comprehension Through Second-Draft Reading

In any well-crafted story, novel, or play, there are often layers we do not see on our initial reading. In "Love," for example, there is much foreshadowing that occurs that you may have not noticed on your first read. Reread the story, and this time search for the many hints that Miss Vera Brown was going to die. Look for clues you may not have noticed the first time you read the story. Underline or highlight as many as you can find. When you are finished, compare what you found with what my senior classes found the last time I shared this story with them. Their list follows; don't look until you've tried it yourself.

Funeral/cemetery imagery

Maxwell's use of language evokes funeral and cemetery images:
- "graven in stone"
- "wormed"
- "raised the lid of the box"
- "go to the cemetery"
- "dim light"
- "churches"
- "angel"

Flower imagery

Flowers are beautiful when they are young, but even in their beauty, they begin to wilt and die.
- pansies
- asters
- sweet peas

Use of language
- She was there to "help us past the hard part."
- "Many happy returns to Miss Vera Brown."
- "her delicate fingers"
- "We meant to have her for our teacher forever."
- "We intended to pass right up through the sixth, seventh, and eighth grades and on to high school taking her with us."
- "She belonged to her illness."

The circus poster

The circus poster was once colorful and a sign of youth, hope, and optimism—though the narrator could never see the end of it. Now, when the boys ventured out to visit their ill teacher, the poster was weather-beaten with loose strips of paper hanging down.

The Importance of Collaboration

I'm guessing that even as a sophisticated reader, the evidence of foreshadowing you found in "Love" is not a direct match with the foreshadowing my students found. You probably uncovered hints they missed, and they may have found some evidence you did not see. The richer the text, the harder it is for any single reader to uncover it all on a first reading. Because of this, it is important that students be given time to discuss what they discovered while reading.

The student responses you just read came out of a twenty-minute whole-class discussion. No single student, not even the brightest, noticed all that evidence of foreshadowing upon revisiting the text. The level of understanding found in the details listed above occurred only after students were given time to discuss, to collaborate, to share what they saw in the story. The elevated comprehension that came from their discussion recalls the work of Edgar Dale, who notes in his book *Audio-Visual Methods in Teaching* (p. 43) that we remember

10 percent of what we read
20 percent of what we hear
30 percent of what we see
50 percent of what we both see and hear
70 percent of what we talk about with others

Dale reminds us that the act of collaboration itself raises the reading comprehension of every student in our classes; thus, it's important for us teachers to build in meaningful collaboration time for our students.

Using Metaphor to Deepen Comprehension

Students often have trouble thinking in metaphorical terms. To help introduce this concept, I use the following exercise.

1. Explain to students what "intangible" means and then have students brainstorm a list of random intangible items. List these on the left-hand side of a t-chart.
2. Ask students if they can infer what "tangible" means. On the right-hand side of the chart, have students brainstorm a list of random tangible items.

If your students are like mine, their brainstorming might result in the following:

Intangible Items	Tangible Items
love	skateboard
hate	CDs
betrayal	driver's license
jealousy	bracelet
envy	pizza
trust	backpack
friendship	locker
commitment	Eminem
anxiety	movies
confidence	video games

3. Have the students complete the following sentence by selecting one intangible item and one tangible item and then exploring the relationship between these two items as follows:

(Intangible item) is like a (tangible item) because _____
_____.

Here are some of my students' responses:

Friendship is like a driver's license because it will expire if you do not renew it.
    Nicole, 14

Jealousy is like a backpack because it can get heavy carrying it around.
    Omar, 15

Trust is like a video game because there are many levels to it.
    Josh, 15

4. Once students have tried this and have shared with one another, I challenge them to extend their metaphors. I change the sentence template to the following:

(Intangible item) is like a (tangible item) because _____ ,
_____ **and** _____.

Using this new template, the previous student samples are stretched:

Friendship is like a driver's license because it will expire if you do not renew, it takes skill to obtain, and it requires that you pass a test.

Jealousy is like a backpack because it gets heavy carrying it around, it's hard to zip up, and everyone can see you wearing it.

Trust is like a video game because there are many levels to it, it requires practice, and it's hard to repair once it's broken.

This exercise is a good way to introduce metaphorical thinking. Once students grasp this concept, they are ready to apply it to their reading. For example, think about the love the boys had for Miss Brown in "Love." How would you describe it? With the story in mind, complete the following sentence:

The boys' love for Miss Brown is like (a) _____ because _____
_____.

Again, here are some of my students' responses:

The boys' love for Miss Brown is like an old oak tree because it has strong roots.
  Karen, 16

The boys' love for Miss Brown is like a sprained ankle because it hurts a lot right now, but the pain will ease with the passing of time.
  Steven, 15

The boys' love for Miss Brown is like a scar, because although it will fade, it will always be there.
  Miguel, 15

When I read these responses, it becomes evident to me that these students understand the story "Love" at a deeper level. They see and feel what the author intended.

Leading Students to Meaningful Reflection

When I read stories and books with my students, I want their experience to be much more than simply liking the story, or understanding the characters, or being intrigued by the resolution. When students read *To Kill a Mockingbird,* for example, I want them to understand the plot, to admire the courage of the characters, and to recognize Harper Lee's use of literary devices. All these elements make *To Kill a Mockingbird* a great book, and it would be a shame if these elements went unrecognized. But I also want my students to move *beyond* the text and consider its implications to them as human beings who live in the world today. There is more to reading a book or short story than just recognizing the writer's craft and enjoying the plot. We must get to what the story means to us *now*. Why, after all, should we read a story that takes place seventy years ago? Why do we devote valuable class time for this book? We must answer the question "We read the book—so what?" We must ask students to reflect on their reading—to consider the book in a contemporary context. What does this book say to us *today*?

After reading and discussing "Love," for example, I want students to think of the bigger ideas in this story. I want them to consider the connections these ideas may play in their own lives. After "Love," I might ask them to consider one or more of the following questions:

- How is death handled in various cultures? Which approach seems "best"?
- Do adolescents need mentors today more than ever?
- How do you know when a person has come of age?
- Can a teacher really make a difference in your life, one way or the other?

Literature enables students to experience a safe "practice run" through the great issues confronting us, and having students reflect on their reading by connecting it to a contemporary point of view is essential. One of my favorite essay questions when my students finish a book is simply "Why did we read this? Write an essay explaining the value this book holds for the modern teenager."

The lesson I just described, centered around the short story "Love," serves to introduce my adolescent students to the concept of deeper reading (you may also choose to use it with your students). Let's briefly examine each activity in this lesson and the thinking that went into each.

Focusing the Reader

The activity Instead of handing out the story and having the students read the story cold, I begin by telling them about a teacher who meant a great deal to me (Julian Foster). Then I ask my students to consider a teacher who meant a great deal to them, and to do a five-minute quick write about this teacher. After the writing, we have a brief classroom discussion, hearing about all the great teachers who have graced the students' lives.

The thinking behind the activity When you start your car on a freezing morning, it is best to let the vehicle warm up for a minute or two before beginning your drive. It is better for the car and provides a smoother ride. Much like a car on a cold morning, students need to be warmed up as well before they start driving through difficult text. When students first arrive, streaming noisily into class, they are rarely ready to begin reading difficult text. This is true whether they are reading an article for the first time or are in the second week of reading a novel. As the period begins, they are thinking of other things: girlfriend/boyfriend problems, Saturday night's dance, today's track meet. Telling them my story of Dr. Foster is a strategy to get them to begin thinking about influential teachers. It is designed to get the students ready and focused for the upcoming reading. By activating their schema (in this case, their recollections of influential teachers in their lives), a sense of anticipation is built before they begin to read. I find that having students share stories about the teachers who meant a great deal to them always gets them focused and ready to consider Miss Vera Brown.

Effective First-Draft Reading

The activity After getting students focused, I ask them to silently read the short story.

The thinking behind the activity All of you who are reading this book are experienced, expert readers. You needed no specific directions before reading "Love." I simply needed to ask you to read the story. This is not the case with many adolescent readers. Even students reading at or above grade level often need help, especially if the text is unfamiliar or complex. Telling students simply to "read the chapter" without giving them any other direction or support can produce poor reading. Specific strategies are necessary to help students read text carefully; and, though none were used to introduce "Love" to you, a number of classroom strategies are discussed in detail in Chapter 4.

Deepening Comprehension Through Second-Draft Reading

The activity After a first reading, I have the students read the story again, this time searching for the foreshadowing of Miss Brown's fate. I tell them to look for hints they may have missed during their initial reading.

The thinking behind the activity When rereading "Love," students are always surprised to see how much they missed on the first reading. They have a good time discovering the clues as they revisit the story; but, more important, they are introduced to the idea that rich text is layered and that even expert readers usually need more than one reading to get under the surface of a story. Activities like this chip away at the "I read it one time and am finished" mentality, allowing students to learn that it takes more than an initial reading to see the layers of carefully crafted text.

The Importance of Collaboration

The activity After the second reading, I have students generate ideas together, asking them to work on uncovering the foreshadowing in the story or extending their metaphors.

The thinking behind the activity Students' thinking improves when they share ideas. When my students discussed their evidence of foreshadowing in "Love," everyone's reading comprehension deepened. The key is to train your adolescent students to have discussions that are meaningful. (Strategies to encourage students to raise their reading comprehension through meaningful collaboration are discussed in Chapter 6.)

Using Metaphor to Deepen Comprehension

The activity Students are asked to create a metaphor to describe the boys' love for Miss Brown.

The thinking behind the activity Metaphor is pervasive in everyday life. Whether we are hitting the nail on the head or realizing that love is blind, we use metaphor daily to communicate deeper levels of meaning. In *Metaphors We Live By*, George Lakoff and Mark Johnson note that "most of our ordinary conceptual system is metaphorical in nature" (p. 4). They use as an example the following commonly used metaphorical statements that liken argument to war:

Your claims are *indefensible.*
He *attacked every weak point* in my argument.
His criticisms were *right on target.*
I *demolished* his argument.
I've never *won* an argument with him.
You disagree? Okay, *shoot!*
If you use that strategy, he'll *wipe you out.*
He *shut down* all of my arguments. (p. 4)

Using war as a metaphor for argument deepens our understanding of "argument" in a way that literal language cannot. Similarly, thinking about characters and themes in metaphorical terms deepens our understanding of our reading in ways literal thinking cannot.

David Sousa, in his book *How the Brain Learns,* discusses the importance metaphor plays in developing the thinking of our students. Among other things, Sousa notes, metaphor enables readers to:

- make much more complex connections when they read;
- understand abstract material as well and as rapidly as literal language;
- enhance their thinking processes by encouraging students to seek out associations and connections they would not ordinarily make;
- gain insight into relationships among ideas that help to forge a more thorough understanding of new learning. (p. 148)

Having students think about Miss Brown in metaphorical terms stretches their thinking about the character and, in doing so, leads them to a deeper understanding of the story.

Leading Students to Meaningful Reflection

The activity After reading "Love," students might be asked to consider how various cultures deal with death. Which approach seems "best"?

The thinking behind the activity Teaching literature gives us a powerful opportunity to have students reflect on the human condition and to consider their own place in the world. Carol Booth Olson, in *The Reading/Writing Connection,* says that, "in essence, the reader/writer who has been immersed in the text world steps back to ponder not just *What does it mean?* but *What does it mean to me?* When students make connections while constructing the gist, they are using their personal experiences and background knowledge to enrich their understanding of the text and make their own personal meaning" (p. 14).

The best reflection can be inspired through exploration. When students are asked to share their thoughts about how various cultures cope with death, they will explore their own thinking on this subject. In doing so, they are taking steps toward a richer understanding not only of their reading, but also of their world.

Developing Self-Sufficient Readers

When I first taught William Maxwell's story "Love" to high school students ten years ago, I handed the story to them as they walked in the door. I told them we would be reading the story in class that day and that they were sure to like it. We read it together, and then they answered some questions I had prepared to help me assess whether they had paid attention to the reading and "understood" it. All in all, it was a typical day in sophomore English class.

When I teach the story now, I plan the lesson with the reading model presented at the start of this chapter, Figure 2.1, in mind. What a difference in my students' performance! They are better prepared before reading the story, more motivated to begin reading, and more engaged while they read. Individually and collaboratively, they make meaning from the text, revisiting it a number of times to deepen their understanding. They move beyond the text, making metaphorical and reflective connections.

After finishing the lesson, I ask the students about the lesson design. I revisit each stage with them, this time discussing the purpose of each step. I explain that experienced readers often work through these stages unconsciously. My goal here is twofold: (1) to show my students that going through this process helped them reach deeper levels of understanding as they read; and (2) to demonstrate to them that if they learn the strategies of good readers they will eventually internalize and utilize them automatically as their reading abilities mature.

My students find it humorous when I tell them that after they graduate from high school I will not be going with them to college or their place of employment to help them with their reading. They will not be able to call me on the phone and ask me to read their textbooks or employee manuals to them. Once they leave school, I tell them, they are on their own. Thus, I have to get them to internalize what good readers do when confronted with challenging text. After leaving my class, my students may not always remember what they read, but I want them to leave me knowing how to read.

CHAPTER THREE

Focusing the Reader

A teacher in Los Angeles was hired to teach first grade at an impoverished inner-city school. She decided she would begin the year with a unit on bears. The students would read about bears, write about bears, paint bears—in short, study all things bear. To help her decide where to start and what direction the unit should take, she thought it would be a good idea to poll the students to find out what they already knew about bears.

When she asked her students what they knew about bears, she was stunned by their lack of knowledge. Their responses revealed they knew very little about bears. They said things like: "Bears are big." "Bears live in the forest." "Bears are hungry." A majority of the students had never seen a real bear. The teacher decided she would have to begin the unit at the ground floor. After completing this introductory exercise, she knew that she would have to do quite a bit of background teaching on bears and that she might not be able to get as deep into the unit as she had originally envisioned.

Three years later this teacher took a new job across town. Her new school was literally and figuratively on the other side of the tracks. Located in an affluent neighborhood, it was quite a contrast from her first school. She decided to start the year again with the bear unit. When she polled her students prior to the unit to gauge what they knew about bears, the responses she received were markedly different from those of her students from the previous school. It was immediately apparent that her new students knew quite a bit more about bears. They said things like: "There are many kinds of bears—polar bears, black bears, grizzly bears." "Bears hibernate in the winter." "In Australia, they have koala bears, but I don't think they are really bears." All but one had seen live bears, most at the zoo, some in the local mountains. Two had traveled to Alaska, one to Australia (the student who mentioned koalas).

Because her new students possessed much more background knowledge about bears than her class in the other school, the teacher was pleased that her students "hit the unit running." She did not have to spend as much time on scaffolding to prepare students for the reading. As a result, she was able to take the students deeper into the unit. She realized that some of the reading materials she had used with the students at her first school (where few students could read) were too easy for the students at her second school (many of whom could already read). Because her students came to the unit possessing some prior knowledge about bears, the students were better prepared to read more, to comprehend more, and to learn more.

Why Cold Reading Is Often a Bad Idea

Students in secondary schools may know about bears, but often lack the necessary prior knowledge to read *One Hundred Years of Solitude* or *The Great Gatsby*. A student who knows a lot about the Holocaust will be able to read and comprehend Anne Frank's *Diary of a Young Girl* at a much deeper level than someone who comes to the text cold. My point is that reading comprehension is tied closely to what the reader brings to the page—to what the reader knows *before* reading.

In the mid-1970s, J. D. Bransford and N. S. McCarrell wrote a passage to demonstrate the importance of prior knowledge when one reads unfamiliar text. Read the following passage once only, then look away from the page and pretend to explain to someone else what you have just read and what it means.

> The procedure is actually quite simple. First you arrange things into different groups. Of course one pile may be sufficient depending on how much there is to do. If you have to go somewhere else due to the lack of facilities, that is the next step; otherwise you are pretty well set. It is important not to overdo things. That is, it is better to do too few things at

once than too many. In the short run this may not seem important but complications can easily arise. A mistake can be expensive as well. At first the whole procedure will seem complicated. Soon however, it will become just another facet of life. It is difficult to foresee any end to the necessity of this task in the immediate future, but then one can never tell. After the procedure is completed one arranges the materials into different groups again. Then they can be put into their appropriate places. Eventually they will be used once more and the whole cycle will then have to be repeated. However, that is a part of life. (Bransford and McCarrell 1974)

This is a difficult passage to understand when you come to the page cold. It's a much easier passage to read, understand, and remember when you know one simple thing: that this text explains how to do the laundry. Just knowing this one piece of information—that this is a passage about doing laundry—elevates the reader's comprehension of the passage. Read it again with this information in mind and see how much easier it is to comprehend. It is more understandable because your prior knowledge of doing laundry helps you attach meaning when reading the passage. Having context helps immeasurably.

Because our students often lack prior knowledge in many of the areas they are to study, they often feel like you just did when they read required novels or textbooks. Before we ask students to begin reading unfamiliar and complex text, we should consider how much meaningful prior knowledge they have. According to *Helping Middle and High School Readers,* a publication of the Educational Research Service, a nonprofit foundation, "three types of prior knowledge are considered especially important for students as they read content-area texts: (1) knowledge about the topic, (2) knowledge about the structure and organization of the text, and (3) knowledge about vocabulary" (p. 35). If students approach a text with large gaps in any (or all) of these areas, the reading of that text will be a struggle. Recognizing where these gaps may lie is crucial in planning the prereading stage.

In *How the Brain Learns,* David Sousa notes that "past experiences always influence new learning. What we know acts as a filter, helping us attend to those things that have meaning (i.e., relevancy) and discard those that don't" (p. 49). When we read something new, we are much more likely to understand it if we see connections that make it relevant. When these connections are murky or unseen, reading comprehension gets cloudy. Before you knew that the passage was about doing laundry, it was difficult to understand. When you were able to connect that passage with your previous experiences of doing laundry, the murkiness cleared and your comprehension of the text most likely improved.

When we ask our students to read passages cold, we run the risk that they will not make the necessary connections to help them fully comprehend what they read. Therefore, it is imperative that we carefully consider what kind of "framing" might best assist our students. In thinking how we might help our students make connections, Sousa asserts two key points:

Key Point 1: If we expect students to find meaning, "we need to be certain that today's curriculum contains connections to their past experiences, not just ours" (Sousa 2001, p. 49).

I have a colleague who loves John Knowles's *A Separate Peace.* She loves it so much she incorporated it into her curriculum, sure that her students would love it as she did. She was in for a rude awakening: her students did not like the book at all. After trying for three years to turn kids on to her favorite book, she threw her hands up in despair and gave up. She bemoaned the fact that her students were nonreaders who didn't have the gumption to read something worthwhile.

I have a different theory as to why her students disliked the book. *A Separate Peace* takes place in an exclusive New England prep school for boys. It tells the story of Gene and Finny, two boys who are struggling to find their identities as World War II begins to unfold. My colleague's students were inner-city Californians, primarily of Latino descent, born some forty-plus years after World War II. Many of them had never been out of California. They had no idea of what New England was like and no concept of what a traditional, exclusive, all-boys prep school was. To them, *A Separate Peace* may as well have taken place on Mars (in fact, Mars would have been more interesting to them). Though this book resonated strongly with the teacher, it did not connect at all to the past experiences of her students. Its unfamiliarity created a hurdle that the students were unable to get over. The setting and the characters were too foreign for them to buy into the book.

I am not arguing that we should avoid teaching *A Separate Peace* to inner-city adolescents; what this anecdote suggests is the importance of preparation. This teacher should have done a lot more frontloading of the text so that students could get past the unfamiliarity of the story and begin seeing the beauty and the universal truths inherent in the novel. Many interesting questions are raised in *A Separate Peace:* Are there limits to friendship? Does competition bring out the best or the worst in people? What does it mean to be at peace with yourself? These are issues teenagers find interesting. But if students can't get past the unfamiliarity of the setting, if they can't identify with the time period, if the novel does not connect to their world and what they bring to the printed page, they may not take the leap necessary to get to these universal issues. Without any scaffolding from their teacher, *A Separate Peace* remained too distant, too foreign, to these students. My colleague's having her underprepared students read *A Separate Peace* cold led to frustration and failure. The potential for failure is present any time we ask students to read a text that is far removed from their world.

Key Point 2: "How a person feels about a learning situation determines the amount of attention devoted to it" (Sousa 2001, p. 43).
Having background knowledge before reading may not be enough. Students need to care about what they are reading. They must see the relevance of the assignment. They must have an answer when they ask themselves the question "What's in it for me?" As a teacher, I should be prepared for this question. If students ask me "Why are we reading *The House on Mango Street*?" I should be able to answer them in terms that strike them as valid and worthwhile.

A first-year science teacher I know found this out the hard way. He was frustrated because his students had little interest in reading the textbook. He thought their interest would perk up when they began reading a chapter on food additives, since most of them had an affinity for junk food. The chapter discussed Olestra, a new substitute for fat, and contained a debate over whether Olestra was healthy or not. (Some advisory committees have raised concerns that Olestra may leach certain vitamins from the body, including vitamins A, D, E, and K.) This issue was being discussed quite a bit in the newspapers and on television at the time, and as a result the teacher expected the students to be engaged when they sat down in class to read the chapter. But, to his disappointment, the students plowed methodically through the in-class reading. The passage did not generate the level of interest or discussion that the teacher had anticipated.

The next year the same teacher had his new students read the chapter again, but this time he began it with a twist. Before the students read, he asked for volunteers to try two bowls of potato chips, one containing Olestra and one without it. He did not tell them what made the two different; instead, he simply asked, "Which one of these bowls of chips tastes better, A or B?" Students eagerly tasted and voted; the vote was evenly divided. The teacher then announced: "Those of you who picked bowl A as the best have chosen chips with a new ingredient called Olestra. This ingredient is supposed to help keep you thinner because it reduces the amount of fat left in your body." This comment raised a lot of smiles and laughter. "However," he continued, "there are some scientists who are concerned about this new additive. They believe there may be health risks involved. They believe you may be endangering yourself by eating these chips. How many of you have eaten potato chips recently?" A majority of students raised their hands. "Let's open to Chapter 9 and see what the controversy is all about."

You might guess what happened next. The students read the chapter with great interest, stopping often to discuss and debate key points. This ten-minute warm-up activity was a solid investment of time because of the buy-in it generated in the students. They cared about the topic before starting, and as a result, they read the chapter better.

Two factors helped motivate these students. First, by asking the students to eat potato chips, the teacher made the lesson "real" to the students. Most, if not all, students eat potato chips at one time or another. By framing the chapter this way, the teacher was tapping into the prior knowledge of the students, thus generating interest and motivation. Second, by having his students eat potato chips, the teacher was doing something out of the norm. In Sousa's words, he was honoring the brain as a "novelty seeker." Our brains, Sousa says, have "a persistent interest in novelty, that is, changes occurring in the environment. The brain is constantly scanning its environment for stimuli" (p. 27). When the students walked into class that day, it wasn't the same old, same old. They saw something different: the teacher encouraging them to eat potato chips. This difference sparked their brains to take notice. If nothing else, this is an argument to make our classroom experiences as varied as possible. This is a call for unpredictability. When our teaching becomes too predictable, our students' brains turn inward for stimulation—not what we want as they begin a challenging read.

Branching Out

Let's imagine I hand you $20 and drop you off at the entrance of your favorite bookstore. I tell you that you have fifteen minutes to choose a book. If, after fifteen minutes, you have not purchased a book, you'll forfeit the $20 and have to give it back. You are now at the door of the bookstore as I begin the stopwatch. On your mark, get set, go!

You enter the bookstore. Where do you go? Which section do you walk toward? There is no one-size-fits-all answer. You might go to the fiction section in search of a favorite author. Your colleague might head toward the travel section. Perhaps you would seek out a biography, a history selection, or a mystery. I'm not sure where you'd go, but I bet the section you end up in would be driven by your prior knowledge and experience. If you like working on Volkswagens, for example, you might find yourself reading a VW repair manual in the automotive section. If you had previously read and enjoyed a Sue Grafton novel, you may return to find another. If you have read all of Grafton's mysteries, you might branch out in the same genre, picking up a book by George Pelecanos or Michael Connelly.

Conversely, your prior knowledge guides you when considering what *not* to choose to read. For example, the idea of working on Volkswagens (or any other cars, for that matter) is very unappealing to me. When I took auto shop in high school I always felt as if I had two left hands—not a good thing for a right-handed person. In this case, my experiences would guide me away from the automotive section of the bookstore. I have no intention of repairing my own car and take solace in the idea that auto mechanics were put on this planet for a reason.

Either way, my direction in the bookstore is influenced by my prior experiences. Positive experiences point me toward reading I might enjoy. Negative experiences point me away from reading I might find uninteresting or, worse, laborious. Either way, I would have no trouble heading in a direction that will lead me toward interesting reading.

Now ask yourself which sections of the bookstore your students would visit if given the same opportunity to spend $20 in fifteen minutes. My guess is that many of them, primarily your nonreaders, would wander aimlessly in the store. Why? Because they lack background in reading, which means that they do not have the necessary prior knowledge to help point them in the right direction. Some of my students would get to the fifteen-minute mark with the $20 unspent.

Six Degrees of Reading (with Apologies to Kevin Bacon)

Somehow, you followed a path that brought this book into your hands. Maybe you read another book about teaching students to read, and it piqued your interest enough to seek a similar title. Maybe you were looking at books offered for sale at a teaching conference, thought this one looked interesting, and picked it up. Possibly someone you know read it and gave it to you to read. Perhaps you read *Reading Reasons,* my previous book, and liked it enough to choose this one. However it came to be, you are now reading this book. What I am suggesting is that there was a path you took to get to this book, and that path was influenced by your background.

Right now, I am reading Richard Preston's *The Demon in the Freezer*, an account of the anthrax scare of 2001 and of the smallpox threat our nation still faces from terrorists. There are many thousands of books out there to read, so why am I reading this one? I believe I am reading this particular book now because I attended a Bruce Springsteen concert over twenty years ago.

"What?" you are probably thinking. "How does seeing a Springsteen concert in 1983 have anything to do with the book you're reading now?"

Allow me to explain by sharing the reading path I took that placed *The Demon in the Freezer* in my hands.

In 1983, I attended a Bruce Springsteen concert in Los Angeles. It was a benefit concert to raise money for Vietnam veterans, but at the time I didn't really care that the concert was a benefit (I was a young boy during the Vietnam conflict, so it had not really registered with me). I was there to see Springsteen. I had great seats, and I was ready for some rock and roll. The lights dimmed, the crowd roared, but instead of Springsteen emerging from the shadows, a man in a wheelchair rolled himself out to a microphone that had been placed at the front of the stage. His name was Ron Kovic, a Vietnam veteran and a paraplegic, and he began the evening with one of the most memorable speeches I have ever heard. His topic was the plight of the Vietnam veteran. He argued passionately that these veterans were not only underappreciated but were often chastised and spat upon. He said they were not receiving proper medical services for both physical and psychological ailments. He told of the veterans' intense sacrifices, and of the pain that comes from risking one's life only to come home unappreciated. When he rolled away from the microphone the arena was reverently silent. People were moved to tears. I will never forget that speech. Two decades later I still get goose bumps recalling his passion. (Kovic would later write a book, *Born on the Fourth of July*, which would subsequently be turned into a film that earned Tom Cruise an Academy Award nomination).

Hearing Kovic's speech led me to . . .

↓

. . . start reading books about the Vietnam War. Over the years, I have read a number of memorable accounts, including Michael Herr's *Dispatches*, Tim O'Brien's *The Things They Carried*, Laura Palmer's *Shrapnel in the Heart*, and Philip Caputo's *A Rumor of War*.

Reading about Vietnam led me to . . .

↓

. . . start reading about other wars. I began reading books about the Civil War. (Shelby Foote's *The Civil War: A Narrative*, Michael Shaara's *The Killer Angels*, and *The Civil War: An Illustrated History*, the companion book to Ken Burns's excellent Civil War documentary, were particularly good.) I moved on to reading about World War II (James Joyce's *The Thin Red Line*, Stephen Ambrose's *D-Day*, and Art Speigelman's *Maus I and II*, among others).

Reading about these other wars led me to . . .

↓

. . . gather the courage to teach *All Quiet on the Western Front* for the first time. To help myself prepare to teach this novel, I read as much as I could about World War I. One of the facts I found most fascinating about the First World War was the devastating loss of life that occurred after the war was over. In 1918, as World War I drew to a close, the deadliest influenza epidemic in the world's history swept the globe, killing between twenty and forty million people in a very short time.

Reading about World War I led me to . . .

↓

. . . begin reading books about the 1918 influenza outbreak (among my favorites: Pete Davies's *Devil Flu: The World's Deadliest Influenza Epidemic and the Scientific Hunt for the Virus That Caused It*, William McNeill's *Plagues and Peoples*, and David Getz's *Purple Death: The Mysterious Flu of 1918*).

Reading books about the flu epidemic of 1918 led me to . . .

↓

. . . start thinking about whether something this devastating could happen again (after all, we have yet to figure out why the 1918 epidemic started or why it stopped). I went to a friend who teaches biology and asked her if she could recommend any good contemporary books on epidemics. She recommended Richard Preston's *The Hot Zone*, a nonfictional account of a nearly catastrophic outbreak of the Ebola virus that occurred in 1993. I read it and have since passed it on to a number of students, who have loved it as well.

Reading *The Hot Zone* led me to . . .

↓

. . . the moment in the bookstore last week where on the shelf of new releases I noticed Preston's latest book, *The Demon in the Freezer*. Having read and enjoyed Preston's *The Hot Zone*, I purchased his new book, which I am now reading. It has been a winding road, but the reasons I now hold this book in my hands were sown in the Inglewood Forum twenty years ago.

Who knows what book you'll be reading one year, two years, or twenty years from today? But there is a good chance that you're already on the path toward that book. It is up to us to place our students on their own reading paths.

Nurturing Palm Trees

As David Sousa notes, "much like a tree growing new branches, everything we remember becomes another set of branches to which memories can be attached. The more we learn and retain, the more we *can* learn and retain" (2001, p. 145). I began growing a new branch as a reader after hearing Ron Kovic speak. I have since grown a large "war" branch, with many offshoots such as Vietnam, the Civil War, World War I, and World War II. As a result of my interest in those areas, I have begun sprouting a new reading branch, a nonfiction biology branch. As I sit down to read *The Demon in the Freezer*, for example, I do not need anyone to motivate me to read. My motivation has sprouted from my past reading experiences. The more branches I grow, the easier it will be to add new ones. All readers have their own branches— and they are varied. Lest you think that all I like to read about is gloom and doom, let me say that I also have a humor branch, a poetry branch, a fiction branch, and a teacher-book branch, among many others.

Let's return to the imaginary bookstore we visited a short time ago. Let's say you enter the store this time to buy a book as a gift for someone you care deeply about. Again, I ask the same question as before: Which section of the bookstore will you visit to pick out this gift book? My guess is that you will carefully consider the person who will be receiving this gift. What are her interests? What does she like to read? What has she particularly enjoyed reading in the past? Which book is right for her? When you ask yourself these questions before purchasing the book, you are really examining the branches of the gift recipient's reading tree. By picking something you know she'll be interested in, you are attempting to sprout off one of her branches. (Amazon.com understands the importance of prior knowledge when it comes to selling books. Whenever you call up a book on their site you also get a section that reads, "Customers who bought this book also bought . . ." In this way, Amazon appeals to its customers' reading branches.)

Growing a branch on a healthy tree is a lot easier than starting from just a seed. For example: sitting on my nightstand at home is a book given to me as a gift. It is David Michaelis's beautiful biography of the artist N. C. Wyeth, complete with reproductions of Wyeth's work. This book has been sitting on my "to read" list for three years now—the longest of any book on that list. Why has it been pushed aside for so long? Because, frankly, it scares me. I have a very limited background in art history. In school, art was a close second to auto shop in Gallagher's Hierarchy of Academic Disasters. I know not a single thing about N. C. Wyeth. The biography is long—over 500 pages in length—quite an investment of time for something I might not find interesting. My lack of background in art makes me think I should read *Art for Dummies* or something similar before I give the Wyeth book a try. Every time I consider it as my next book, other choices scream out, "Read me first! You are much more interested in (fill in the blank) than N. C. Wyeth!" The person who gave me the Wyeth book, by the way, is an accomplished watercolorist with an extensive background in art history. She assures me the book is great. It comes from one of her branches.

Am I suggesting that we never read completely unfamiliar books? Of course not. Eventually I will muster up the courage to give the Wyeth biography a go. But let's not forget that I am an experienced reader with many branches on my reading tree. What about the adolescent who sits in my third-period class and would rather go to the dentist than begin reading *Great Expectations*? That student is a king palm tree, growing tall at an alarming rate, but without developing a single reading branch. When you are branchless, all books in the English curriculum are unfamiliar. Every book to this student resembles a 500-page N. C. Wyeth obstacle.

Literary Tour Guides

Recently I visited the Sixth Floor Museum in Dallas, Texas, which is located in the Texas School Book Depository, the building where Lee Harvey Oswald shot President Kennedy. It is a somber, yet remarkable, exhibit that moves beyond the assassination to include the triumphs and shortcomings of the Kennedy presidency. There are two ways to visit the museum: you may stroll through it on your own, or you may rent headphones that allow you to listen to an audio tour as you snake your way through the artifacts. I had read quite a bit about the assassination prior to visiting the museum (another reading branch), so I did not feel a need to rent the headsets. However, my friend Bob, who went along on the visit, knew little about the assassination and the events leading to it. He decided to rent the audio tour.

Now, Bob is a bright guy. He has an advanced finance degree and runs a successful business. He is outstanding in his field and is in high demand as a consultant. But his expertise in finance was of little use to him when he stepped into the Sixth Floor Museum. It did not prepare him to understand the Kennedy exhibit on a meaningful level. For him, the headsets were a blessing. At each stop in the exhibit the historian on the audiotape would briefly explain the context for each item, often augmenting the narration with original recordings from that era. Hearing this narration provided my friend with the background information necessary to fully appreciate the historical relevance of many of the artifacts. It framed his visit in a way that raised his level of comprehension. Had he made the visit without the audio tour, he would have left with a much less sophisticated level of understanding. It was the scaffolding provided by the narration that made his museum experience much richer.

Bob's experience in the Kennedy museum reminds me of the primary reason why my school district pays my salary: to provide adolescents with expert, guided "tours" through challenging text. They do not pay me to assign books my students can handle easily on their own. After all, if my students could read and comprehend the books without assistance, why would they need me there? As difficult as it may be, my job is to be a tour guide through the complexity of great books.

Recognizing this challenge raises some interesting questions: What criteria should I consider in selecting books for my classes to read? How do I know which books are worthy of whole-class instruction? Which books by their very nature demand a literary tour guide? When considering which books to teach (and which books not to teach), Carol Jago, in *Classics in the Classroom* (2004, p. 47) suggests we choose books that:

- are written in language that is perfectly suited to the author's purpose;
- expose readers to complex human dilemmas;
- include compelling, disconcerting characters;
- explore universal themes that combine different periods and cultures;
- challenge readers to reexamine their beliefs; and
- tell a good story with places for laughing and places for crying.

Looking at this list, one realizes that it is very difficult, if not impossible, for adolescents to extract all this richness on their own. My elder daughter experienced this painful lesson recently in her ninth-grade

English class. She was assigned by her teacher to read John Steinbeck's *The Grapes of Wrath* over the summer prior to her sophomore year. The teacher did not frame the book at all; he just handed it to her and told her to have it read by September. She dutifully took it home and plowed through it; lacking knowledge about the Great Depression and of America's dust bowl, however, she found the book "boring." (This pains me to no end, as I think *The Grapes of Wrath* is a great book.) Though she is a good reader, she struggled with Steinbeck's classic. She could read the words, but the concepts they represented were too foreign to her. She knew the book was supposed to be great, but without a tour guide at her side, she had a hard time recognizing the greatness.

My daughter's frustration in trying to read *The Grapes of Wrath* raises an interesting question: Have you ever returned to a book you did not like as a youngster, but upon rereading it many years later, found it to be much better than you had recalled? (In my case, Pearl Buck's *The Good Earth* comes to mind.) When this happens, remember one thing: the book didn't change—you did. My guess is that when you read the book the second time, you had much more knowledge and experience to help you see it in a new light. A person who reads the same title at the age of fifteen, again at the age of thirty, and again at sixty will see the book differently each time. Why? Because the thirty-year-old reader brings more prior knowledge to the page than the fifteen-year-old reader, and the sixty-year-old reader brings more prior knowledge to the page than the thirty-year-old reader. In essence, a person who reads the same book at three different stages of life will have read three different books.

When we teach difficult literature and challenging nonfiction to our students, we need to work hard to frame the text for them. Remember, adolescents often bring very limited prior knowledge to the page, so we need to be the equivalent of that guided audio tour. We are the headsets—the guides who provide the context necessary for students to appreciate the greatness of the literature.

Framing the Text

As the teacher, what you do (or don't do) before your students read a major literary work will determine their level of motivation and interest. This in turn will have a direct effect on their level of comprehension.

For example, suppose you are scheduled to begin (or continue) teaching a major novel on Monday morning and are convinced that your students will need some framing to help them fully comprehend and appreciate the work. Where do you begin? What kind of strategies can you employ to help your students read better? What can you do to shore up those gaps in the prior knowledge of your students? In the remainder of this chapter you will find ten effective framing activities that I have successfully used to help students to approach challenging text. I've divided these activities into two categories: (1) framing activities to help students before they begin reading a major work; and (2) framing activities to help students after they have already started reading.

Framing Activities to Use Before Reading a Major Work

Web Searches

Before beginning major works, I often assign Web searches. Prior to a class's reading George Orwell's *1984,* for example, I give my students this assignment:

> Next week we will begin reading George Orwell's classic, *1984.* One of the central characters in the novel is named Big Brother. When I search Google for the phrase "Big Brother," over one million examples are found. Obviously, the phrase "Big Brother" has become a permanent part of our culture, and it might help us when we begin reading the novel if we understand what this phrase means and how it's used. By next Friday, please complete the following "Search for Big Brother" assignment:
>
> > Search the Internet for references to "Big Brother." You might use Google.com or Yahoo.com to assist your search.
> >
> > Find references to Big Brother in at least three different genres. You may choose from the following, or find other categories:
> > *   Books (other than *1984*)
> > *   Newspapers
> > *   Magazines
> > *   Music
> > *   Poetry
> > *   Business
> > *   Art or theater
> > *   Television or film
> > *   An organization or business
> > *   Speeches

- Essays
- Humor (jokes, cartoons)
- Letters to the editor
- Editorials
- Political cartoons

Try to find examples from different genres that seem to be addressing the idea of "Big Brother" in the same manner, theme, or idea. Try to find examples that your classmates will not find.

Print these examples and include a paragraph of your own, explaining what you think the phrase "Big Brother" means. Explain how you think this meaning cuts across the different genres you have selected. Bring the examples and your explanation to class Friday. Be prepared to discuss and share in groups.

On the due date, students get together in groups and share their Big Brother examples and their ideas on what the phrase might mean. After each small group has had time to share, a person from each group is randomly chosen to share a "big idea" with the entire class, and I write their ideas on the overhead for the whole class to see. I also take the students' Big Brother examples and turn them into a collage on the bulletin board.

This activity is an effective warm-up to the reading of *1984* because the discussion that ensues from the Web search is student-generated and always rich. It allows many of the book's themes—oppression, totalitarianism, invasion of privacy—to surface and be discussed prior to the students' reading the novel. This strategy could be adapted to fit any book that might be unfamiliar to readers. For example, students beginning Wiesel's *Night* might search "genocide"; students preparing for Hawthorne's *The Scarlet Letter* might search "witch trials."

Anticipation Guides

Anticipation guides, developed by J. E. Readence, T. W. Bean, and R. S. Baldwin (1985), can be used to frame the major ideas and themes that students will find in the book they are about to begin. These guides help them understand that as long as books have been written, literature has expressed universal truths about the human condition. In reading *Romeo and Juliet,* for example, students will discover that many of the issues in this four-hundred-year-old play are still relevant to them today.

Before having them open to Act I of *Romeo and Juliet,* I often ask students to consider the issues they are about to encounter in their reading.

Anticipation Guide for *Romeo and Juliet*		
Before Reading		After Reading
1-2-3-4-5-6-7-8-9-10	Violence can solve problems.	1-2-3-4-5-6-7-8-9-10
1-2-3-4-5-6-7-8-9-10	Long-term neighborhood feuds can be solved peacefully.	1-2-3-4-5-6-7-8-9-10
1-2-3-4-5-6-7-8-9-10	Teenage love is real love.	1-2-3-4-5-6-7-8-9-10
1-2-3-4-5-6-7-8-9-10	There are times when secrets must be told.	1-2-3-4-5-6-7-8-9-10
1-2-3-4-5-6-7-8-9-10	Love at first sight is possible.	1-2-3-4-5-6-7-8-9-10
1-2-3-4-5-6-7-8-9-10	"Luck" is a figment of someone's imagination; there is no such thing as luck.	1-2-3-4-5-6-7-8-9-10
1-2-3-4-5-6-7-8-9-10	Your parents should have the final say in whom you date.	1-2-3-4-5-6-7-8-9-10
1-2-3-4-5-6-7-8-9-10	You are the pilot of your own life. There is no greater force determining your outcome. You determine your own outcome.	1-2-3-4-5-6-7-8-9-10
1-2-3-4-5-6-7-8-9-10	Suicide is never a reasonable option.	1-2-3-4-5-6-7-8-9-10

1	2	3	4	5	6	7	8	9	10
strongly disagree			somewhat disagree			somewhat agree			strongly agree

Figure 3.1

I express these issues in provocative statements and ask students to what degree they agree or disagree with them. Figure 3.1 presents an anticipation guide for *Romeo and Juliet,* the left-hand side of which students complete before reading the play.

After recording their opinions on the various statements, students use the items on the anticipation guide as starting points for discussion (and often writing and debate). These discussions get them thinking about the big ideas they will soon discover in the play. Upon completing the reading, the students revisit the anticipation guide and complete the right-hand side. Sometimes reading the work solidifies beliefs they already had, but often they find that significant shifts in their thinking have occurred as a result of their reading the work. Students complete the unit by choosing one statement from the anticipation guide that speaks especially to them—a "hot spot," one might say—and use this statement as the basis of an essay.

Theme Spotlights

While anticipation guides prompt students to think about many of the ideas they will encounter in a text, the theme spotlight assignment focuses students' attention to one major theme to be studied. Figure 3.2 is an example of a theme spotlight for *Dr. Jekyll and Mr. Hyde,* though this strategy can be easily adapted to any major work.

By inspiring rich discussion and passionate writing, theme spotlights help prepare students to consider the big ideas in the work they will read. They may also suggest further activities. For example, students who complete the *Dr. Jekyll and Mr. Hyde* theme spotlight might then chart the degrees of evil found in the book.

Focus Poems

One way to prepare students for a major literary work is to let them read thematically related poetry beforehand. From these poems, students are asked to make inferences about the major work they are about to read.

Figure 3.2

Theme Spotlight for *Dr. Jekyll and Mr. Hyde*

While reading *Dr. Jekyll and Mr. Hyde,* we will be examining the nature of evil. One of the ideas presented in the novel is that there are varying degrees of evil. Do you agree?

Below you will find twelve examples of evil, all taken from actual events. Please rank them in order from 1 to 12, with 1 the most evil and 12 being the least evil.

Degrees of Evil

_____ A con artist swindles elderly people out of their life savings.

_____ A racist police officer shoots a suspect and then frames him.

_____ An inmate in a concentration camp becomes an assistant to his captors, helping them beat prisoners to make them work harder.

_____ An unmarried woman continues to use crack cocaine during her pregnancy even after learning it could cause birth defects in her unborn child.

_____ A doctor assists terminally ill patients to commit suicide.

_____ Two boys open fire in a high school, killing several and wounding many others.

_____ A tobacco industry executive lies to a congressional committee about the addictive qualities of smoking even after his research shows thousands of people each year will die from smoking addiction.

_____ An attorney vigorously defends a client against a murder charge even when it's clear that his client is guilty.

_____ Two white men tie a black man to the back of a pickup truck and drag him to his death.

_____ A disgruntled man bombs a federal building, causing the deaths of hundreds of unsuspecting people.

_____ A scientist develops a biological weapon that could kill thousands.

_____ A man hijacks an airplane and flies it into the Pentagon, killing everyone on the plane and many military and civilian personnel on the ground.

Focus Poem for *All Quiet on the Western Front*

Dulce et Decorum Est
Wilfred Owen

Bent double, like old beggars under sacks,
Knocked-kneed, coughing like hags, we cursed through sludge,
Till on the haunting flares we turned our backs
And towards our distant rest began to trudge.
Men marched asleep. Many had lost their boots
But limped on, blood-shod. All went lame: all blind;
Drunk with fatigue; deaf even to the hoots
Of tired, outstripped Five-Nines[1] that dropped behind.

Gas! GAS! Quick, boys!—An ecstasy of fumbling,
Fitting the clumsy helmets just in time;
But someone still was yelling out and stumbling
And flound'ring like a man in fire or lime . . .
Dim, through the misty panes and thick green light,
As under a green sea, I saw him drowning.
In all my dreams, before my helpless sight,
He plunges at me, guttering, choking, drowning.

If in some smothering dreams you too could pace
Behind the wagon that we flung him in,
And watch the white eyes writhing in his face,
His hanging face, like a devil's sick of sin;
If you could hear, at every jolt, the blood
Come gargling from the froth-corrupted lungs,
Obscene as cancer, bitter as the cud
Of vile, incurable sores on innocent tongues,—
My friend, you would not tell with such high zest
To children ardent for some desperate glory,
The old Lie: Dulce et decorum est
Pro patria Mori.[2]

1. *Five-Nines:* Shells containing poison gas
2. *Dulce . . . Mori:* It is sweet and honorable to die for your country

WWI Inferences

- Men were pushed beyond exhaustion.
- Morale was low.
- They were ill-equipped.

- Gas warfare was used.
- Men were gassed.
- Men "drowned" on land.

- Chemical weapons produce horrifying deaths.

Figure 3.3

For example, in preparing to teach *All Quiet on the Western Front*, it may become readily apparent that students know very little about World War I. This lack of knowledge can make it difficult for them to get into the novel. To help bridge this knowledge gap before they begin to read, students are given packets of poetry written during or about the war. They are asked to read all the poems more than once and to begin generating a list of things they can infer about World War I simply from reading the poetry. In Figure 3.3, for example, students were able to gain insight about World War I from reading Wilfred Owen's "Dulce et Decorum Est." In addition to "Dulce et Decorum Est," other Owen poems that are excellent to help students understand World War I include:

"Miners"
"Greater Love"
"Apologia Pro Poemate Meo"
"Futility"
"Sonnet"

The World War I poems of Siegfried Sassoon and Isaac Rosenberg are also excellent. Among my favorites of Siegfried Sassoon's poems are:

"They"
"The Rear Guard"
"The General"
"Glory of Women"
"Everyone Sang"
"One Passing the New Menin Gate"

Isaac Rosenberg's poems include:

"Returning, We Hear the Larks"
"Break of Day in the Trenches"
"December 30th"
"Louse Hunting"
"Dead Man's Dump"

These poems and others can be found by simply searching "World War I poetry" on Google or any other search engine.

K-W-L-R Charts

Before beginning a major work that may be foreign to students, it is often beneficial to have them begin a K-W-L-R chart (adapted from Ogle 1986), which activates and builds on their prior knowledge. Before reading, begin by having students identify what they know ("K") about the topic. For example, in teaching John Hersey's nonfictional work *Hiroshima*, I begin by writing the word "Hiroshima" on the board and asking the students what they know about it. I note their responses in the "K" column of the K-W-L-R chart (see Figure 3.4). I write down everything the students brainstorm, even if what they "know" is incorrect (note that one student thought that Hiroshima is in China). If students challenge the incorrect knowledge, I put their challenge in the "K" column as well. I am

K-W-L-R Chart for John Hersey's *Hiroshima*			
K	*W*	*L*	*R*
The U.S. dropped a nuclear bomb there.	How many died?		
	How many survived?		
Or was it an atom bomb?	How did the survivors cope?		
It was dropped from a plane.	Why did we drop the bomb?		
Lots of people died.	Who dropped it?		
Some survived.	How was it dropped?		
It's a city in China.	Where did we drop others?		
China? Wasn't it Japan?			
It was during WWII.	Did it end the war?		
	How does the bomb work?		
	Who made the decision to drop the bomb?		
	Did the enemy have nuclear weapons too?		
	How have nuclear weapons changed since WWII?		
	Who possesses them now?		

Figure 3.4

a recorder, and I try not to interfere with my students' brainstorming because I want to gauge what they know and what they don't know before we begin reading the book.

After we list everything the students know about the topic, I have students brainstorm what they want ("W") to know by the time we finish reading Hersey's book. From our initial "K" brainstorm, what new questions have popped into their minds? Where are their knowledge gaps? We list these in the "W" column (again, see Figure 3.4).

As they read the book over the next two weeks, students search in the text for the answers to their questions. They begin charting this in the "L" column (indicating what they have learned while reading). Upon completing the book, we look to see which questions remained unanswered. For example, students asked, "How does the bomb work?" This question, not addressed in the book, remains unanswered. We also brainstorm new questions that arise from the reading. These unanswered questions, both from the initial "W" stage and from the questions generated after reading the book, become the basis for post-reading research ("R"). The questions are assigned to groups of students, and the students are given one week to find the answers. The following week each group gives a five-minute presentation to the rest of the class answering their assigned research question. These are questions students are interested in finding answers to because they are the ones who generated the questions. The assignments grew organically from their curiosity generated from the reading and honor both what they know and what they want to know.

Web searches, anticipation guides, theme spotlights, focus poems, and K-W-L-R charts are all excellent tools to raise students' knowledge before they tackle unfamiliar text. Here are some additional ideas for preparing students:

- Read a related story or article as a warm-up.
- Role-play some of the issues to be found in the reading.
- Share a current event that touches on the same central idea.
- Create an art experience to help students begin thinking in the direction of the text to be read.
- Show a clip from a related film, video, or DVD.
- Bring an authentic artifact to class.
- Use guided imagery exercises to help students visualize.
- Listen to music relevant to the text.
- Play or read relevant speeches.
- Line up guest speakers who have related experiences.

Framing Activities to Use While Reading a Major Work

Suppose that, thanks to your scaffolding, your students are ready and eager to read *Hamlet*; they have agreed to start a journey through Shakespeare's masterpiece with you. You open the book to Act 1, Scene 1, and because you have already taught a number of introductory lessons to help frame the play, the initial class reading goes well. Now you are faced with a different challenge: once the work as a whole has been adequately framed, you must now consider framing each day's lesson *within* the unit. When students in my third-period class walk out of my room after reading a bit of *Hamlet,* they do not immediately go home, hunker down in the fetal position, and concentrate intensely so as not to lose their train of thought until we resume our discussion the next day. Quite the contrary: when they come into class the next day it's sometimes seems as though we have never even started the play. Teenagers have a tendency to dwell on other things during the twenty-three hours between classes. As a result, I can say from experience that the following directions are a recipe for disaster: "Yesterday we read Act 1, Scene 1. Open up your books and let's start Scene 2."

Instead, I have found it useful to invest a couple of minutes to refocus my students before they resume reading. Here are some strategies to help students refocus on a daily basis while they are midstream in a literary work.

Daily Focus Questions

When students walk into my class they find a daily focus question on the board. The purpose of this question is to get students' heads back to where they were when we left off the day before. While I take roll, they respond to the focus question. There are two types of focus questions:

1. *Text-dependent questions* may ask students to revisit yesterday's (or last night's) reading. I call these "text dependent" questions because they require the students to have read the text before they can answer the question; in other words, their ability to answer is dependent on their reading and comprehending the text. Here are some examples of text-dependent questions I might use during the reading of *Hamlet:*
   - What aspects of Scene 1 establish that something is wrong (rotten) in Denmark?
   - What does Hamlet's first soliloquy tell us about him?
   - Explain the significance of the following passage: "The play's the thing/Wherein I'll catch the conscience of the King."

   Students who have not read the text or participated in class will be unable to answer these questions. Many of these questions are culled from the previous day's reading; often they have been discussed thoroughly in class. My goal is not to catch students in a mistake, but rather to have them spend a moment answering a question that will bring them back to where we left off the day before. These questions can also serve as reading checks if the reading was assigned for homework.

2. *Text-independent questions* may ask students to consider a big idea that will help them "set the table" for what will be found in the reading they'll do in class that day. These questions are not specifically from the previous day's reading; instead, they serve to prepare students for some of the big ideas and themes they are soon to encounter. While reading *All Quiet on the Western Front,* for example, students might be asked some of the following questions before key chapters:
   - Where is God during wartime?
   - Who profits from war?
   - If the president asks you to go to war, would you go with no questions asked?

   These questions prepare students for the themes they will find in passages they are about to read. They serve to "prime the pump" before reading commences.

The Word Game

Rather than ask a question, one way to focus students is simply to write a single word on the board and have them explain the significance of that word to the chapter they read the day (or night) before. For example, if they read Chapter 1 of *Animal Farm* the previous night, they might find the word "song" on the board when they arrive in class. They would be asked to write a paragraph explaining the significance of this word in Chapter 1. Students who had read the chapter would be able to discuss Old Major leading the barnyard animals in a chorus of "Beasts of England," a song written to stir up unrest in the animals.

What's nice about this word game is that not only does it serve as a reading check, it also warms up the students. It's also easy to change the word every couple of periods to keep students honest.

Interrupted Summary

Before beginning the day's reading, I often generate an oral summary of the chapter we read the day before. One way to do this is to conduct what

I call an interrupted summary. Choose a student at random and give that student a starter sentence. For example, if today we are to read Chapter 3 of *Lord of the Flies,* I might choose Matthew to lead off the class discussion by feeding him the following line: "Matthew, today we are going to read Chapter 3 of *Lord of the Flies.* Before we begin, let's review Chapter 2. As you recall, Chapter 2 starts with Ralph calling a meeting to order by blowing the conch. What happened next?"

Matthew stands up and begins summarizing the previous day's chapter. When he completes a sentence or two, I interrupt him by calling out another student's name. That student then picks up where Matthew left off and continues the oral summary. Everyone in the class pays close attention because they do not know when the next interruption will occur or who will be called on to continue the summary.

As we get deeper into *Lord of the Flies,* we may alter the interrupted summary activity. I might ask a student to stand and tell me everything he or she knows thus far about a character—for example, Simon. After a moment, I'll interrupt by choosing another student who must add additional details, while being careful not to repeat earlier information. Or I'll start with the student whose desk is closest to me and snake around the room. Students who cannot add information may say "Pass" and sit down. The process continues until there is one Simon expert standing (or until enough discussion has been generated to move on to the next chapter). Instead of identifying character traits, this game can be played by asking students to discuss symbolism, foreshadowing, theme, as well as other literary elements.

One Question and One Comment

Here is an excellent strategy to get students to revisit a chapter or passage that they find particularly challenging. Students are asked to come to class with one question and one comment generated from their reading assignment. They can meet in small groups to share what they have come up with, but I prefer this as a whole-class activity. During the class discussion, every student is required to share at least one question or one comment about the reading. I begin with a random row or table of students and ask the first person to tell us his or her question or comment. The next person can answer the question, respond to the comment, or branch out with his or her own question or comment. This activity never fails to generate an in-depth discussion about the reading assignment and helps those who have struggled with the text to gain meaning they would have otherwise been unable to attain. Even excellent readers learn something new during this conversation.

Word Scramble Prediction

Before we read a climactic chapter, I want students to predict what might happen. To help them a bit (and to pique their curiosity), I give them a list of words they will find in the chapter they will read. For example, prior to reading Chapter 28 of *To Kill a Mockingbird,* I'll provide the following list of words to the students:

dark   afraid   kitchen knife   "Run!"   useless   kicking
dying   trembled   reeling   jerk backwards   dead

Students read the word scramble and are given five minutes to write a prediction of what will happen in the chapter. Students then volunteer to read their predictions out loud, and after we have heard a number of them, I say, "Let's see whose prediction is closest. Open to Chapter 28 and let's read." This activity never fails to make students focus intensely as they read.

The Perils of Assumicide

All of the activities I've just described are designed to help teachers from suffering from "assumicide"—the death of a book that occurs when it is assumed that students possess enough prior knowledge, connections, and motivation to make higher-level reading possible.

Have you ever had the following happen to you? A student complains over and over that the book the class is reading is boring; then suddenly, when they are finished, he or she says something like, "You know, that book really wasn't that bad." My theory as to why this happens is that the student didn't have the requisite background to appreciate the book at first. The book was too foreign, too distant. But as the student gradually got used to the world of the book, he or she was able to establish meaningful connections. These connections, which often kick in when the student is near the end of the book, allow him or her to begin to appreciate the work.

Students come to books with various gaps in their knowledge—about the topic, the setting, the time frame, or the vocabulary found in the text. If these gaps are too wide, the chances that they will have a rich and positive experience with that text are diminished. As teachers, we have to shake off any remnants of assumicide by planning framing lessons to address these gaps *before* our students attempt the challenging reading. In doing so we give our students a better chance to appreciate the great works of literature and nonfiction.

Framing a chapter or book, however, is just the beginning. In Chapter 4 we consider effective strategies to help students with the actual reading of challenging works.

CHAPTER FOUR

Effective First-Draft Reading

In *Keeping a Head in School: A Student's Book About Learning Abilities and Learning Disorders,* Mel Levine discusses the different attention channels we have in our brains and how it's necessary when attempting a difficult task to make sure we are "tuned" to the right attention channel. I found this particularly true one morning last week as I drove to school.

Getting into my car, I knew that a particularly troublesome day was looming: a parent was going to meet with me before school started to discuss her child's unhappiness with a report card grade, my principal wanted to meet with me during my planning period to discuss a "budget concern," a visitor was coming into my classroom to observe a lesson, and I was woefully behind in grading the stack of essays on my desk—a stack that seemed to be growing faster than the push for a California gubernatorial recall. In addition to this I was about to spend the day with 175 adolescents.

Preoccupied with the day's hurdles, I hurriedly pulled into the faculty parking lot. As I turned off my ignition, I suddenly thought with a jolt: How in the heck did I get here? I knew I had driven the 15.3 miles to work, and had in fact driven three freeways to get there. But I had no specific memory of actually driving to work. My mind was so preoccupied with the upcoming day's events that I remembered little more than getting into my car at home and—what seemed like the next moment—getting out of my car in a different city. How I arrived safely was a mystery to me, for I had no memory of turning, stopping, accelerating, or negotiating traffic. I had driven on autopilot; and although I am reasonably sure I obeyed most traffic laws, I wouldn't swear to it. Preoccupied with what was in store for me that day, my mind was set on its "upcoming day at school" channel instead of its "driving" channel, where it should have been.

Sometimes my reading resembles my drive to work that morning; I am so preoccupied that I do not focus on the task at hand. Have you ever read a page in a book or a magazine and, as you neared the end of the page, stopped and thought to yourself, "What the heck did I just read?" More than likely, when this happens your mind was not set on its "reading" channel. Though you were reading the page, you may have been thinking about filing your taxes, taking your car to the mechanic, or finding time to get to the gym. When I finished my drive to work that morning I couldn't tell you a thing about it, though I did make the drive. Sometimes when I finish reading a page, I can't tell you a thing about it either, though I know I read the page.

The fact that this happens to every good reader I know illustrates an important point: coming to text in the right frame of mind is not a reading issue; it's a *concentration* issue. Even good readers experience comprehension problems when they are not properly focused on the reading task at hand. Regardless of reading ability, your understanding of the text is directly affected by your frame of mind when you sit down to read. Even proficient readers will not comprehend their reading if their minds are not tuned to the reading task at hand. Before thinking about how to help students read challenging text, we must first make sure they are in the right frame of mind before they begin to read. How do we do this? By letting students know that it is normal for all readers to be occasionally "off channel" while reading. Being "off channel" is not the problem; the question is what good readers do when their reading minds are "off channel." To help my students prepare for a challenging text, I suggest that they ask themselves three questions:

1. Have I chosen a place to read that will enable me to give my full concentration to the reading task at hand?
2. Have I set aside enough time to give this reading the attention it deserves?
3. Have I cleared my mind of other issues and turned to the "reading" channel of my brain?

Once students are in the correct frame of mind to read, there are things we can do to help them make sense of difficult text. Before I ask students to read challenging or unfamiliar material, I ask myself: Have I adequately framed the text to help shore up my students' lack of prior knowledge and experience (as discussed in Chapter 3)? In short, are they ready to go?

First-Draft Reading

When students read Toni Morrison's *Beloved* for the first time, it is unrealistic to expect them to "get it" immediately. The novel is simply too complex for them to grasp on an initial reading. Before starting a novel of this complexity, I try to lower students' anxiety by telling them that the initial reading is a "first-draft" reading. I share with them an Anne Lamott passage from *Bird by Bird,* where she discusses the trouble professional writers have in writing first drafts:

> Almost all good writing begins with terrible first efforts. You need to start somewhere. Start by getting something—anything—down on paper. A friend of mine says that the first draft is the down draft—you just get it down. The second draft is the up draft—you fix it up. You try to say what you have to say more accurately. And the third draft is the dental draft, where you check every tooth to see if it's loose or cramped, or decayed, or even, God help us, healthy." (p. 25)

What Lamott writes about the difficulties of the early stages of writing applies equally to the early stages of reading. When my students read a difficult work for the first time, this is the "down" reading draft. My hope is that they get the basics down—familiarizing themselves with the characters, recognizing significant plot points, getting used to the language and structure of the novel. Once students have achieved a basic understanding of the text, they are ready to undertake a second, deeper reading—the "up" draft. In a way, it's like getting used to the cool water in a swimming pool before beginning a rigorous workout. Before the real swimming begins, students first need to become acclimated to the water.

Assuming I have done an adequate job framing the text, and assuming my students have prepared themselves to read by tuning their minds to the correct "reading" channel, what can I do to help make their first-draft reading as meaningful as possible? As my students embark on any new literary work, I consider four key questions:

1. Have I provided my students with a reading focus?
2. Are my students willing and able to embrace confusion?
3. Can my students monitor their own comprehension?
4. Do my students know any fix-it strategies to assist them when their comprehension begins to falter?

Let's take a closer look at each of these questions.

Question 1: Have I Provided My Students with a Reading Focus?

Each of us has our own private hell. Here's mine: It was three days before Christmas last year and I still needed to buy a gift for my wife. I had not a clue as to what to get her. I thought to myself, "No problem. I'll just jump into my car and drive to the local mall." I figured I'd just walk around the mall, browse a bit, and keep moving until the ideal gift grabbed me.

Three hours later, after what seemed like seven hundred miles of walking, I was still looking for that gift. I had slowly and painfully come to the realization that weaving aimlessly through the mall may not have been the best shopping strategy. The perfect gift never emerged. In fact, the opposite occurred: everything started to look the same. By the end of the afternoon I was more confused than when I had entered the mall. A sense of hopelessness began setting in, prompting thoughts of the ultimate bailout—buying a gift certificate. Because I value my marriage, I forced myself to reject that idea and trudged onward in search of the right gift.

If ever I become a contestant on *Fear Factor* and am given a choice between drinking a blended worm concoction or spending three hours in a mall during the holiday season, you, dear reader, now know which one I'd choose. However, as dreadful as that experience was, it taught me a valuable lesson in shopping strategy. To increase my shopping success and lower my frustration level, I have learned to plan *before* leaving the house. Having an idea of what I am looking for before I venture to the mall will shorten my shopping time and reduce frustration.

This lesson came in handy recently when my wife's birthday rolled around. Prior to running off to the mall, I carefully considered what gift she might desire. Before getting in my car, I conducted exhaustive research on possible gift ideas ("exhaustive research" being a euphemism for asking my daughters, "What do you think your mom would like for her birthday?"). After considering the possibilities, I came to the conclusion that my wife would like a new leather winter coat for her birthday.

This time, my shopping experience was much more pleasant than my Christmas disaster. Rather than walking through the vast acreage of the mall, I drove straight to her favorite clothing store. I parked near the entrance and entered the store. I was on a mission. I knew my purpose for being there and I was focused on the task at hand—so much so that I did something completely out of character: I asked a salesperson for help. She politely walked me directly to the section of the store that had leather coats and answered a few of my questions. Fifteen minutes later, I was on my way home with gift in hand. No fuss, no muss.

My shopping experiences remind me of my students and the approaches they take in reading difficult text. The first shopping trip (when I was wandering aimlessly before Christmas, hoping a gift would find me) is analogous to how poor readers approach an unfamiliar book. They begin by wandering through the text without purpose. They do not have a particular "store" in mind and aimlessly "walk around" the book, hoping the meaning will find them. When that doesn't happen, a sense of hopelessness sets in, and they begin wishing they were doing anything other than trying to make sense of this text.

I want my students to have a game plan when they begin reading a major work. I have learned that students have a much easier time with comprehension if they approach the text with a specific purpose in mind. To borrow from the shopping analogy once again, I want students to know which store they are looking for before they start reading. I do not want them wandering aimlessly through the text; rather, I want them to have a focus before they begin to read. I find that providing a focus point lowers students' anxiety, assists their comprehension, and gives them confidence to approach a work they might otherwise shun.

How do I provide such a focus? How do I help my students establish a purpose for their reading? Much depends on the level of the text and the abilities and attitudes of my students, but I have found that the following six activities can be used with a variety of texts to help students make the most of their first-draft reading.

Text Frames with Gaps

Here's an activity that provides a framework for students but that also requires their input. Students are given outlines of the upcoming chapter, but the outline has some gaps in it. For example, if students were reading

Act 1, Scene 1, of *Romeo and Juliet,* they might be given the following text frame:

Romeo and Juliet—Act 1, Scene 1
- Sampson and Gregory, two of Capulet's servants, fight with Abram and Baltazar, who are servants from the rival house of Montague.
- Tybalt, a quick-tempered Capulet, enters the fight.
-
- The Prince enters and, enraged, stops the fight.
- The Montagues express concern about their son, Romeo.
- Romeo confesses to Benvolio that he is in love with a girl who is indifferent to him.

When students begin reading Shakespeare for the first time, the unfamiliarity of the language makes it a challenging task. To help them gain their footing, I provide them with a nearly completed outline of what they will encounter in the day's reading. Notice that for Act 1, Scene 1, most of the summary is provided for them—only the third point is missing. This allows students to immediately comprehend the play, but requires them to pay close attention, because they have to figure out what belongs as the third point. In this example, the missing bullet might be written as follows:

- Benvolio, a Montague, tries to stop the fight but gets drawn into it.

As the students become more familiar and confident with the play, I provide fewer bulleted details, requiring them to provide additional key plot points. For example, my text frame for Act 3, Scene 1, might look like this:

Romeo and Juliet—Act 3, Scene 1
-
- Tybalt and other rivals arrive. Tybalt wants to find Romeo.
- Romeo arrives. Tybalt calls him a "villain."
- The Prince enters and, enraged, stops the fight.
- Romeo says he now "loves" Tybalt.
-
-
-

By Act 5, students have become much more proficient at reading Shakespeare, so at this stage I ask them to provide all of the bulleted statements.

Using Text Frames with Gaps is an excellent way both to help students focus as they read hard text and assist them in establishing surface-level understanding. True, this activity has a bit of a worksheet feel to it, but sometimes activities like this are necessary to help students begin to make sense of challenging first-draft reading. As they grow more comfortable with the text, the scaffolding is slowly withdrawn. Text Frames with Gaps helps students get acclimated to the text and, in doing so, serves as a stepping-stone to deeper reading.

This activity is not limited to novels and plays; it can be used with virtually any type of reading, including magazines, newspapers, and textbooks. For example, a Text Frame for a chapter in a social studies textbook on the events leading to America's involvement in World War II might look like this:

Chapter 2: The War Begins
- German troops occupy Paris.
- France surrenders.
- Hitler begins an all-out attack on Britain.
- America considers its options.
- The Japanese attack Pearl Harbor.
- The U.S. declares war.

To provide focus, the history teacher could remove specific bulleted items and have the students fill them in as the class reads that particular section of the textbook.

Turn Headings or Titles into Questions Prior to Reading

One way to encourage students to develop their own purpose for reading is to have them create questions based on the chapter title or heading. In the World War II example just given, students might find the following heading in their text: "Minorities in Uniform." This heading might prompt them to write some questions:

- Were the armed forces segregated?
- How many minorities served?
- Were minorities disproportionately represented?
- Which minority groups participated? In what numbers?

Students then read the passage with a purpose, hoping to find the answers to their questions.

This activity is also effective to use with chapter titles in novels. For example, Chapter 9 of *Lord of the Flies* is titled "A View to a Death." Before reading this chapter, my students and I engaged in a whole-class brain-storm and came up with the following questions:

- Will someone die in this chapter?
- If so, who is most likely to die? Why?
- What clues can you identify to support your prediction?
- How will this person die? Will it be an accident or a murder? Is there foreshadowing?
- Whose death would have the most damaging impact on the boys on the island?
- How will the death change the course of the story?

Some questions may remain unanswered even after the students complete their reading. That's O.K. What's important is that by creating these questions, students have generated a focus for their reading. After brainstorming questions, students are then motivated to search for the answers, and so will be much more likely to pay close attention as they read.

Twenty Questions

The first chapter of a book is usually the most confusing for students, and it's the place where an immature reader is most likely to lose focus. To promote the idea that good readers consciously work through early confusion, I ask students to generate Twenty Questions after reading Chapter 1 of any text. Here are the questions that William, age seventeen, wrote after reading the first few pages of *1984*.

1. How can clocks strike thirteen?
2. What are "Victory Mansions"?
3. What is "Hate Week"?
4. Who is Big Brother?
5. What is a telescreen?
6. Who belongs to the "Party"?
7. Why do party members wear uniforms?
8. What does "INGSOC" mean?
9. What is the Ninth Three-Year Plan?
10. Who are the "Thought Police"? Why are they called this?
11. Which countries are found in Oceania?
12. What is Airstrip One?
13. What do the following slogans mean?
    - War Is Peace.
    - Freedom Is Slavery.
    - Ignorance Is Strength.
14. What is the Ministry of Truth?

15. What is the Ministry of Peace?
16. What is the Ministry of Plenty?
17. What is the Ministry of Love?
18. Why are products like gin and cigarettes called "Victory Gin" and "Victory Cigarettes"?
19. How could it be that "nothing is illegal"?
20. What is the "Two Minutes Hate"? What function does it serve?

That's an awful lot of confusion after having read only the first few pages. George Orwell's *1984* is ideal for this assignment because the author is intentionally trying to disorient the reader. However, Twenty Questions works with any book where the first chapter is particularly confusing to students. Having them generate questions early on teaches adolescents to read closely and helps them focus as they read the rest of the book. Before they are finished with the novel, their early questions should be answered. By the time he reaches the end of *1984,* for example, William's early confusion will have dissipated, and he should be able to answer most, if not all, of his initial questions. Twenty Questions nicely reinforces some important ideas: that confusion is natural when one reads complex text, that competent readers are not deterred by initial confusion, and that hanging in there when the early part of the book is tough is what good readers do.

Focus Groups

Often when students are reading a major work, I will place them in groups and provide each group with a specific focus. For example, I may have each group focus on and chart a specific literary element as they progress through the work. Here are focus groups I set up for Rudolfo Anaya's *Bless Me, Ultima:*

Group	Focus
Group 1	Focus on how setting (time and place) is used to develop emotional effect.
Group 2	Chart any evidence of the author's use of foreshadowing/hints. How does this foreshadowing add to the overall effect of the novel?
Group 3	Track how the author uses language (description, imagery, metaphor, irony, humor) to make the story richer.
Group 4	Identify the major and minor conflicts in the story. Pay attention to how the author develops these conflicts.
Group 5	Identify the major and minor themes found in the novel. Pay attention to how the author develops these themes.
Group 6	Identify the major and minor symbols found in the novel. Pay attention to how the author develops these symbols.
Group 7	Chart the dream sequences in the novel. Pay attention to how the author uses these dreams to develop the themes of the novel.

Each group is responsible for charting its assigned focus area, which helps them focus as they read. Periodically, they share their findings with the entire class; everyone takes notes from the groups' presentations.

Focus groups can also be used to track features other than literary elements. For example, my focus groups for reading *Hiroshima,* John Hersey's nonfictional account of the dropping of the atomic bomb, might be as follows:

Group	Focus
Group 1	Miss Toshinki Sasaki
Group 2	Dr. Masakazu Fujii
Group 3	Mrs. Hatsuyo Nakamurs
Group 4	Father Wilhelm Kleinsorge
Group 5	Dr. Terufumi Sasaki
Group 6	Reverend Kiyoshi Tanimoto

Each group tracks and keeps notes on one of the six survivors. If students are reading fiction, they can track specific characters; if reading a history or science book, they can track actual people or events.

Character Charts

When students are reading a work with many characters, the use of Character Charts helps them keep the characters straight. Figure 4.1, for example, is a character chart made by Michael, a ninth-grade student, as he read Barbara Kingsolver's *The Bean Trees.* Students fill out the grid as they progress through the work. When completed, the chart can also be used as a graphic organizer to help students prepare for writing an essay on the work. Sometimes I even use a character chart as an exam.

Shift Charts

Another way to provide focus for students is to have them center their attention on characters in the book who undergo significant change. Using a Shift Chart, shown in Figure 4.2, students write adjectives describing the character early in the novel, providing passages from the text (with page numbers) as evidence. After the character has undergone change, they choose different adjectives to describe the character after the change. In the center of the chart, they note what caused the change to the character.

Figure 4.1

Character Chart for *The Bean Trees*

Character	Taylor	Turtle	Lou Ann	Estevan	Esperanza
Relationship of the character	Main Character "Mother" of Turtle	"child" of Taylor	Roommate and Friend of Taylor	Lives with Mattie Husband of Esparanza	Lives with Mattie Wife of Estevan
Strength of the character	Tough and Doesn't let anyone push her around Does what she thinks is right	She keeps on going	compassionate	Coping with loss of daughter	Taking care of Turtle
Weakness of the character	Sometimes Gives up	Self-defense	Shy and doesn't stand up for herself	He gives Taylor the wrong impression	Missing Ismene
Defining moment for the character	Deciding to fight for Turtle	When she buried her doll in the dirt	Deciding not to go back to Angel	kissing Taylor at the church	Trying to commit suicide
Essential question for the character	How will you protect Turtle?	who molested you?	Why do you have low self-confidence?	Will you ever consider dating Taylor?	Would you like to have another baby?
Symbol for the character			Rules		5 4 3 2 1 Bomb!

These activities—using text frames, turning titles into questions, generating questions, setting up focus groups, and employing Character Charts and Shift Charts—provide students with a focus as they read. It gives them something to hold on to as they venture into first-draft reading. To return to the shopping metaphor, if the students know the specific store they are going to in order to begin their shopping, then the vastness of the entire mall does not seem as overwhelming.

Figure 4.2

Shift Chart

Character _____

Early Traits _____ Later Traits _____

		What Caused the Shift?		

Question 2: Are My Students Willing and Able to Embrace Confusion?

When my reluctant adolescent readers are confronted with a difficult reading assignment, their "strategy" is simply to give up! They complain that the reading is too hard or too confusing, and that they don't understand what is going on in the story. They are experts at surrender, with hopes that their teacher will bail them out. They have assumed a learned helplessness.

Unfortunately, students often see reading as an all-or-nothing proposition—they think that readers either get it immediately or they don't. We have hoodwinked them into believing that we, as teachers and adults, are trouble-free readers, capable of reading any difficult book at a single glance, comprehending it at a level that would make Harold Bloom proud. We know, of course, that this isn't the case. Often, before we step foot into our classroom with the intention of teaching a challenging book, we have done extensive homework. How many times, for example, do we turn to the notes provided in the special teacher's edition of the text? How often do we review our scribbled marginalia from last year's experience? How many of us have done background reading of literary analysis or read other ancillary support material before starting a new book with our students? And yet, unfairly, we often expect our students to "get" the text almost instantly! And we are advanced readers to begin with; most of our students are not.

My students do not realize that their teachers often struggle immensely with text. They do not see that when I am confronted with extremely difficult reading, I employ a number of strategies to help me through the hard parts. They do not see this because I have become expert at hiding this struggle from them. This, I have come to believe, is a disservice to my students. Rather than hiding my reading difficulties from them, I should make these struggles visible so they can see that reading can be hard for adult readers as well. They must come to realize that all readers become confused when they are reading in unfamiliar territory. For example, I am resigned to that fact that I will always struggle with Joseph Conrad's *Heart of Darkness*, which seems to have literary allusions hidden in every line. This, despite the fact I have read it three times. I understand the novel, in a way, but I also know I don't *really* understand the novel. *Heart of Darkness* is hard for me.

My first task as my students begin reading, therefore, is to get them to understand that confusion is natural, even necessary, when we read something challenging. Sheridan Blau, in his excellent book *The Literature Workshop*, says that the only things worth reading in an academic class are those things we do not understand. Blau argues that recognizing when we are confused is actually a sign of increased comprehension and that as readers we should welcome and embrace confusion. Learning begins when we encounter confusion.

Students do not understand this concept. They think that they are supposed to sit down and read *Great Expectations* once and understand it. They are dismayed when they become confused, and they often see their inability to immediately work through the hard parts as a reason to give up. They shy away when the reading turns hard. My task, beginning the first day of school, is to begin breaking this attitude down. My students need to expect confusion as they begin reading, and they need to recognize that this confusion is natural and necessary. I am not concerned that they will encounter confusion; I am concerned, however, about what they will do when they encounter the confusion.

Question 3: Can My Students Monitor Their Own Comprehension?

I recently had this dialogue with a student:

Michael: I tried to read the homework last night, but I didn't understand it.

Me: Which part of the reading did you not understand?

Michael: All of it.

Sound familiar? If I had a dollar for every time I've had this conversation, I'd be able to afford Fleetwood Mac tickets. Though I have had this conversation innumerable times, I would venture to guess that *in every case,* the student's claim that he or she didn't understand any of it was false. When students say they didn't understand the reading, they usually mean one or more of the following:

- They were not in the right frame of mind to read.
- They had not identified a purpose for reading.
- They were not aware of the exact point when their comprehension began to falter.
- They had no idea what to do when they started to lose meaning.
- They are making a not-so-subtle plea for "reader's welfare" (a term coined by Karen Feathers in her 1993 book *Infotext*)—hoping that the teacher will provide them with the meaning without their having to expend any real reading effort.

Allow me to return to a driving metaphor again. Have you ever set out for an unfamiliar place and started getting that feeling you were driving in the wrong direction? You started your journey "knowing" where you were going, but somewhere along the way you became aware of that first initial prickling of dread—that creeping feeling that you might be heading the wrong way. This hint of dread slowly becomes a more solid feeling of being pretty sure you have taken a wrong turn somewhere. Finally, if you are unfortunate enough to continue heading in the wrong direction, you reach the conclusion that you are for sure, no doubt about it, hopelessly lost. My own experiences in getting lost has led me to the conclusion that there are three degrees of "lostness": (1) a little bit lost, but no need yet for assistance; (2) knowingly lost, but with a bit of help could recover; and (3) hopelessly lost—also known as, "Hello, is this AAA?"

Careful drivers don't let the problem get that far. When they feel themselves getting lost, they take corrective measures before the situation gets out of hand. When they first get the feeling of "Uh, oh. I think I'm heading in the wrong direction," they either stop to consult a map or ask someone for directions. They realize that if they continue to drive without reflecting where the wrong turn was, the situation could get out of hand. These drivers know that to continue to drive aimlessly would be foolish and in no way would offer promise of finding their way. Before becoming desperately lost, these drivers take action to correct the problem.

Careless drivers, by contrast, refuse to consult a map or ask directions. They believe the problem will work itself out if they just continue to drive. They let the situation get too far out of hand; and by the time they come to accept the fact that they need help, they often need a global positioning system to find their way home. (Special note: the gender designations for good versus poor drivers depicted in this analogy are purely coincidental and in no way reflect the real world. All names, characters, and incidents inferred are fictitious. No identification with actual friends, colleagues, neighbors, spouses, family members, and potential book buyers is intended or should be inferred).

These degrees of lostness can also be applied to readers. When reading a challenging work, students often can sense that they are getting lost. Like drivers entering unfamiliar territory, they need to take action before the situation turns hopeless. They need to recognize and pay attention to that little prickling in their brains when they feel they are beginning to get a little bit lost.

A Little Bit Lost

Are we not all a little bit lost when we read unfamiliar books? The difference between a good reader and a poor reader is that a good reader will tolerate being a bit confused for a while, trusting that the confusion will eventually clear, while a poor reader will become preoccupied with thoughts such as, "Uh-oh. I don't understand exactly what's happening here. This is getting too hard." Poor readers have less tolerance for getting lost.

Recently I read John Case's *The First Horseman,* a fictional biomedical thriller about the race to prevent a terrorist cell from releasing a deadly virus. I got a little bit lost reading the first three paragraphs of the novel:

> Tommy was nervous. Susannah could tell because she knew he liked to talk, and yet he hadn't said a word for nearly fifty miles. Not that she could blame him. She was nervous too. And excited. And scared.
>
> It was dusk when they got off the Taconic Parkway, switching on the headlights as they traveled through rolling farmland, a Ralph Lauren landscape where the houses were so perfect you just knew they were owned by doctors and lawyers. They were "mini-estates," or enclaves with

names like "Foxfield Meadows," and they didn't really grow anything except maybe sun-dried tomatoes and arugula.

As they passed the Omega Institute, Susannah wondered aloud—what's *that*? And the driver, Tommy, made a sound like a duck—*kwak-kwak-kwak!* So both of them laughed (a little too loud), and Susannah thought, Some kind of New Age thingie. (p. 1)

Huh? Even as a good reader, I was already confused. Before I finished a single page, a number of questions had emerged:

1. Who is Tommy?
2. Why is he nervous?
3. Why isn't he talking? Is something serious about to happen?
4. Who is Susannah?
5. Why is she nervous, excited, and scared?
6. Where is the Taconic Parkway? In the United States? What city?
7. Why are they exiting there?
8. Why the mention of affluence?
9. What is arugula?
10. What is the Omega Institute?
11. When Susannah wonders aloud, "What's that?" what is she referring to?
12. Why is Tommy making a sound like a duck?
13. Why did they laugh "a little too loud"?
14. What does the phrase "New Age thingie" mean?

After reading only three paragraphs, there were already fourteen things I did not understand! As a reader, I had to decide to live with this level of ambiguity, trusting that the author would answer my questions in due time. To return to the driving metaphor, sometimes I know that I'm a little lost, but I have learned to recognize when it's not serious. I'm familiar enough with the neighborhood (in this case, the genre) that I know if I keep driving I will figure out where I am. I do not need to ask others for directions. Rather then get hung up in the confusion, I continued to "drive" my way through *The First Horseman* until I found my way.

Carol Jago, author of *With Rigor for All*, suggests this notion of being a little bit lost when she discusses "good enough" reading. Jago tells her students that all readers struggle when they encounter unfamiliar texts and that it is not always essential that they understand every word or concept. Readers sometimes have to live with some ambiguity as they try to piece together meaning. Students need to recognize that even though they won't initially understand everything in a passage, their reading may be good enough—that being a little bit lost is not unusual. Comprehension when reading is not an all-or-nothing proposition. There are gray areas.

Sometimes, however, too much ambiguity sets in and the potential for a reader's getting hopelessly lost occurs. When readers start getting into territory where their reading may *not* be "good enough," they should try to figure out exactly where their comprehension is breaking down. When a student says she didn't understand the reading, I ask her what parts she didn't understand. When she replies that she didn't get any of it, I ask her if she understood the first word. When she says, "Yes," I ask her if she understood the first sentence. If she replies "Yes" again, I ask her if she understood the first paragraph. I continue this process with the student until we find the exact place where comprehension begins to break down. The idea is to pinpoint the intersection where the wrong turn was taken.

When students tell me they do not understand the reading, what they are really telling me is that there are *parts* of the reading they do not understand. Teaching students to identify the precise areas where they began having trouble is the first step to helping students cope with their confusion. Much like driving, we don't want to wait until we are hopelessly lost in our reading before taking any corrective action. If we can be alert to the exact moment we get lost, before we go too far down the wrong road, our confusion is much easier to deal with. Later in this chapter I discuss how to correct the problem; but before we fix the problem we must determine where it exists. Here are a number of ways to help students do just that.

Scoring Comprehension

To help students get an idea of where their comprehension problems are located, I ask them to read an excerpt from a *Parade Magazine* article entitled, "The Search for Other Worlds" by David H. Levy. I break the article into sections, and as they read each section, I ask them to score their level of comprehension on a scale of 1 to 10, with 1 meaning you have little or no understanding and 10 meaning you thoroughly understand the text.

In sharing this piece with both adolescents and adults, I have never had a single reader score a "10" for every section of the text. Once they have scored themselves on each section, readers can focus their attention on the passages that received the lowest scores. (The act of scoring itself helps readers focus.) This activity can be adapted to any novel as well as to non-fiction. Depending on the reading abilities of your students, you could have them score every paragraph, or every page, or every chapter. The better your readers, the longer the sections you can have them score. Remedial students might score every paragraph, while advanced students might score every page.

Color Coding

Another effective way to teach students to monitor their reading comprehension is to have them color-code the text. To do this, I give each student two highlighters, one yellow and one pink. I ask them to read a difficult passage with the highlighters in hand, and highlight every single word in the text. They use the yellow highlighter for words, phrases, sentences, or entire passages they understand; they use the pink highlighter for everything they do not understand.

I wouldn't ask my students to do the color-coding assignment without doing it myself; and I invite you to try the exercise by color-coding the Steven Pinker passage found in Figure 4.3. (This passage is not one I'd use with adolescents; I chose it to help adults see the value of this exercise.) Remember to highlight every word, pinpointing exactly where your comprehension breaks down. If you were in a classroom with other adults, I would then place you in groups and have you discuss your trouble spots.

Color-coding comprehension has many benefits:

- It provides the reader with a focus.
- It motivates the reader to concentrate in order to come up with as few pink-highlighted passages as possible.
- It shows the reader where to slow his or her pace.
- It alerts the reader to the importance of context in trying to make meaning.
- It encourages the reader to revise his or her comprehension while reading.

Because we cannot replace schoolbooks every year, we cannot have students write scores or color code in their books. Using sticky notes is one way to get the same results without physically marking the books. Students can score themselves, note where their comprehension falters, or write questions on the slips as they read. They can remove the notes after

Figure 4.3

> ### A Passage for Color Coding
>
> Some cognitive scientists have described language as a psychological faculty, a mental organ, a neural system, and a computational module. But I prefer the admittedly quaint term "instinct." It conveys the idea that people know how to talk in more or less the same sense that spiders know how to spin webs. Web-spinning was not invented by some unsung spider genius and does not depend on having had the right education or on having an aptitude for architecture or the construction trades. Rather, spiders spin webs because they have spider brains, which give them the urge to spin and the competence to succeed. Although there are differences between webs and words, I will encourage you to see language in this way, for it helps to make sense of the phenomena we will explore.
>
> Thinking of language as an instinct inverts the popular wisdom, especially as it has been passed down in the canon of the humanities and social sciences. Language is not more a cultural invention than is upright posture. It is not a manifestation of a general capacity to use symbols: a three-year-old, we shall see, is a grammatical genius, but is quite incompetent at the visual arts, religious iconography, traffic signs, and the other staples of the semiotics curriculum. Though language is a magnificent ability unique to Homo sapiens among living species, it does not call for sequestering the study of humans from the domain of biology, for a magnificent ability unique to a particular living species is far from unique in the animal kingdom. Some kinds of bats home in on flying insects using Doppler radar. Some kinds of migratory birds navigate thousands of miles by calibrating the positions of the constellations against the time of day and year. In nature's talent show we are simply a primate with our own act, a knack of communicating information about who did what to whom by modulating sounds we make when we exhale.
>
> From Steven Pinker, *The Language Instinct: How the Mind Creates Language* (New York: Perennial, 2000), pp. 18–19.

each chapter, attach them to a sheet of notebook paper, and turn them in as evidence of their having interacted with the text. I often ask students to choose one of their sticky notes and write a reflection to be turned in with it.

Trouble Slips

Create trouble slips (Feathers 1993, p. 135) by cutting scrap paper into bookmark-size strips. Provide each student with a number of strips. As they read, have them make notes on their bookmarks, flagging those words and passages that are giving them the hardest time. They may want to line the bookmark up with the text and draw arrows to show the trouble spots. Asking students to keep trouble slips for their homework is a good idea. The next day, when they meet in groups, the slips provide instant conversation starters as the students ask each other for clarification on their trouble spots.

Sentence Starters

To find out where students are having comprehension problems, have them complete the following sentence starter:

I don't understand . . .

If they are reading a particularly difficult passage or chapter, I might have them write at least three "I don't understand . . ." statements. I then have the students get in small groups or with a partner to share their statements and help each other clear up confusion. Here are some other sentence starters that have proven useful in prompting students to focus on their reading:

- I noticed . . .
- I wonder . . .
- I was reminded of . . .
- I think . . .
- I'm surprised that . . .
- I'd like to know . . .
- I realized . . .
- If I were . . .
- The central issue(s) is (are) . . .
- One consequence of _____ could be . . .
- If _____, then . . .
- I'm not sure . . .
- Although it seems . . .

All of these activities—scoring comprehension, color-coding the passage, creating trouble slips, and using sentence starters to interact with text—helps teach students to monitor their comprehension. They encourage students to become more aggressive readers, which helps prevent them from driving too far down the wrong road. They teach students to be active, aggressive readers when the reading gets hard.

Once we have taught students to pinpoint where their comprehension breaks down, how do we help them fix the problem?

Question 4: Do My Students Know Any Fix-It Strategies to Assist Them When Their Comprehension Begins to Falter?

Read the following quote and explain what it means:

> There are known knowns. There are things we know that we know. There are known unknowns. That is to say, there are things that we know we don't know. But there are also unknown unknowns. There are things we don't know we don't know.
> *Donald Rumsfeld,* Newsweek *(2003, p. 113)*

Got it? How many times did you have to read this quote before you were confident that you understood it? My guess is that you had to read it more than once in order to grasp it. This is not, unfortunately, how my students approach passages they do not understand. Generally, they read it once and come to the often erroneous conclusion that it is simply too hard for them to understand.

If we are to teach students how to improve their comprehension, the first lesson we need to teach them is that rereading is the principal strategy good readers use. Does this mean a student has to read a novel in its entirety four times to ensure comprehension? No, but it does mean that there will be troublesome passages or specific sections that demand rereading. Students who have learned to monitor their comprehension (for example, by using the activities described in the previous section) can identify troublesome passages; it's there where they should reread.

When a student approaches me and tells me he does not understand a particular passage, I always ask two questions: (1) Where, *exactly,* do you feel you do not understand? and (2) How many times have you read it? I want to reinforce the idea that before you tell me you don't understand something you've read, you should have identified where the problem is and have made an effort to reread the trouble spot.

When my students learn to reread the hard parts, they are taking the first step toward clearing up the confusion they are encountering, at either the word level or the sentence level.

Rereading at the Word Level

Recently I asked David, a ninth-grade student, how well he thought he did on the vocabulary section of the CAT-6, a standardized, state-mandated exam.

"Not so good," he said.

"Why not?" I asked.

"There were lots of words on there I didn't know."

"What did you do when you were asked about a word you didn't know?"

"Guessed."

"Did you have a strategy for guessing?"

"Yes. I picked 'C' for the ones I didn't know."

Unfortunately, David's admission that he blindly guessed is not atypical. When students lack word attack know-how, they take uneducated guesses. To avoid this, I teach them two word attack strategies.

Word Attack Strategy 1: Search Prefixes/Suffixes/Roots for Partial Meanings

Although it has gone out of fashion in some schools, I believe that rote memorization has its place. It can be useful, for example, to have students memorize the meanings of the most common prefixes, roots, and suffixes. I am not advocating some of those word dissection programs where students are asked to memorize hundreds and hundreds of prefixes, roots, and suffixes. The amount of time spent on these programs takes away from reading time, which is where the most effective vocabulary acquisition occurs. But students can benefit from knowing—that is, *memorizing*—some of the "staples."

I teach in the Anaheim Union High School District, and for years we have had what has become known as the "30–15–10 list" (see Figure 4.4). Quite simply, this list contains the thirty most common prefixes, the fifteen most common roots, and the ten most common suffixes—a very manageable total of fifty-five. I require that my students memorize these meanings, five at a time, and I check and recheck until I am convinced that the students have learned all of them. I spend very little class time on this activity; all of it is done as homework.

When students have memorized the 30–15–10 list, they will not be at a loss, for example, when asked to define the word *malpractice*. They'll know that *mal* means bad, and they can then take a very educated guess at the correct answer. When they encounter the word *unenviable*, they can piece together what they know about the word: *un* means *not*, and *able*

Figure 4.4

The 30–15–10 List

Prefix	Meaning	Example
a, ab, abs	away, from	absent, abstinence
ad, a, ac, af, ag, an, ar, at, as	to, toward	adhere, annex, accede, adapt
bi, bis	two	bicycle, biped, bisect
circum	around	circumference
com, con	together, with	combination, connect
de	opposite, from, away	detract, defer, demerit
dis, dif, di	apart, not	disperse, different
epi	upon, on top of	epicenter
equi	equal	equality, equitable
ex, e	out, from, forth	eject, exhale, exit
hyper	over, above	hyperactive, hypersensitive
hypo	under, beneath	hypodermic
in	in, into, not	inject, endure, incorrect
inter	between, among	intercede
mal, male	bad, ill	malpractice, malevolent
mis	wrong	mistake, misunderstand
mono	alone, single, one	monotone, monopoly
non	not	nonsense
ob	in front of, against	obvious
omni	everywhere, all	omnipresent
preter	past, beyond	preternatural
pro	forward	proceed, promote
re	again, back	recall, recede
retro	backward, behind, back	retroactive
se	apart	secede
sub	under	subway
super	greater, beyond	supernatural, superstition
trans	across, beyond	transcend, transcontinental
un, uni	one	unilateral, unity
un (pronounced uhn)	not	unhappy, unethical

Root	Meaning	Example
bas	low	basement
cap, capt	take, seize	capture, capable
cred	believe	credible
dict	speak	predict, dictionary
duc, duct	lead	induce, conduct
fac, fact	make, do	artifact, facsimile
graph	write	autograph, graphic
log	word, study of	dialog, biology
mort	die, death	mortal, mortician
scrib, script	write	transcribe, subscription
spec, spect	see	specimen, aspect
tact	touch	contact, tactile
ten	hold	tenacious, retentive
therm	heat	thermostat, thermometer
ver	true	verify

Suffix	Meaning	Example
-able, -ible	able to (adj.)	usable
-er, -or	one who does (n)	competitor
-fy	to make (v)	dignify
-ism	the practice of (n)	rationalism, Catholicism
-ist	one who is occupied with	feminist, environmentalist
-less	without, lacking (adj)	meaningless
-logue, -log	a particular kind of speaking or writing	prologue, dialog
-ness	the quality of (n)	aggressiveness
-ship	the art or skill of (n)	sportsmanship
-tude	the state of (n)	rectitude

means *able to*—so even if they can't figure out that the root is *envy*, they still would have a better chance of answering the question correctly than the student who blindly selects choice C. Good readers look for familiar word parts, and our students must be able to do this.

Word Attack Strategy 2: Figure Out Sound-Alikes
Sometimes students are confronted by unfamiliar words that are not covered on the 30–15–10 list. When this occurs, I encourage my students to pick the word apart in order to see if any of the parts sound familiar. For example, students may come across the word *patricide*. Very few adolescents know this word, but they may be familiar with the suffix -*cide*. Ask them where they have heard this suffix before and they will come up with other words, such as *suicide, homicide,* and *genocide.* When these connections are made, students then can derive at least a partial meaning for the word and can take an educated guess as to its actual meaning. Using sound-alikes is an effective strategy for bilingual students, who can sometimes make these connections from one language to another.

Rereading at the Sentence Level

In Figure 4.5 you will find six words. You probably will not know the definition of every one of them. All will be found in a passage you will soon read. Before reading the passage, however, note your prediction of what each word means in the "before reading" column of Figure 4.5.

When I share these six words with teachers, there usually are at least one or two words they have trouble clearly defining. Why? Because the words are not high-frequency words and there is no context provided to help the reader. Let's see what happens to your predictions after you read these words in context. The six words are embedded in the first three paragraphs of William Styron's brilliant novel *Sophie's Choice*. Read the following paragraphs, paying close attention to the six words (they appear late in the passage, giving you the opportunity to develop some flow before you encounter them). After you have read the passage, revisit your predictions and revise them as appropriate once you have seen the words in context.

In those days apartments were almost impossible to find in Manhattan, so I had to move to Brooklyn. This was in 1947, and one of the pleasant features of that summer which I so vividly remember was the weather, which

Figure 4.5

	Predicting Meaning	
Word	*Prediction Before Reading*	*Prediction After Reading*
wan		
covet		
alacrity		
euphemism		
emolument		
coolie		

was sunny and mild, flower-fragrant, almost as if the days had been arrested in a seemingly perpetual springtime. I was grateful for that if for nothing else, since my youth, I felt, was at its lowest ebb. At twenty-two, struggling to become some kind of writer, I found that the creative heat which at eighteen had nearly consumed me with its gorgeous, relentless flame had flickered out to a dim pilot light registering little more than a token glow in my breast, or wherever my hungriest aspirations once resided. It was not that I no longer wanted to write, I still yearned passionately to produce the novel which has been so long captive in my brain. It was only that, having written down the first few paragraphs, I could not produce any others, or—to approximate Gertrude Stein's remark about a lesser writer of the Lost Generation—I had the syrup but it wouldn't pour. To make matters worse, I was out of a job and had very little money and was self-exiled to Flatbush—like others of my countrymen, another lean and lonesome young Southerner wandering amid the Kingdom of the Jews.

Call me Stingo, which was the nickname I was known by in those days, if I was called anything at all. The name derives from my prep school days down in my native state of Virginia. The school was a pleasant institution to which I was sent at fourteen by my distraught father, who found me difficult to handle after my mother died. Among my other disheveled qualities was apparently an inattention to personal hygiene, hence I soon became known as Stinky. But the years passed. The abrasive labor of time, together with a radical change of habits (I was in fact shamed into becoming almost obsessively clean), gradually wore down the harsh syllabic brusqueness of the name, slurring off into the more attractive, or less unattractive, certainly sportier Stingo. Sometime during my thirties the nickname and I mysteriously parted company, Stingo merely evaporating like a **wan** ghost out of my existence, leaving me indifferent to the loss. But Stingo I still was during this time about which I write. If, however, it is perplexing that the name is absent from the earlier part of this narrative, it may be understood that I am describing a morbid and solitary moment in my life when, like the crazy hermit in the cave on the hill, I was rarely called by any name at all.

I was glad to be shut of my job—the first and only salaried position, excluding the military, in my life—even though its loss seriously undermined my already modest solvency. Also, I now think it was constructive to learn so early in life that I would never fit in as an office worker, anytime, anywhere. In fact, considering how I had so **coveted** the job in the first place, I was rather surprised at the relief, indeed the **alacrity**, with which I accepted my dismissal only five months later. In 1947 jobs were scarce, especially jobs in publishing, but a stroke of luck had landed me employment with one of the largest publishers of books, where I was made "junior editor"—a **euphemism** for manuscript reader. That the employer called the tune, in those days when the dollar was much more valuable tender than it is now, may be seen in the stark terms of my salary—forty dollars a week. After withholding taxes this meant that the anemic blue check placed on my desk every Friday by the hunchbacked little woman who managed the payroll represented **emolument** in the nature of a little over ninety cents an hour. But I had not been in the least dismayed by the fact that these **coolie** wages were dispensed by one of the most powerful and wealthy publishers in the world . . . (pp. 3–4)

Now that you have read the words in context, go back to Figure 4.5 and see if you'd like to revise any of your predictions for the six words.

How'd you do? My guess, based on the number of times I have shared this exercise with teachers, is that reading the words in the context of the passage helped you come up with at least a partial definition of one or more words of which you were initially unsure. Reading the passage also helps you change or fine-tune your prereading predictions. If you learned a new word or two reading those three paragraphs, imagine how your vocabulary might expand if you read the entire 576-page novel. (For definitions of the six words, see the bottom of this page.)

Teaching Context in the Classroom

One way I try to reinforce the importance of context in comprehending unfamiliar words is by having students begin class by working on a three-

---

Here are the definitions of the six words in Figure 4.5. *Wan:* lacking natural color; pale. *Covet:* to desire eagerly. *Alacrity:* prompt and cheerful willingness. *Euphemism:* the use of a mild or indirect expression instead of one that is harsh or unpleasantly direct. *Emolument:* salary, fee, or wages. *Coolie:* a laborer who does hard work for very little pay.

minute sponge activity. When students enter the classroom they find a sentence on the board with an unfamiliar word in it. (A good source for these sentences is Linda Carnevale's *Hot Words for the SAT I*.) Here are some examples:

- Harry followed Sally around, <u>slavishly</u> attending to her every need.
- The teacher <u>berated</u> Jonathan for shouting an obscenity in class.
- A <u>fastidious</u> dresser, Annette looks as though she just stepped out of a fashion magazine.

If the word is particularly difficult, I might give students two sentences containing the same unfamiliar word:

- Maggie blossomed once she left the house and became <u>autonomous</u>.
- While others worked on research teams, Eddie did the experiments <u>autonomously</u>.

When students arrive in class, they open their notebooks to a warm-up section—a page containing three columns. They then read the sentence, copy it onto the left-hand column, and predict the meaning of the highlighted word. After students have made their predictions and have had a chance to discuss their predictions, we look up the word in the dictionary, and they write that definition in the third column. For example:

Copy the sentence here	Predict meaning	Actual meaning
Maggie blossomed once she left the house and became autonomous.	responsible for herself	adj. independent

This exercise takes no more than three minutes and helps students learn that good readers use context to help them when comprehension breaks down.

There is a big difference between assigning reading and teaching kids how to read more effectively. I can help my students make the most of their initial reading by:

- helping them overcome gaps in their prior knowledge and background by providing the necessary framing of the text.
- making them conscious about approaching the text with their minds tuned to their reading channels.

- planning strategies that help students approach the page with a specific reading focus in mind.
- reinforcing the notion that confusion is natural and should even be welcomed.
- teaching them to monitor exactly when and where their comprehension begins to falter.
- modeling strategies to help them fix their comprehension when it gets shaky.

With repeated modeling, I expect that my students will, first consciously and then unconsciously, begin using the strategies good readers use to make sense of their first-draft reading—or, as Anne Lamott might call it, their reading "down" draft. Let's now turn our attention to the "up" draft—second-draft reading, where students move beyond the literal interpretation of the text toward uncovering deeper meaning.

CHAPTER FIVE

Deepening Comprehension Through Second-Draft Reading

Recently my wife, Kristin, and I rented *The Sixth Sense,* a film we had heard good things about but hadn't seen when it was playing in the theaters. The movie is essentially a ghost story, with lots of good jolts and a surprise ending. Allow me to amend that by saying *I* was surprised by the ending—Kristin calmly informed me that she had figured out the ending thirty minutes before the final credits rolled. "Impossible!" I said, not wanting to admit that she had outsmarted me. She then slowly and methodically pointed out the many hints embedded in the first half of the film that allowed her to predict the ending. (I'll refrain from stating the ending here out of respect for those of you who have yet to see the film. I still haven't forgiven Gene Siskel for giving away the surprise twist in *The Crying Game* in his review.)

The next day I watched *The Sixth Sense* again, this time with my radar alert to any and all hints as to how the film would end. I was surprised to see how many clues I had missed during my first viewing and how seemingly inconsequential scenes took on entirely new importance the second time around. Having a basic understanding of the film freed up room in my brain to focus on the subtleties on the repeat viewing and as a result I became aware of a higher level of craft in the filmmaking—a level I had initially missed. I walked away from the film the second time with a much richer and deeper "reading" of it.

This raises an interesting question: If seeing *The Sixth Sense* a second time allowed me to appreciate the film on a more complex level, does this mean I did not understand the film the first time I saw it? No, of course not. After all, I came away from that first viewing with an understanding of the plot points, the major conflicts and themes, and the resolution. But there is richness to that film—a depth—that I was unable to appreciate during my first viewing. The complexity of the film made it impossible for me to immediately "get" it. I was in surface-level mode the first time around; I did not attain a deeper appreciation of the film until I was able to revisit key scenes with some entry-level viewing experience under my belt. The more complex the film, the more worthwhile a second viewing becomes.

Much like "reading" a complex film, reading a complex book requires the reader to revisit it if a deeper appreciation is to be developed. Most adolescents simply cannot read *Beloved* or *Macbeth* one time and "get it." The benefit comes, as R. J. Tierney and P. D. Pearson note in their article "Toward a Composing Model of Reading," from multiple readings in which one's comprehension is refined. Students need to return to the text to help them overcome their initial confusion, to work through the unfamiliarity of the work, to move beyond the literal, and to free up cognitive space for higher-level thinking. They need both a "down" reading draft to comprehend the basics and an "up" reading draft to explore deeper meaning.

Students come to us with an "I read it—I'm done" mentality. It is up to us to show them the value of second-draft reading.

Second-Draft Reading

If I want students to buy into the idea that rereading is often necessary to move beyond surface-level comprehension, I have to demonstrate this in terms they understand. I need to teach them that good readers *infer* when they read; that is, they see and consider things that are not literally on the printed page. The ability to infer is essential for every excellent reader, but unfortunately I have found it to be a difficult concept for many of my students to grasp. They are more comfortable seeing and thinking about their reading in literal terms. This presents both bad news and good news for teachers of adolescents: the bad news is that many of our students begin the year unable to see beyond the literal; the good news is that the ability to infer can be taught.

I try to ease my students into the concept of inference. For example, I may read them the following and have them hypothesize where the narrator is sitting:

> I can't believe I have been sitting here among all these sick people for over an hour waiting for them to call my name. Why do they overschedule so many patients? I hope I am called next, for I don't know how much longer I can tolerate this sore throat.

Students have no trouble telling me the narrator is sitting in a doctor's office or a hospital emergency room. When I ask them how they could possibly know this, since the words "doctor's office" or "emergency room" are not in the passage, they tell me that there are enough hints in the passage that they can figure out where the narrator is sitting. I ask them to identify the words in the passage that gave them these hints; they can say without hesitation that the hints are found in the words *sitting, sick people, waiting, patients,* and *sore throat.* Giving students a few obvious examples like this, or, better yet, having them write examples of their own for their peers to guess helps introduce them to the idea of inference.

From there we move on to passages that are not as obvious. I ask them to read the following:

> Humpty Dumpty sat on a wall,
> Humpty Dumpty had a great fall.
> All the King's horses and all the King's men,
> Couldn't put Humpty together again.

I ask them how many of them have heard this before. Every hand rises. Then I say, "It may surprise you to hear that Humpty Dumpty is not really about an egg. What do you think it might *really* be about?" Every time I have asked this question, the students' reactions are the same:

1. They look at me like I'm crazy.
2. I look back at them like I'm not crazy.
3. They come to the realization that I'm not kidding—that my question is serious.
4. Almost on cue, they return to the page to read the nursery rhyme again. This, of course, is the point of this exercise—getting them to

return to the text and to consider it at a deeper, previously unseen level.

5. Lightbulbs begin to turn on and they begin theorizing.

Very rarely do my students come up with the answer. In fact, even historians are unsure of the origins of this rhyme. Here are three leading theories:

1. The rhyme refers to King Richard III, who fell from his horse in the Battle of Bosworth Field. Richard was surrounded by enemy troops in the battle and butchered on the spot.
2. The rhyme refers to Charles I of England, who was toppled by the Puritan majority in Parliament. The King's army could not restore his power and he was subsequently executed.
3. "Humpty Dumpty" was the name of a powerful cannon during the English Civil War. It was mounted on top of St. Mary's at the Wall Church in Colchester in 1648. The church tower was hit by enemy fire and was knocked off, sending the cannon tumbling to the ground. It could not be repaired.

Though students do not know these historical references, this exercise teaches them that meaning can often be found beneath the surface of text and to truly appreciate higher levels of comprehension they need to revisit the passage and start digging. In reading "Humpty Dumpty," for example, just knowing there was more to the nursery rhyme than meets the eye compelled them to go back and read it again. Usually during this second reading, the students see it in a new light and come to the conclusion that maybe the poem is about a fallen leader. It is not important that their inferences be exactly historically correct for the purposes of this lesson. After all, aren't adult readers' inferences sometimes wrong? This doesn't mean we should stop inferring—rather, it suggests that inferring correctly takes much practice, and the more we infer the better we get at it. With my students, what is important in studying "Humpty Dumpty" is that they learn to see different levels of text and that they practice making inferences.

After Humpty Dumpty, my students and I move on to Dr. Seuss. I read them *Yertle the Turtle*. Yertle is a turtle who wants to rule as far as he can see. He climbs on the backs of other turtles to get a view of the entire pond. Not satisfied with ruling the pond, he orders other turtles to join the stack so he can see the entire farm. His goal is not only to rule the turtles, but also to rule all the other farm animals. Still, this is not enough for

Yertle, who wants to rule the land beyond the farm. He commands more and more turtles to bear the weight of the stack, until finally, the turtles underneath him can take it no more. They collapse and Yertle lands face first in the mud. He has lost his grip of tyrannical power and is finished as their leader.

I tell the students that this is a children's classic, but—you guessed it—it's not really about a turtle. After they wrestle with that idea for a few minutes, I give them a hint: the book was written in 1952. I ask them to consider who Yertle might really be, given the historical context. Someone always correctly identifies Yertle as Hitler.

Students get a kick out of deriving meaning that is not directly spelled out for them. Through Humpty Dumpty and *Yertle the Turtle* they begin to learn that developing the ability to infer is intellectually challenging and rewarding. Once students have internalized the basics of drawing inferences, they can use these basics throughout the year as we read works of literature. Reminding them that Yertle is not really a turtle comes in handy when I want to introduce them to the idea that Simon from *Lord of the Flies* is not just a boy (he's a Christ figure) or that *To Killing a Mockingbird* is not really about killing a mockingbird. Just telling my students that they are "only seeing turtles" is enough to get them to begin probing deeper.

What Does It Not Say?

After Humpty and Yertle, then it's off to real-world text. I use articles, graphs, and charts in the newspaper for practice. Here, for example, is a recent bit of information I shared with students:

Influenza-related deaths have increased dramatically since the 1970s.

Influenza Deaths	Influenza Deaths
1977	1999
Approximately 18,000	Approximately 65,000

I asked my students to read the table and list everything it tells them on the left side of a t-chart. After completing the left side, we get to the really interesting question: What does the chart *not* say? I ask them to brainstorm their responses in the right-hand portion of the chart. (See Figure 5.1.)

Underneath these two columns, I then have students consider the following question: What might have caused such a dramatic rise in flu-related deaths? I chart their inferences and we discuss them as a class. In

Figure 5.1

> ### **Analyzing Flu Information**
>
> | *What Does the Chart Say?* | *What Does the Chart Not Say?* |
> |---|---|
> | 1. Influenza deaths have increased dramatically since the 1970s. | 1. What caused such a dramatic rise in deaths? |
> | 2. In 1977, there were approximately 18,000 flu-related deaths. | 2. Deaths where? In the USA? |
> | 3. In 1999, there were approximately 65,000 flu-related deaths. | 3. Who is the source of this information? |
>
> *What caused such a dramatic rise in flu-related deaths?*
>
> What I think:
> - There are more strains of flu than ever before.
> - There are nastier strains of flu today than there were twenty years ago.
> - People do not have good medical care.
> - The vaccines don't work anymore.
> - There are more people than there were twenty years ago.
> - There are more elderly people than ever, and they are the most vulnerable.

doing so, I am trying to train my students not only to notice what is said, but also to infer what is left unsaid. I want them to be aggressive, active readers, capable of looking under the surface of the literal. More and more, it seems to me that students come to me willing to accept whatever they read at face value. I want them to know that this is a dangerous way to read your way through life. I want them to realize that every time something is said, something remains unsaid, and that every time something is written, something remains unwritten.

To further help students see the unwritten, I present them with the table shown in Figure 5.2. I teach in Orange County, California, and in this county there are 568 schools located in twenty-six separate school districts. Every year, students throughout the county are assessed on state-mandated exams. The schools are then ranked on an Academic Performance Index (API). The higher a school's API, the better. The table in Figure 5.2 lists the ten schools in Orange County that had the lowest API scores in 2002.

When students are asked what this table tells them, they are able, without much difficulty, to generate a list like the following:

What the Table Says

- Which ten schools in Orange County had the lowest test scores.
- The grade levels of these schools (elementary/middle school/high school).

Figure 5.2

10 Lowest Orange County API Scores, 2002		
School	*School District*	*API Score*
Valley High School	Santa Ana Unified	484
Lathrop Intermediate	Santa Ana Unified	487
Carver Elementary	Santa Ana Unified	500
Monte Vista Elementary	Santa Ana Unified	501
Century High School	Santa Ana Unified	504
Hoover Elementary	Santa Ana Unified	512
Davis Elementary	Santa Ana Unified	515
Garfield Elementary	Santa Ana Unified	518
Key Elementary	Anaheim Elementary	518
Kennedy Elementary	Santa Ana Unified	524

- Their numerical API scores.
- The school district where each school is located.
- That one district, Santa Ana Unified, had nine of the ten schools.

This table was printed in our local newspaper without any further explanation. This broke my heart for the teachers and administrators working in these schools because, clearly, this table leaves much unsaid. I am concerned that the general public, much like my students, will not look below the surface of this table and ask themselves the key questions: What does this table *really* mean? What's *not* being said here?

Even if you have never heard of any of these schools, and even if you have never been to southern California, I'm guessing you could accurately infer much about these low-scoring schools—information not found in the table printed in the newspaper:

What the Table Doesn't Say
- There is a very high percentage of non-English-speaking students at these schools.
- There is a high mobility rate among students at these schools; students come and go frequently.
- These schools are located in low-income neighborhoods.
- The schools suffer from high absenteeism.
- The students come from print-poor home environments; they have limited access to books, magazines, the Internet, and other forms of print.
- Some of these students live in print-poor communities; they have limited access to bookstores and libraries.
- Many of these students do not have a quiet place to study at home.

- The education level of the students' parents is low.
- The classrooms are overcrowded and underfunded.
- These schools may have a higher percentage of teachers who are inexperienced or who are teaching with preliminary teaching credentials.
- This table does not tell the reader the API scoring range. If these are poor scores, what do good scores look like? Without context, how do we really know these scores are low?
- Though these scores are low, how do they stack up with scores in previous years? Are the scores rising?

(For those teachers working at one of these "bottom"-ranking schools, let me add a little rant: I have visited a number of schools in the past three years, from the highest-ranking school in the county to some of the lowest-ranking, and I have found that some of the finest teaching is in the lower-ranked schools. Rather than blame these teachers and threaten school takeovers, we should be saying "thank you" and offering financial rewards for experienced teachers who choose to teach under such adverse conditions. Memo to Fox television executives: Instead of making national heroes out of singing waitresses and truck drivers, maybe the next *American Idol* series could focus solely on heroic urban educators.)

Clearly, in the case of the information shown in Figure 5.2, there is more than meets the eye. In this case, what is not said is as important as what is said. When my students are first shown this table, they do not consider the unsaid. They have to be taught how to read between the lines—to uncover the deeper meaning they might initially gloss over. Those who simply take this table at face value do not see the real picture. Sharpening students' inference skills with exercises like the ones presented in this chapter is sure to help them realize that Coleridge's "Rime of the Ancient Mariner" is not simply about a bird.

Three Key Questions

Sheridan Blau says that there are really only three questions we need to ask students after they have read something, and that these three questions encompass three different levels of thinking. The three questions are:

1. What does it say?
2. What does it mean?
3. What does it matter?

What Does It Say? What Does It Mean?

The first question—"What does it say?"—is asking for literal-level comprehension. Students must be able to answer this level of question before moving on to the other two. A literal understanding is a prerequisite for uncovering deeper meaning in the text—foundational to answering the second question, "What does it mean?"

Take Chapter 1 of William Golding's *Lord of the Flies*, for example. The first line of the novel reads: "The boy with fair hair lowered himself down the last few feet of rock and began to pick his way toward the lagoon" (p. 5). This is our introduction to Ralph, one of many boys stranded on an island after a plane crash. At first, Ralph appears to be much like the other boys stranded on the island. It isn't until we reread the first two pages that we notice hints that Ralph will eventually come to represent fairness. Not only is "fair" used to describe his hair in the opening line, but Golding also uses "fair" nine times in the first two pages to describe Ralph. Not once in my fifteen years of teaching this book has a student pointed this out after an initial reading. However, when I ask my students to revisit the first two pages and look carefully at Golding's diction, they are always surprised to "discover" the word "fair" nine times—a clue they had initially missed. Recognizing Golding's overuse of the word "fair" leads to some natural questions: Why does Golding do this? What is he trying to achieve in the readers' minds? When students start asking these kinds of questions, they begin getting down into the "What does it mean?" level of thinking.

To further illustrate the difference between the thinking required in Blau's three questions (What does it say? What does it mean? What does it matter?), read the following passage from Chapter 24 of *To Kill a Mockingbird*. In this excerpt, Tom Robinson, wrongly accused of rape, has been killed while attempting to escape from prison. Atticus, Tom's attorney, comes home and breaks up the meeting of the Missionary Society with the bad news:

> The front door slammed and I heard Atticus's footsteps in the hall. Automatically I wondered what time it was. Not nearly time for him to be home, and on Missionary Society days he usually stayed down town until black dark.
>
> He stepped in the doorway. His hat was in his hand, and his face was white.
>
> "Excuse me, ladies," he said. "Go right ahead with your meeting, don't let me disturb you. Alexandra, could you come to the kitchen a minute? I want to borrow Calpurnia for a while."

He didn't go through the diningroom, but went down the back hallway and entered the kitchen from the rear door. Aunt Alexandra and I met him. The diningroom door was opened again and Miss Maudie joined us. Calpurnia had half risen from her chair.

"Cal," Atticus said. "I want you to go out with me to Helen Robinson's house—"

"What's the matter?" Aunt Alexandra asked, alarmed by the look on my father's face.

"Tom's dead."

Aunt Alexandra put her hands to her face.

"They shot him," said Atticus. "He was running. It was during their exercise period. They say he just broke into a blind raving charge at the fence and started climbing over. Right in front of them—"

"Didn't they try to stop him? Didn't they give him any warning?" Aunt Alexandra's voice shook.

"Oh yes, the guards called for him to stop. They fired a few shots in the air, then to kill. They got him just as he went over the fence. They said if he'd had two good arms he'd of made it, he was moving that fast. Seventeen bullet holes in him. They didn't have to shoot him that much. Cal, I want you to come out with me and help tell Helen." (p. 238)

Consider this passage with Blau's first question in mind: What does it say? A student summary might look like this:

Tom Robinson, an African-American man, tries to escape from prison. He is shot seventeen times and killed. Atticus breaks the news to his family and to Calpurnia, the caretaker of his children.

Most of my students are able to produce a similar answer to the question "What does it say?" The problem occurs when they don't read *beyond* their initial interpretation. To help students dig deeper, I ask them to read the passage again with the following question in mind: "What does it mean?" This is the point of the lesson in which they look at me like I have three heads. They usually respond by asking me something along the lines of, "What do you mean, 'What does it mean?'?"

I prod them a bit: "You told me that Tom tried to escape. He ran, was shot, and died. Why do you think he did that? He still had an appeal pending in court. Why do you think he tried to escape before his appeal was heard? Why did he take what appears to be a foolish risk before exhausting his last chance at possible freedom? Didn't he still have a chance of being given a new trial?" I have asked students this year after year, and the responses are the same:

"He gave up hope!"

"He wasn't going to get a fair trial and he knew it!"

"'Tom knew the system was rigged against African-Americans!"

"The unfairness of his trial finally made Tom snap!"

"How can you know this to be true?" I ask. "It doesn't say anywhere in that passage that Tom gave up hope or that he knew he wouldn't have a chance of having a fair trial. How can you come up with that conclusion *if it's not actually written into that passage*?"

Students are not allowed to get away with the typical answers I receive:

"It's obvious that's why he ran."

"I just know that's why he did it!"

"Wouldn't you try to escape as well, Mr. Gallagher?"

Instead, I ask students to support their statements by returning to the text and providing strong textual evidence. In this case, they would be required to cite passages in the book that illustrate the depth of racism in Maycomb, Alabama—specific examples that would reasonably lead the reader to believe that Tom had indeed abandoned hope.

Reading at the "What does it mean?" level certainly promotes a higher-level interaction with the text, but if I have my students stop there, I am still shortchanging them. It is not enough that my students have read and enjoyed *To Kill a Mockingbird* (or any other novel), nor is it enough that they can walk away from the novel able to discuss the plot points, or recognize the themes, or identify the author's use of foreshadowing. While I certainly want my students to be able to do these things, if that's all I require of them, then in essence they haven't done more than read and appreciate a great story. That's a start, but I want more than that.

What Does It Matter?

We have our students read great works of literature to give them an opportunity to think deeply about the issues that will affect their lives. After students are able to answer the two questions "What does it say?" and "What does it mean?" they are ready to get to the heart of why they read the book: What does it matter? Why, in 2004, are we still reading *To Kill a Mockingbird* forty-four years after it was written? If I am a student living in California, why should I read Toni Morrison's *Jazz,* which takes place in Chicago sixty years ago? Why read *The Scarlet Letter* when the Salem witch trials occurred in 1692? What do we say when a student asks, "Why are we reading this book?"

We teach these great works because we want our students to do more than appreciate a good story. We want to provide them with what Kenneth Burke calls "imaginative rehearsals" for the world they will soon inherit.

Reading great literature provides young people with a practice ground to explore these issues, and by asking them "What does it matter?" we help students see the relevance of the great themes found in classic literature. Though the world has changed drastically since many of these works were written, there is much about the human condition that has remained unchanged, and recognizing these universals enables students to carefully consider their place in society. Asking "What does it matter?" is an excellent way to get students to think beyond the story and consider its themes in a contemporary light.

One could argue that asking "What does it matter?" becomes the reason we read great books in the first place. For example, in the *To Kill a Mockingbird* passage where Tom Robinson gives up hope and recklessly tries to escape from prison, I ask the students if African-American men today still feel that same sense of hopelessness. I give them some of the following statistics (from the Human Rights Watch organization):

- Blacks today comprise 13 percent of the national population, but account for 49 percent of those in prison.
- Nine percent of all black men are under some form of correctional supervision (in jail or prison, on probation or parole). This compares with only 2 percent of white adults.
- One in three black men between the ages of twenty and twenty-nine was in jail or prison, or on parole or probation in 1995.
- One in ten black men in their twenties and early thirties is in prison or in jail.
- Thirteen percent of the black adult male population has lost the right to vote because of felony disenfranchisement laws.
- Nationwide, black men are 8.2 times more likely to be incarcerated than white men.

Today, in Alabama, which serves as the setting for *To Kill a Mockingbird,* black men comprise 26 percent of the state's population, but account for 65 percent of the state's prison population. According to U.S. Census data, for every 100,000 white adults living in Alabama, 236 are in prison; for every 100,000 blacks living in Alabama, 1,271 are in prison.

While I want my students to appreciate Harper Lee's classic and to feel close to its many memorable characters, I believe it is most important to use their reading of *To Kill a Mockingbird* as a springboard for them to consider some of the critical issues in their own lives. To that end, I ask students questions such as these:

- Why is the incarceration rate for blacks so much higher in our country than for whites?
- Why is it that in every single state in our country the percentage of black prisoners exceeds the percentage of black citizens?
- Do black Americans today feel the same sense of hopelessness that Tom Robinson felt? If so, are these feelings justified?
- Have we achieved racial equality in our society?
- If Martin Luther King Jr. were alive today, would he believe his dream has been fulfilled?

Reading *To Kill a Mockingbird* with the "What does it matter?" question in mind prods students to think about injustice, to argue about these issues, to defend their points of view. To get students to this point, we must push them to read beyond the classic at hand, and to read outside the traditional English canon. To augment *To Kill a Mockingbird,* for example, my students will read passages from Ralph Ellison's *Invisible Man,* Zora Neale Hurston's *Their Eyes Were Watching God,* and Richard Wright's *Black Boy.* They will analyze the speeches and writings of Martin Luther King, Jr., and Gandhi. They will read the poetry of Langston Hughes and Jimmy Santiago Baca. They will read current newspaper and magazine articles. Taken together, these pieces help my students move beyond the core work being read in class by adding relevancy and significance to the unit. "What does it matter?" is a question I always ask my students after reading *To Kill a Mockingbird,* but not until they have had the opportunity to examine a number of more contemporary viewpoints. Multiple viewpoints give our students those "imaginative rehearsals" they need before they leave the shelter of our schools and are confronted with issues in the real world.

Strategies to Achieve Deeper Comprehension

Once our students have completed an initial reading of the text, how do we structure lessons to encourage them to return to the text to deepen their comprehension? How do we move students beyond the "I read it— I'm done" mentality? How do we get them to revisit the text to consider "What does it mean?"

In this section are eight effective ways to help students deepen their understanding by encouraging them to move beyond the surface "What does it say?" question and to consider the deeper "What does it mean?"

question. (Chapter 8 contains strategies to help students generate "What does it matter?" thinking.)

Say/Mean Chart

A simple t-chart is an effective tool to prompt students to higher-level reading. On the left side of the chart, students are asked to write what the passage says (literal comprehension); on the right side, they record what they think the passage means (inferential comprehension).

A nice way to introduce this chart is by sharing some of the quirky statistics found in "Harper's Index," a monthly compilation of interesting statements found in *Harper's* magazine (available online at Harpers.com). Here, for example, are some of the statements from the May 2003 index:

- Last calendar year in which the Dow Jones Industrial Average gained in value: 1999.
- Last period in which the Dow declined for four consecutive years: 1929–1932.
- Percentage change since 1968 in the real value of the U.S. federal minimum wage: -37.
- Number of words the *New York Times* has devoted to the shuttle disaster per resulting death: 28,500.
- Number of words the *Times* devoted to 1998's U.S. Embassy bombings in Africa per resulting death: 163.
- Percentage of employed U.S. mothers who think full-time mothers look down on them: 66.
- Percentage of full-time mothers who think employed mothers look down on them: 73.
- Number of U.S. doctors per pharmaceutical sales representative in 1995 and 2002, respectively: 19 and 9.

Students choose one of these statements and together we put together our t-chart. Figure 5.3 presents the results of a recent class brainstorm.

This t-chart activity can be used with any type of challenging text, including magazine articles, poems, short stories, novels, and plays. I use it to help students deepen their comprehension of political cartoons, a type of reading with which they often struggle. When reading a political cartoon, "What does it say?" takes on a new light because what is "said" is often done so pictorially. I ask students to list every image and all the words they see in the cartoon.

Figure 5.3

A Brainstormed T-Chart

What Does it Say? *(Literal)*	*What Does It Mean?* *(What Can We Infer?)*
Number of U.S. doctors per pharmaceutical sales representative in 1995 and 2002, respectively: 19 and 9.	Drug companies are flourishing. There must be money to be made to hire so many salespersons.
	As technology advances, more drugs become available.
This says that in the last few years the number of people selling legal drugs per doctor has more than doubled.	Doctors are prescribing more drugs than ever.
	People in our culture may be more readily turning to prescribed drugs.
	Drug companies are spending a lot more on advertising, creating a much greater "need" for their products.

Multi-Layered Time Lines

When students are reading a difficult work for the first time, it can be helpful to have them develop a time line of events. This activity is especially useful for a novel or play that has an intricate plot or many characters to keep track of. For example, Figure 5.4 shows a time line for Act 1, Scene 1, of *Hamlet*.

First, I simply ask students to tell what happened in the story. Once students have the basic characters and plot points down, I encourage them to revisit the text by adding layers to the time line. For example, in the next

Figure 5.4

Time Line for *Hamlet,* Act 1, Scene 1

What Happened?

Francisco and Bernardo are standing watch at the castle. Horatio and Marcellus come to relieve them.	The ghost of King Hamlet appears and leaves without speaking. Horatio has a bad feeling about the ghost's visit.	We learn that King Hamlet had killed Fortinbras in battle and that young Fortinbras has sworn revenge.	The ghost reenters and exits again without speaking.	Horatio, shaken by the ghost's appearance, is off to tell Prince Hamlet what he saw.

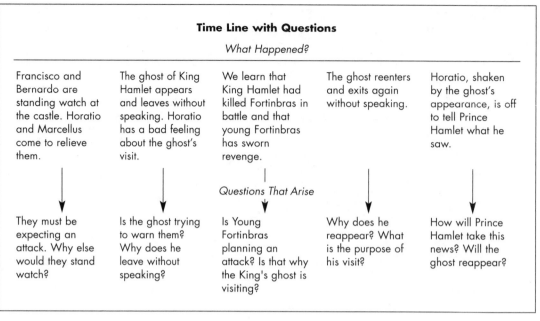

Time Line with Questions

What Happened?

| Francisco and Bernardo are standing watch at the castle. Horatio and Marcellus come to relieve them. | The ghost of King Hamlet appears and leaves without speaking. Horatio has a bad feeling about the ghost's visit. | We learn that King Hamlet had killed Fortinbras in battle and that young Fortinbras has sworn revenge. | The ghost reenters and exits again without speaking. | Horatio, shaken by the ghost's appearance, is off to tell Prince Hamlet what he saw. |

Questions That Arise

| They must be expecting an attack. Why else would they stand watch? | Is the ghost trying to warn them? Why does he leave without speaking? | Is Young Fortinbras planning an attack? Is that why the King's ghost is visiting? | Why does he reappear? What is the purpose of his visit? | How will Prince Hamlet take this news? Will the ghost reappear? |

Figure 5.5

layer they might note the questions that have arisen from their initial reading (see Figure 5.5). A third layer could have them make predictions, with these predictions supported by passages from the play (see Figure 5.6).

A number of other layered time lines can be devised to help students move beyond the literal meaning of the text. Here are two other suggestions:

- *A what/why time line.* In this time line, the first layer chronicles what happened; the second layer explains why it happened.
- *Character time lines.* Following a specific character, students chart a triple-layer timeline: (1) what the character does; (2) why the character behaved that way; (3) what the character feels about the chain of events.

Literary Dominoes

Have you ever lined up dominoes in elaborate formations and then knocked them all down by pushing the first domino? The first one falls and knocks the second one down, which falls and knocks the third one down—starting a chain reaction that winds its way all the way through the dominoes until none is left standing. As a child I would build elaborate formations that would fork into different directions, climb up and

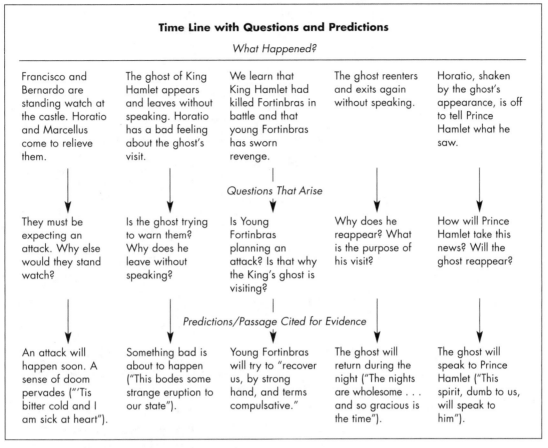

Time Line with Questions and Predictions

What Happened?

Francisco and Bernardo are standing watch at the castle. Horatio and Marcellus come to relieve them.	The ghost of King Hamlet appears and leaves without speaking. Horatio has a bad feeling about the ghost's visit.	We learn that King Hamlet had killed Fortinbras in battle and that young Fortinbras has sworn revenge.	The ghost reenters and exits again without speaking.	Horatio, shaken by the ghost's appearance, is off to tell Prince Hamlet what he saw.

Questions That Arise

They must be expecting an attack. Why else would they stand watch?	Is the ghost trying to warn them? Why does he leave without speaking?	Is Young Fortinbras planning an attack? Is that why the King's ghost is visiting?	Why does he reappear? What is the purpose of his visit?	How will Prince Hamlet take this news? Will the ghost reappear?

Predictions/Passage Cited for Evidence

An attack will happen soon. A sense of doom pervades ("'Tis bitter cold and I am sick at heart").	Something bad is about to happen ("This bodes some strange eruption to our state").	Young Fortinbras will try to "recover us, by strong hand, and terms compulsative."	The ghost will return during the night ("The nights are wholesome . . . and so gracious is the time").	The ghost will speak to Prince Hamlet ("This spirit, dumb to us, will speak to him").

Figure 5.6

down stairs (made from other dominoes), and bend around corners. If I set them up properly, I could set off a chain reaction that would not stop until the last domino fell.

In a way, the plots of novels, plays, and stories are like dominoes. A happens, which causes B to happen, which in turn causes C to happen—a process that continues until the reader reaches the resolution. To illustrate this domino effect in literature to my students, I begin by reading the Dr. Seuss Cat in the Hat classic, *Because a Bug Went Ka-Choo!* In this story, an incredible chain of events begins when a bug sneezes, causing a seed to fall out of a tree. The seed hits a worm on the head, who in his anger then kicks a tree. The tree drops a coconut and bops a turtle in the head. The turtle falls in the lake and splashes a hen, and before you know it, things quickly spin out of control. The chain of events culminates with an entire city in an uproar. And all because a bug, the first domino in the series, went *ka-choo.*

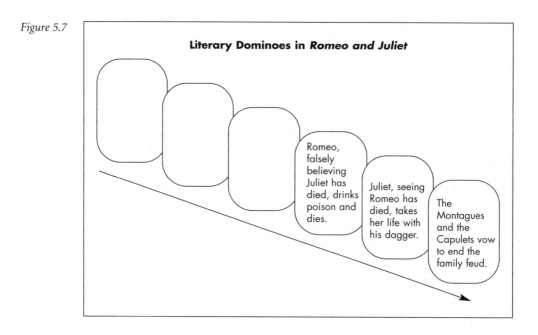

Figure 5.7

Literary Dominoes in *Romeo and Juliet*

Romeo, falsely believing Juliet has died, drinks poison and dies.

Juliet, seeing Romeo has died, takes her life with his dagger.

The Montagues and the Capulets vow to end the family feud.

It's interesting to have students consider challenging literature from a domino point of view. When I introduce this concept, I often start from the last domino and begin working backward. At the end of the novel or play, a resolution has been reached, and I want my students to consider the events that led to that resolution. For an example, see Figure 5.7 for what the last three dominoes in *Romeo and Juliet* might look like. Instead of supplying students with dominoes A, B, and C, this example begins with dominoes X, Y, and Z. The last domino indicates that the long-lasting feud between the rival Montagues and Capulets has finally ended. Why? Because the death of their beloved children has jolted the families to their senses. And why did their children die? Juliet committed suicide after waking to find her lover, Romeo, dead. Why did Romeo die? Because he drank poison after erroneously thinking Juliet was dead. Much like dominoes knocking one another over, Romeo's death led to Juliet's death, and Juliet's death led to a truce between the families. One event led to the other.

After providing students with the last three dominoes in the chain, I ask them to back up and consider what the dominoes might look like throughout that led to the ending of the play. We know it ends in tragedy, but what specific actions lead to this conclusion? Much like the bug whose *ka-choo* set of a chain of events that led to havoc in the city, students are asked to identify all the key events in the chain that led to the deaths of Romeo and Juliet.

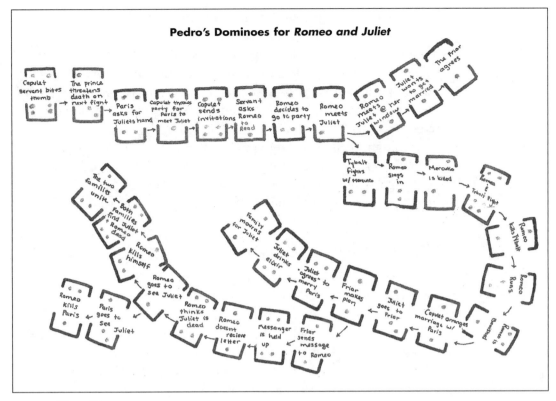

Pedro's Dominoes for *Romeo and Juliet*

Figure 5.8

Figure 5.8 shows Pedro's *Romeo and Juliet* dominoes. What is interesting about Pedro's dominoes is that they are not lined up in a straight line. His dominoes are nonlinear—much like the chain of events in the play.

This domino activity is an excellent way to prompt students to review the plot points of any major work. It requires students to:

- comprehend (understand the plot)
- analyze (properly order and connect events)
- synthesize (modify by answering "What if . . . ?")
- evaluate (rank importance of plot points)

Students will not have identical sets of plot points on their dominoes, and this leads to interesting discussions about what was important and what was not in the plot. Setting up these literary dominoes is an excellent way to help students answer the question "What does it say?"

To move their thinking to the "What does it mean?" level, I ask students to write their "dominoes" in order on index cards. This allows me to ask a number of questions that require below-the-surface thinking:

- If you were to line up your dominoes of plot events, would they be in a straight line, or would there be curves and offshoots? What does your domino trail look like? How sophisticated is the plot structure?
- Of all the dominoes leading to the tragedy, which *single domino* do you think was the key? Which domino carried the most weight in leading to the tragedy? Explain your answer and cite text references to support your response.
- Flip to domino number seven (or choose any other random number). If you were to remove this domino from the chain—if this specific event did not happen—how would the outcome of the play have been different? Explain your answer and cite text references to support your response.

Flip Side Chart

Someone once said that everything is a problem. If you win the lottery, you pay higher taxes and become saddled with long-lost relatives looking for gifts. If you are awarded first prize in a poetry contest, some of your colleagues will envy you. If you drive a beautiful new car, you will pay higher insurance. Every positive has a negative. Everything has a flip side.

Though this may be a rather pessimistic way of looking at the world, it can help students become critical readers, particularly when they are reading nonfiction. In this morning's newspaper, for example, there are a number of stories that have a flip side:

The Story	The Flip Side
The president declares that the major fighting in Iraq is over and the Iraqis have been liberated.	American soldiers continue to be ambushed. Anarchy reigns in the cities.
Mortgage rates for homebuyers are at a thirty-year-low.	Housing prices are at an all-time high.
You can buy a new camcorder with no payments and no interest for one year.	An interest rate of 19.6 percent is calculated from the beginning of the loan if you do not pay in full within the first twelve months.
The Mighty Ducks hockey team made it to the Stanley Cup finals for the first time in franchise history.	They lost the series in seven games to the New Jersey Devils.
The U.S. Congress passes the Patriot Act, enabling law enforcement to more effectively fight terrorism.	Some innocent people are held indefinitely against their will.

Unfortunately, many of my students read at face value only. Teaching them to consider the flip side of what they read allows them to sharpen their ability to dig under the surface of text.

Positive-Negative Chart

A positive-negative chart is an excellent way to have students track specific literary elements in a novel or play. Figure 5.9 is an example of such a

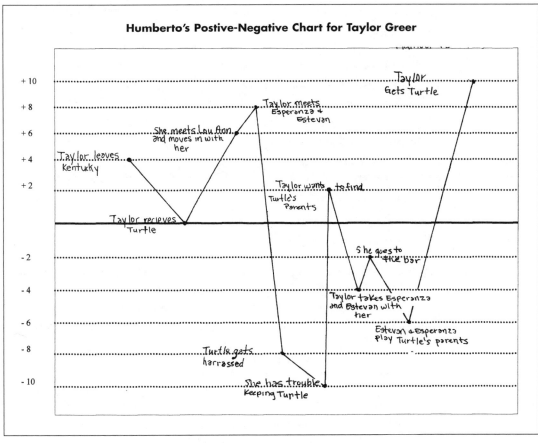

Humberto's Postive-Negative Chart for Taylor Greer

- Taylor Gets Turtle (+10)
- Taylor meets Esperanza & Estevan (+8)
- She meets Lou Ann and moves in with her (+6)
- Taylor leaves Kentucky (+4)
- Taylor wants to find Turtle's Parents (+2)
- Taylor recieves Turtle
- She goes to the bar (-2)
- Taylor takes Esperanza and Estevan with her (-4)
- Estevan & Esperanza play Turtle's parents (-6)
- Turtle gets harrassed (-8)
- She has trouble keeping Turtle (-10)

Figure 5.9

chart, created by Humberto, a freshman, for a character in *The Bean Trees* by Barbara Kingsolver. There are a number of ways to create such a chart:

- *Positive versus negative behavior by the character.* Have students chart a character's behavior, both positive and negative. For example: When Pip steals food for the convict in *Great Expectations,* is that positive or negative behavior? How positive or how negative is it? How does this compare to his other behaviors?
- *Positive or negative influence other characters have on the main character.* Students pay attention to the influence other characters have on a given character. Example: In Rudolfo Anaya's *Bless Me, Ultima,* how much influence does each character have on Antonio? Who has the most positive influence? Who has the most negative influence? Rank the degree of positive and negative influence the following characters have on Antonio: Ultima, his father, his mother, Tenorio, Cico, and Narciso.

- *Highest or lowest point in the story.* Using this strategy, students mark the high and low points of the story for a given character. Example: In Barbara Kingsolver's *The Bean Trees,* students chart the travails of Taylor Greer as she makes her cross-country journey. As they read, students make judgments as to which events mark Taylor's high and low points. This is not always as easy as it seems. For example, is it a high point or low point in Taylor's life when Turtle, a three-year-old Native American girl, is thrust into her arms?

Positive-negative charting activities work best when students are able to share, discuss, and argue about them.

Paragraph Plug-Ins

Robin Turner, a colleague of mine, developed this strategy to help students make sense of difficult reading. After an initial reading, students are asked to complete a "paragraph plug-in." Here is an example of a plug-in that students are given after reading Chapter 1 of *The Grapes of Wrath*:

> The novel begins with an atmosphere of _____. The men and women are feeling several emotions, including _____ and _____. We're also introduced to _____, who has just been released from _____. As he hitches a ride back to his childhood home, he becomes upset at a truck driver's _____. We find out that he was in prison for _____ years because of his crime, _____. Steinbeck's use of diction in this passage can best be described as _____.

Notice that some of the plug-ins require students to consider surface-level, "What does it say?" questions ("We find out that he was in prison for _____ years"), while other plug-ins require deeper reading ("The novel begins with an atmosphere of _____").

This activity, which can be done individually or in small groups, helps students by providing a partial outline to direct them through challenging text. Though it has a fill-in-the-blank feel to it, Paragraph Plug-Ins prompt students to reread and, in doing so, enables them to begin thinking at different levels. Giving students this activity has resulted in higher-level discussion in my classroom; my students have been able to clear up confusion.

As students proceed in the text, the paragraphs can be gradually withdrawn, then eventually eliminated, as students become able to achieve deeper reading on their own.

Reading Symbols

Students can also write their reflection in logs as they work their way through a book. To encourage students to move beyond simply summarizing, Robin Turner asks his students to do the following as they read:

- *Make predictions.* Students predict what will happen next, supporting their predictions with specific references to the text.
- *Recognize when the author uses literary devices.* Students analyze the techniques used by the author.
- *Make connections.* Students make connections from either real life or from other books, films, poems, and stories.
- *Make judgments.* Students judge the characteristics and behavior of the characters.
- *Challenge the text.* As they read, students challenge the author or any of the characters.

After writing their reflections, students trade logs and look for evidence of the elements. To assist them, Turner has developed a symbol for each of these elements:

Element	Symbol
Prediction	P
Literary terms	LT
Connections	C
Judgments	J
Challenges	?

As students read their partners' logs, they draw the appropriate symbol in the margin whenever one of these elements is encountered. For example, Maria is reading Eric's reflection and she notices that he has made a connection to another literary work. She writes "C" in the margin to let Eric know that she has recognized his deeper reading. The goal of each student is to receive his or her reflection log back with many such symbols written in the margins—evidence that their reflections were thoughtful. (Turner also encourages his students to use an "S" when the reflection consists of too much summarizing.)

This strategy works on two levels: (1) it motivates the reader to move beyond surface-level understanding when writing a reflection, and (2) it teaches the peer-responder to actively search for deeper-level reading in the reflection. When students trade logs, they get a double dose of deeper reading reinforcement.

Figure 5.10

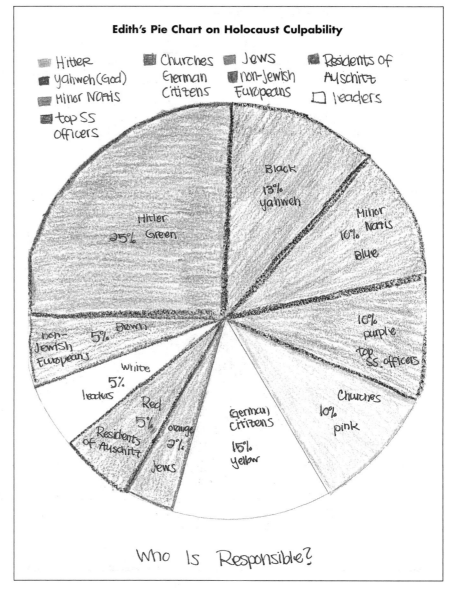

Edith's Pie Chart on Holocaust Culpability

Hitler
yahweh (God)
Minor Nazis
top SS officers
Churches German Citizens
Jews
non-Jewish Europeans
Residents of Auschitz
leaders

Black 13% yahweh

Minor Nazis 10% Blue

Hitler 25% Green

10% purple top SS officers

non-Jewish Europeans 5% Brown

white 5% leaders

Red 5%

orange 2%

Jews

German Citizens 15% yellow

Churches 10% pink

Residents of Auschitz

Who Is Responsible?

Responsibility Pie Charts

Another way to help prompt deeper thinking is to ask students to consider which characters or people are most responsible for the book's outcome. My freshmen just completed Elie Wiesel's *Night,* a nonfictional account of the Holocaust. At the end of the unit, they were asked to brainstorm the various people and groups who played a role in the genocide of World War II. It is easy for students to simply blame Hitler, but I want them to realize that he needed a lot of help to murder millions of people. As a class, we brainstormed all the people and groups who played a role in the Holocaust; students then created pie charts to visually represent culpability. In Figure 5.10, Edith has assigned percentages of responsibility to various individuals and groups. The real value in this assignment comes when students are asked to defend their charts.

Responsibility pie charts can work with any book that carries a strong ending: Who shared responsibility for the deaths of Romeo and Juliet? For the fall of Hamlet? For the treatment of Hester Prynne? For the demise of Piggy? Who was most to blame? Who was indirectly responsible? Having students consider these questions prompts them to revisit the text and to consider the consequences of the actions (or inaction) of others.

The eight activities described in this chapter demonstrate to students the value of revisiting text. Deeper meaning emerges when difficult text is reread, and these strategies, through repeated modeling, help to break students from their "I read it one time and I don't get it" mentality.

CHAPTER SIX

The Importance of Collaboration

Someone once said there is not a single book on Earth that is completely understood by any one person. Every one of us comes to the printed page with different prior knowledge and experiences, with different viewpoints and biases, with different insight and blind spots. Though we can "comprehend" text the first time we read it, deeper comprehension is more likely to occur when we discuss our reading with others. I have learned this lesson ninety-one times in the past ten years. Allow me to explain.

Ten years ago I started a faculty book club at the high school where I teach, and today we have thirty-three members who read a book a month. The books we have read and discussed have encompassed a wide range of subject matter, from the dangers inherent in climbing Mount Everest (Jon Krakauer's *Into Thin Air*) to the dangers inherent in attending an inner-city Los Angeles high school (Miles Corwin's *And Still We Rise*). We have examined life from a biologist's point of view (Lewis Thomas's *Lives of a Cell*) and death through the eyes of an oncologist (Jerome Groopman's *The Measure of Our Days*). We have read books where God seemed absent (Helena Maria Viramontes's *Under the Feet of Jesus*) and where God was ever present (Anne Lamott's *Traveling Mercies*). It has been a varied and interesting ten years of reading.

The "rules" of our book club are simple: we meet the last Friday of every month at lunch to eat pizza and discuss the month's selection. The discussions are informal, and there is no attempt to try to elevate them to the level of a Harvard graduate seminar. We have been meeting long enough so that disagreement is welcomed, and many of our discussions are spirited. One of the best things about the club is that it has fostered a collegiality among faculty members who may not have otherwise interacted with one another.

Over the past decade, we have met ninety-one times to discuss ninety-one books, and every single time I have come away from the discussion with a deeper understanding of the book. It is impossible to have discussions like these, with colleagues from various curricular areas—from art to mathematics, from science to home economics—and not gain a deeper understanding of the books. Ninety-one times I have walked out the door at the end of the book club meetings with ideas I would never have generated from reading the book on my own.

My experiences in the book club have taught me a valuable lesson when it comes to teaching difficult works in my classroom: collaboration plays a key role in elevating reading comprehension. Even though I am a good reader, I learn something new every time I am afforded the opportunity to discuss a book with my peers. Conversing with others helps me to establish connections and enables me to generate new insight in my reading.

Students need help to make such connections. Do you remember how confused you felt the first time you tried to read something really challenging, perhaps James Joyce's *Ulysses* or William Faulkner's *The Sound and the Fury*? Even though you may have read the book on your own, you might have welcomed the opportunity to discuss your reading with others. Sometimes after I have taught a novel for a number of years, I forget how hard it was when I first encountered it. I have to remind myself that the adolescents sitting in front of me may be struggling mightily, and then I remember how important a role collaboration can play in raising their levels of comprehension.

Now think of a time early in your career in which you were faced with teaching a challenging work for the first time. Did you ever seek outside help (academic analysis, web research, notes in a teacher's edition) to augment your comprehension? I have done this many times. In my first year of teaching, for example, I actually purchased and read *Cliff's Notes* for the novels I was preparing to teach. Why did I do this? Because even though I can read and "understand" each novel, learning the thoughts of other readers deepened my understanding and better informed my teaching. Even as a teacher, collaboration helps me to embrace the confusion.

For students, many of whom may not be good readers, the opportunity to collaborate—to have meaningful conversations when reading the hard stuff—becomes even more critical. If I, as an adult with many years of experience to draw from, can benefit from collaboration, doesn't it stand to reason that adolescents, who often lack prior knowledge and reading motivation, can reap even more benefits from participating in meaningful talk? My book club experience has taught me the importance of discussion in raising reading comprehension. I need to recognize this when planning lessons that I hope will elicit deeper reading from my students. If I ask my students to read challenging books, I must provide time for challenging discussion.

No Hitchhiking

Perhaps the following will sound familiar. You place students in groups of five and give them ten minutes to identify and discuss the central theme found in whatever novel you are teaching. A few minutes into the exercise you begin your walk around the room to see how your students are doing. You approach the first group, expecting to witness teamwork that would make a flying trapeze team proud. Instead, you see the following:

Student 1 is earnestly trying to complete the task.
Student 2 is half-heartedly trying to help student 1.
Student 3 is applying yet another coat of makeup.
Student 4 wants to derail the group by talking about the party at his house Saturday night.
Student 5 is pretending to participate while trying to complete her algebra homework on the sly.

Unfortunately, simply putting students into groups and giving them time to talk will not automatically result in higher-level thinking. Adolescents, when given the chance, will often "hitchhike" in groups—that is, go along for the ride and not pay for the gas. To make our groups as effective as possible, we need to consider how to structure them; and, once they are structured, we must give careful thought as to which strategies will best generate meaningful discussion among all group members. These considerations are interrelated: having an interesting task will not generate better thinking if the group is not collaborating; and a group that collaborates well will not generate deeper thinking if the task is not taken seriously.

Grouping students in a way that encourages meaningful discussion requires teachers to consider two key questions: (1) What conditions are desirable to help create effective groups? and (2) Once groups are created, which strategies are most effective in creating higher-level thinking?

Building Effective Groups

To prevent hitchhiking and to ensure active participation from all group members, consider the following factors when building discussion groups.

Size Matters

Generally speaking, the smaller the size of the groups the better. My favorite number for groups is three because this few a number will encourage participation from everyone in the group. Sometimes groups larger than three are necessary, but larger groups are good and bad. Larger groups can be good, because they increase students' chances for higher-level thinking, especially if the task is extraordinarily challenging. After all, the more brains, the more brainpower. But large groups can be more problematic because it can be difficult to ensure active participation from every group member. When students are placed in groups of five or six, it is easier for individual members to find places to hide. In general, I prefer groups of three because this size eliminates hiding places and reduces hitchhiking.

Occasionally I want each student to collaborate with a single partner; but I prefer that they not choose the same partner repeatedly. To nudge students to work with different partners, I have them fill in an appointment clock (see Figure 6.1). Students are asked to write the name of a different student at each time slot on the clock. For example, if John writes Amanda's name at three o'clock on his appointment clock, Amanda writes John's name at the same time on her clock. Then, when I want students to pair up quickly, I might ask them to take out their appointment clocks and meet with their three o'clock (or whenever) partner. This brings freshness to partnering by providing twelve possible partners for collaboration instead of having students repeatedly meet with the person sitting next to them.

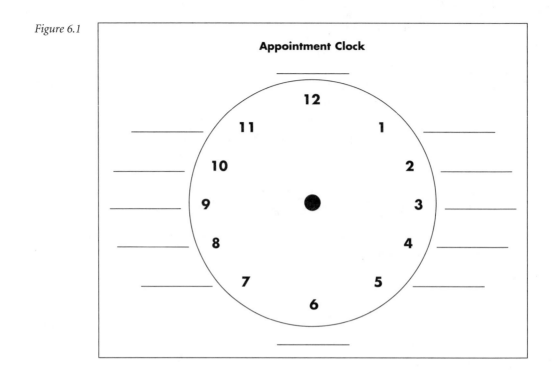

Figure 6.1

Ethnicity and Gender

There are three things in this world that teachers can count on: death, taxes, and freshman students' walking into class the first day of school and segregating themselves by gender. Without direction from me, the boys will cluster on one side of the classroom and the girls will group themselves on the other. This is not a desirable setting for collaboration. Numerous studies have found that boys and girls interact differently with those of their own gender than they do with the opposite sex. Tann (1981), for example, found that groups of girls were more likely to be consensus seeking than groups of boys. Bennett and Dunne (1992) found that girls are more likely to think abstractly, but they are less likely to talk in groups where they are outnumbered by boys. For these reasons I try to mix gender in every group. Because a difference in gender can bring a difference in viewpoint, it is important that both be represented when students collaborate.

Ethnicity is also a factor. I teach in a high school of 1,600 students on a campus where over forty languages are spoken. This multiethnic, multilingual setting provides an opportunity for students to learn from the variety of rich experiences and perspectives brought into the classroom. A student who grew up in a war-torn country might bring a different per-spective to *All Quiet on the Western Front,* for example—a perspective far different from that of a student who grew up in Anaheim. (I am reminded of the time my class read Tim O'Brien's Vietnam saga, *The Things They Carried.* In one group I had a student whose family came from South Vietnam. In the same group sat a student whose family came from North Vietnam. Now *that* was an interesting discussion!) I want to honor the experiences my students bring to the discussion, and I want my students to hear as many different perspectives as possible. Mixing both gender and ethnicity when formulating groups helps me do this.

Time and Task

Once students are assigned the group task, it is important to make sure they understand it. Before they actually start working, I always choose a student at random to repeat the task orally to the class. This gives students a chance to ask questions or seek clarification before the group work begins.

Even when the task is clear, students are sometimes slow to get started. To prompt them to begin immediately, I set a time limit. When I am not sure how long it will take students to complete the task, I try to err on the side of not giving them enough time. For example, if I think the task will take approximately ten minutes, I give them eight. I can always adjust and give them extra time if they are working diligently. Trouble occurs when students are given too much time to complete the task at hand. I want the message to be clear that there is no time to be wasted and that the groups need to get started immediately. If getting a slow start becomes a habit, I may occasionally use an overhead timer so that students can literally see the time being counted down. (These timers are available online at www.newmanagement.com.)

Specific Roles

At the beginning of the school year, students often do not know how to have meaningful group discussions. They may understand the task and be motivated to complete it, but they often have trouble sharing their think-ing in groups. To help them generate meaningful discussion, educators and researchers have developed a number of models in which specific roles are assigned to students in groups. The breakthrough book on the subject of student discussion is *Literature Circles* by Harvey Daniels. In this book Daniels created the following student roles to encourage group talk:

Role	Description of Role
Discussion director	Develops a list of discussion questions and facilitates the group discussion.
Literary luminary	Locates a few special passages for the group to discuss.
Illustrator	Draws, diagrams, sketches, paints some sort of visual representation related to the reading.
Connector	Finds a connection between the book the group is reading and the world outside.
Summarizer	Prepares a brief summary of the reading.
Vocabulary enricher	Searches for important words.
Travel tracer	Tracks where the action takes place and notes changes.
Investigator	Digs up information on a topic related to the book.

Daniels found that providing students with specific roles proved beneficial in prompting meaningful talk. Having a role provides each student with a focus and gives the group a framework so they can "hit the ground talking."

A similar framework to help students create rich talk is the reciprocal reading model (Palincsar and Brown 1984). Here the text is "chunked" (broken into sections) by the teacher and the students assume the following roles:

Role	Description of Role
Questioner	Asks questions about what has been read in the text thus far.
Summarizer	Discusses a brief summary of the reading.
Clarifier	Searches for unclear words or passages; asks others for clarification.
Predictor	Predicts what will happen next and supplies a rationale for that prediction.

These roles encompass the skills (questioning, summarizing, clarifying, predicting) that good readers employ. The reciprocal reading model makes these skills visible to the students.

Assigning specific roles for discussion may help those students who come to us at the beginning of the year unable or unwilling to participate in meaningful group discussion, but there are dangers inherent in such models. Assigning specific roles may actually limit thought and may lend artificiality to students' discussions. I once heard Harvey Daniels express horror as to how his literature circle roles were being rigidly adhered to without any room for students to deviate from the "scripted" discussion.

The idea, of course, is to provide students with models of what good readers do when they sit down to discuss text. When my colleagues participate in our faculty book club discussions, we do not have a "vocabulary enricher" or "literary luminary" because we are mature readers and have already internalized how to have a rich discussion. We don't need guidelines. Providing models—literature circles, reciprocal reading roles, and other structures—should be seen as training wheels for guiding talk for novice readers. Once students begin to understand what good readers talk about, these training wheels should be gradually withdrawn. For example, as the year progresses I may group my students with less restrictive roles, such as the following:

Role	Description of Role
Facilitator	The facilitator's job is to lead the discussion, keep track of time, and to keep the group focused and on task.
Recorder	The recorder's job is to record the group's thinking.
Reporter	The reporter's job is to share the group's thinking to the class.

Though I may start the year by assigning specific roles to help drive student discussion, I hope to end the year with my students able to carry on a meaningful discussion without imposed structures in place. Come April or May, my instructions may simply be, "Get in groups and have a fifteen-minute meaningful conversation."

In a way, teaching students how to make meaning in a group setting without teacher intervention is akin to teaching someone how to swim. A person who does not know how to swim will at first cling to the side of the pool. Eventually, with lots of modeling and encouragement from the swim instructor, the reluctant swimmer will venture out into the water and begin practicing. After the swimmer gains a certain level of proficiency, the instructor can bow out and let the person swim on his or her own. The instructor scaffolds the instruction until the instructor is no longer needed.

This instructional scaffolding—where teachers take students through zones of development—is based on the work of Lev Vygotsky, an early twentieth-century Russian psychologist. Vygotsky labeled what a child can do alone without any assistance the zone of actual development (ZAD). In the example above, the untaught swimmer's ZAD consisted of little more than being able to get in the pool and cling to the side. We want to move this swimmer to a zone where instruction takes place and where real learning can occur—the zone of proximal development (ZPD), the cognitive region that

> lies just beyond what the child can do alone. Anything that the child can learn with the assistance and support of a teacher, peers, and the instructional environment is said to lie within the ZPD. A child's new capacities can only be developed in the ZPD through collaboration in actual, concrete, situated activities with an adult or more capable peer. With enough assisted practice, the child internalizes the strategies and language completing this task, which then becomes part of the child's psychology and

personal problem-solving repertoire. When this is achieved, the strategy then enters the student's zone of actual development, because she is now able to successfully complete the task alone and without help and to apply this knowledge to new situations she may encounter. (myread.org)

With the proper assistance of a teacher within an environment that fosters learning, the nonswimmer becomes a swimmer, and swimming now becomes part of the swimmer's new ZAD. A person who can now swim unassisted may be ready, with the help of a teacher, to progress to a new ZPD (for example, how to do the butterfly stroke).

When we place students in groups and provide a structure for them to shape their conversations, we allow them to internalize the strategies and language used in rich, meaningful discussions. We use structure to help students through their zones of proximal development. In time, they internalize these collaborative strategies, and thoughtful discussions become part of the students' zones of actual development.

Accountability

Students in groups work better when they are held accountable for their collaboration. Accountability can be applied to individuals as well as groups.

Individual accountability occurs when each student in the group has to produce a product—for example, one student takes notes on interesting vocabulary; a second student shares written responses to the most interesting passages; a third student comes up with a metaphor for the passage. Sometimes students have the same job. For example, I may ask students to keep a record of their discussion, including bulleted items to represent the input of every student in the group. Instead of one person's keeping a master sheet, every student is required to keep his or her own set of notes.

Remember the story "Love" from Chapter 2, where I asked students to search for the foreshadowing of Miss Vera Brown's death? In a group situation, my instructions might be as follows: "Now that you have uncovered evidence of foreshadowing, get in your groups and share ideas. Create a master list with as much evidence as possible. Among the three of you, how much foreshadowing can you uncover? You have nine minutes before your group will be asked to share your findings with the rest of the class. Everyone in the group will turn in his or her own list, even if they are identical to your teammates'. I will choose each group's presenter at random, so make sure everyone in the group is prepared to share. John, before we begin, explain the directions back to me . . . Good. Let's get started."

Group accountability occurs when the group as a whole produces one product. For example, I may put students in groups and give each group one overhead pen and one overhead transparency. I will then give them seven minutes to symbolically represent the main character in Chapter 3 on the transparency. Even though the group is producing a single product, each member is held accountable because they know that they will be required to share their group's work, and they also know that the person selected to stand in front of the class to do so will be chosen at random. When randomly choosing who will speak for each group, I may use one of the following criteria to determine the presenter:

- The person who was born closest to our school.
- The person with the longest hair.
- The person with the shortest last name.
- The person with the most siblings.
- The person with the longest fingernails.
- The person born farthest from my birthday.

One benefit of creating goofy selection criteria such as these is that they require students to get to know each other. If I cannot generate random selection criteria on the spot, I ask students to number themselves in their groups and then I pick a number at random within the range of the number of students in the group. I sometimes use a hand-held lottery number generator to do the same thing (also available at www.newmanagement.com). When students know they may be randomly selected to represent their group's thinking, they are much more apt to participate.

Rules to Govern Collaboration

Once students are assigned tasks and understand their accountability, they need to be aware of certain rules of group work before they begin. My rules for collaboration, adapted from the work of Smith, Johnson, and Johnson (1981), are as follows:

1. No hitchhiking. Everyone participates.
2. Be critical of ideas, not people. Disagreement is necessary and can be healthy if handled maturely.

3. Remember that we are all in this together. We are a community of learners.
4. Restate what someone said if it is not clear.
5. If there are two sides to an issue, try to understand both sides.
6. Listen to everyone's ideas, even if you do not agree with them. It often takes more skill to listen than it does to share.
7. Let all ideas emerge.

Careful planning is required when it comes to constructing effective collaborative groups. A teacher has a lot to consider: How big should the groups be? How do I mix gender and ethnicity? How do I get students on task in a reasonable time? Should I assign specific roles? How do I eliminate hitchhiking and create accountability for all group members? All of these issues are important when constructing groups, but they are only half the battle. If we want students to use the power of collaboration to raise reading comprehension, not only must we factor in all of the above issues, we must also present students with challenging and interesting tasks. I could have the perfect group size, with a nice blend of gender and cultures, a clearly defined task, and focused individual accountability, but all of this will be for naught if the group collaboration doesn't promote higher-level thinking.

Ten Strategies to Promote Higher-Level Thinking in Small-Group Settings

Douglas Barnes and Frankie Todd note, "Small groups of students, working together, can advance learning in ways not available when a teacher talks to the entire class" (1995, p. 1). Assuming I have done a good job creating groups, how do I then prompt students to advance their learning? How do I help them tap into the power of collaboration? In the remainder of this chapter I suggest ten ways I have found effective in promoting higher-level thinking in small-group settings.

Silent Exchange

I learned the activity I call "Silent Exchange" from Jeff Wilhelm, who presented it at an NCTE meeting in Baltimore. Students read a passage or chapter and then write a question at the top of a sheet of paper. The question should be open-ended, not one that can be answered with a simple yes or no. In groups of five, students pass their papers to one another, read the question at the top of each page, and have two minutes to write a response to that question. There is no talking at this point. The teacher announces when two minutes are up and the responders stop writing, sign their names, and pass the paper to the next person in the rotation. This continues, two minutes at a time, until each person receives his or her own paper back. When the rotation is complete, each student has a number of written responses to his or her question. Students are given time to read all the responses and then the groups are "opened" for discussion.

Save the Last Word for Me

In an activity created by Kathy Short, Jerome Harste, and Carolyn Burke, each student copies a passage that he or she finds thought-provoking and writes it in large letters on a sheet of paper. Taking turns, each student silently holds up his or her passage so the other group members can read it. Taking turns, each group member verbally responds to the passage being displayed. The group members might try to guess why the passage was chosen, or they might discuss why the passage is important to the development of the chapter. After every group member has had a chance to share his or her thinking about the passage, the person who selected the passage (who hasn't yet spoken) tells why it was chosen. The person who selected the passage gets the last word, responding to the previous comments and adding his or her own thoughts. The group then moves to the next passage, held up by another member of the group, and the process is repeated.

Trouble Slips

In an activity I call "Trouble Slips," students are given slips of blank paper, roughly the size of bookmarks (Feathers 1993). As they read, they take note of their trouble spots in the text—places where their comprehension begins to falter. When students arrive in class the next day they are placed in groups and asked to share their trouble spots with their peers. Together, they try to work through the confusion. This teaches students that confusion is normal; and, through discussions with their peers, students are often able to deal with their confusion without the assistance of the teacher.

Kylene Beers, in her excellent book, *When Kids Can't Read, What Teachers Can Do,* uses other forms of bookmarks to help students make sense of text. Among them:

- *Mark my word.* Students use bookmarks to record interesting or unusual words. Periodically, students are placed in groups to talk about their words. Students are then asked to try to use some of their chosen words in subsequent writing.
- *Marking time.* Bookmarks are used to mark setting changes. This is an excellent strategy to use with works that contain multiple shifts in time and place.
- *Character bookmarks.* Students can track the characteristics of specific characters, noting key actions, dialogue, foreshadowing, and other literary elements.

Any of these bookmarks, when brought to collaborative groups, will prompt students to participate in meaning-making discussions.

Double-Entry Journals Plus

Many teachers are familiar with the double-entry journal, but teachers often miss the opportunity to use these journals to prompt meaningful discussion. In the traditional double-entry journal, students draw a vertical line down the page, creating a t-chart. On the left side of the chart, they copy a passage they find compelling. On the right side, they write a response to the passage. When completed, a student's entry may look like the example found in Figure 6.2.

Notice how in Figure 6.2 the sheet of paper containing the double-entry journal makes use of the space in the lower left-hand corner beneath the transcribed passage. This space is used for notes taken during group share. For example, Cassandra shares both her passage (from *1984*) and her response with her group. The other students in her group then summarize her main point in a sentence on each of their own papers. This process is continued until all members of the group have had a chance to share. Cassandra has written sentences summarizing what her three partners said, thus providing evidence that she actively listened.

SOAPS

SOAPS is a strategy devised by The College Board, and much like literature circles or reciprocal reading, it provides students with roles to help

Figure 6.2

Cassandra's Double-Entry Journal Plus, on *1984*

#8 Hot Spot

"there was the routine | This quote stuck out like a sore
of confession that had to be | thumb to me. Here Winston was
gone through: the groveling on | living in a world were people
the floor and screaming | were tortured until they confessed
for mercy, the crack of broken | to their crimes, which of course they
bones, the smashed teeth and | would do even if it was untrue. It
bloody clots of hair." | sounds alot like today with Bush's
"Nobody ever escaped | new plan on terrorists. His plan
detection, and nobody | is to hold suspected terrorists without
ever failed to confess." | phonecalls, a lawyer, his constitional
      Dej 87 | rights, and forms of torture are then
•See's "I love you" as | performed to get what they want out
hope for Winston and | of him. This is what our government is
the dark haired girl | telling us their doing, but how do we
    James | know their not in their braking bones
•See's the quote about | or smashing teeth in like Winston is
the movie being watched | telling us they will do. This is by far
in the beginning, with the | a scary quote to read; could I or my
boy dying, scary because | children be the next prole turned into the
their showing no remorse. | Thought Police?
    Jorge |
•Picked quote where |
Winston + Julia (Dark haired) |
held hands in the crowd |
as prisoners went by. |
   Thought it was |
brave of them to do that |
    Tara |

---

them discuss text. SOAPS is an acronym; each letter of the acronym represents a role:

Letter	Role
Subject(s)	Identifies the subject and the main idea(s).
Occasion	Discusses the context of the text; considers setting, circumstances, events, the era, the historical or cultural context.
Audience	Identifies the intended audience and discusses why this audience was targeted.
Purpose	Analyzes what the author's purpose was for composing the piece.
Speaker	Determines the tone of voice in the piece; discusses why this tone was used.

If students were to complete a SOAPS after reading the first three chapters of *To Kill a Mockingbird*, for example, they might discuss the following:

Subject(s)	The racism of the South. How schools often get in the way of education. Neighborhood urban legends.
Occasion	The book was written in 1960, prior to the civil rights movement. Racism was still prevalent in America.
Audience	Perhaps Lee wanted a broad audience to see the ugliness of poverty and racism. She may have hoped her book was read by blacks and whites, liberals and conservatives, racists, and lawmakers.
Purpose	Exposes the ugliness of racism and poverty, and explores the ignorance sometimes fostered by a lack of education.
Speaker	The tone varies. At times it is gentle, sarcastic, hopeful, humorous.

SOAPS can be used to help students discuss nonfiction as well.

Mystery Envelopes

Hand each group a "mystery envelope." Inside is an index card with a question for the group to answer. Here are some examples of mystery questions:

- What is the single most important word in this chapter? Why?
- Which character has changed the most so far? Is the change good or bad? What caused this change?
- What lesson(s) have we learned from a specific character?
- This chapter doesn't have a title. What should the title be? Why?
- Which minor character played the most important role in this book? Why?
- Why did we read this book? Why spend four weeks reading it? What value does it hold for the modern reader?
- What techniques did the author use in this chapter to hold the readers' interest?
- What is the central theme of this passage/chapter/book?
- Why did the author write this passage/chapter/book?
- Which character is most (least) believable? Why?
- Revisit the chapter and search for foreshadowing. Was the foreshadowing obvious or was it well hidden?
- How does the author use setting to advance the story?

The groups may be given the same question or different ones. Each group shares their answers, with all students taking notes as a group shares.

Group "Exams"

Many publishers produce study guides for the novels they publish, and as part of these study guides a standardized, multiple-choice exam for the novel is usually included. Generally speaking, I am not fond of using multiple-choice exams for assessment; if I want to gauge my students' understanding I have them produce essays or responses to open-ended questions. But I have found that multiple-choice exams can be useful review tools in group settings to help students prepare for the "real" assessment (the essay).

Prior to assigning the essay, I place students in groups and give them forty-five minutes to complete a one-hundred-question, multiple-choice exam. This is an open-book and open-notes exercise, and students within each group are encouraged to talk freely, though they may not confer with any other group. Each group is given one Scantron answer sheet to complete, and all members of the group will receive the same score. I tell the class that the team that gets the most items correct will get the best prize possible. They roll their eyes because they know their "prize" will simply be the satisfaction that they did well. (I tell them I don't want to cheapen their intellectual reward by giving them some cheesy item as a prize.)

Giving the multiple-choice exam this way is an excellent group activity. It gets students to discuss surface-level questions and gives them an opportunity to clear up any misunderstandings about the novel. It also serves as a nice review of the book. Later, when they sit down to write an essay that requires a higher-level understanding of the text, they will do so with any basic questions cleared up. They have to know what the novel says before they can analyze what it means, and this exercise helps them brush up on the fundamental elements.

You could also try a variation of this activity: Put students in groups and give them an essay question. In ten minutes, they have to turn in a complete outline as to how they would answer the essay question. Usually I do not have students write the actual essay. Putting the outline together sparks rich group discussion about the text. Each group then shares its outline with the rest of the class, and students take notes on the different approaches. Occasionally, I will then surprise them with the same essay question the next day—this time for real.

Group Open Minds

At a given point when they are midway through a novel, students are grouped and asked to analyze a character using an open mind. They are directed to draw metaphorical representations to illustrate what is going on in the character's head. In a novel with multiple characters, each group may work with different characters. The groups then share their thinking with the class as a whole, explaining why they chose their specific metaphors to represent the character's thinking. Each student is then asked to choose one character and an accompanying metaphor and write a brief explanation as to why that metaphor captures that character.

Conversation Log Exchanges

This next suggestion is group work of a different sort. Let's assume, for illustrative purposes, that three of my classes—periods one, two, and three—are reading the same novel. I purchase one set of composition books (which I dub Conversation Logs) and number each one. I then consider my students in all three classes and assign a number to each student in the three classes, giving the same number to one student from first period, one person from second period, and one person from third period, making sure to consider the grouping strategies discussed in the first half of this chapter. Each set of three students will share a Conversation Log. I distribute the numbered logs to my first-period class. These students are given time periodically to create written responses to the novel. They may write anything they want, but if they get stuck, I try to help with suggestions like these:

- If you're confused, write down your questions and ask for clarification.
- Challenge the text by asking pointed questions.
- Make connections from this text to other texts, or to other films, music, art, real-world situations . . .
- Identify the writer's craft. Discuss the literary techniques used. How does the writer draw you in?
- Make a prediction and *give evidence* for your prediction.

At the end of reflection time I collect the logs. When the second-period students arrive, I spread the logs out on a central table and the students, who know their predesignated number, pick up their numbered logs. I keep a master sheet that identifies which student goes with which log; but no names are allowed in the logs and students are not allowed to give clues to their identities. The written conversations must be solely about the reading.

After the students have completed the novel and have finished writing in the logs, I allow them to reveal their identities. I ask each person who contributed to the conversation to draw a highlighted line along the margin of every one of his or her comments (we use a different color highlighter for each period). That way, I can see at a glance who took the logs seriously and who hitchhiked. I ask each student to place one sticky note in the book with his or her name on it, marking the exact spot where the student thinks his or her highest level of thinking is evinced. These selected passages are the ones I read and assess; I do not read the entire logs.

I have also used a related activity to get students to "talk" about literature—though it would not be considered group work in the traditional sense. Rather than pass conversation logs between classes, I designate a computer in the corner of the classroom as the place students may have their conversations. As we begin reading, I open a blank Word document on the screen and ask one student to begin the conversation by writing a reflection. As we progress through the novel, every student is required at one time or another to walk over to this computer and respond to the ongoing conversation about the novel. This is a good way to engage students who finish five minutes early—they can go to the computer and join the conversation.

Theme Triangles

Theme Triangles can be used after students have finished the novel. In this two-week project, students in each group must identify what they believe to be the central theme in the novel. Each group writes its theme in a complete sentence. ("Racism," for example, is not a theme. "Remarkable courage is needed to stand up to the evils of racism" is a theme.) Once each group has settled on a theme, they must do the following:

1. Analyze how the theme is developed in the novel. (This, in itself, takes more than one class period.)
2. Each group chooses a film to watch that addresses the same theme. (They may not watch a film of the novel they have just read.) Students choose appropriate films and obtain their parents' permission prior to viewing the films. Everyone in the group is responsible for watching the film on his or her own time, with special attention paid to the theme. (This creates many movie gatherings at the homes of my students.)
3. Each group finds one more example of the theme in some other medium or genre. I tell them that this third example must be found in the modern world. Students can consider poems, songs, art, books, and speeches—any source that underscores this theme in the modern world.

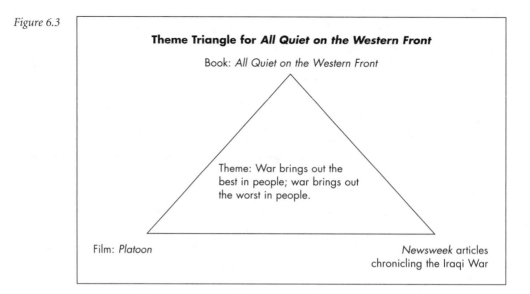

Figure 6.3

Theme Triangle for *All Quiet on the Western Front*

Book: *All Quiet on the Western Front*

Theme: War brings out the best in people; war brings out the worst in people.

Film: *Platoon*

Newsweek articles chronicling the Iraqi War

Figure 6.3 is an example of a theme triangle that one group of senior students put together after reading *All Quiet on the Western Front.*

Each group is then asked to prepare a ten-minute presentation in which they discuss the importance of their theme in the novel and demonstrate how it relates to the other two points of their triangle. I do not give students much more direction than that because I do not want to stifle their creativity. Over the years students have given lectures, produced skits, made films, created art, written songs, and created interpretive dance to convey the universality of their themes.

Talking to Learn

Creating collaborative groups helps students to embrace the confusion that they will encounter when they read challenging works. As Barnes and Todd note, "Neither adults nor children deal eagerly with challenging new ideas, for it is not comfortable to have existing ideas disturbed. Schooling, however, unlike learning in everyday life, is (or should be) designed to give students the opportunity to talk their way with some thoroughness through the dilemmas of learning. It would not be an exaggeration to say that a teacher's central task is to set up situations that encourage students to work on understanding. If schools and colleges are not doing this, they are failing their students" (p. 12).

Giving students an opportunity for group discussion prompts them to confront their confusion and teaches them that they are responsible for making their own meaning. Real meaning making occurs when the teacher has carefully considered how to formulate groups and has taken care to give students a task they will see as intellectually motivating and challenging. This creates a paradox: the more skilled the teacher is in setting up these conditions, the less the students will need the teacher to spoon-feed them the answers.

When I use the activities described in this chapter to elicit meaningful student discussions, I do so with one overarching goal in mind: ultimately, I want my students to have the ability to meet in groups and carry on meaningful discussions without direction from me. By the end of the school year, after they have seen model after model of how good readers discuss books, I place students in groups and simply ask, "What is it you want to talk about?" Instead of generating prompts and activities for students, I begin to back off and trust my students to shape their own discussions as they explore their thinking.

Isn't this why good readers join book clubs? We know that there is power in collaboration, and that even proficient readers can benefit greatly from the insight of others. Students need to discover this power as well. At the beginning of the year, I structure the discussions for them. By June, I want them both to understand the importance talking plays in raising their reading comprehension and to have internalized what good readers do when they sit down to talk.

CHAPTER SEVEN

Using Metaphor to Deepen Comprehension

Take a look at the following quotes:

> Now I don't want to get off on a rant here, but, these days, truth in media has been pushed further into the backseat than loose change during a shuttle launch.
> *Dennis Miller*

> For too long, the citizens of the Middle East have lived in the midst of death and fear. The hatred of a few holds the hopes of many hostage. The forces of extremism and terror are attempting to kill progress and peace by killing the innocent. And this casts a dark shadow over an entire region.
> *President George W. Bush*

> Up in the mornin'
> Work like a dog.
> It's better than sittin'
> Like a bump on a log.
> *John Prine "It's a Big Old Goofy World" (Original title: "When the World Was Flat as a Pancake, Mona Lisa Was Happy as a Clam")*

> Like David vs. Goliath, our mattresses refuse to back down!
> *A newspaper ad for beds*

Life is like playing a violin in public and learning the instrument as one goes on.
Samuel Butler

We live in a world of metaphor, and those who can appreciate it are richer for it. I want my students to experience this richness. Beyond that, I want them to develop their ability to think metaphorically as a means of reaching deeper levels of comprehension. By doing so, I hope I am leading them to a deeper appreciation of literature.

How can I teach *Romeo and Juliet,* for example, without recognizing Shakespeare's use of metaphor? When Romeo sees Juliet for the first time, her beauty floors him. Romeo does not simply say, "Wow! She is so pretty, she sure stands out from all the rest!" Instead, Romeo remarks that Juliet

doth teach the torches to burn bright!
It seems she hangs upon the cheek of night
As a rich jewel in an Ethiop's ear—
Beauty too rich for use, for earth too dear!
So shows a snowy dove trooping with crows
As yonder lady o'er her fellows shows. (1:5, lines 45–50)

By describing Juliet as a rich jewel against an Ethiop's ear, or as a white dove among crows, Shakespeare is creating unforgettable imagery that helps the reader better understand Juliet's beauty and the intensity of Romeo's feelings. By taking something we know (what a white dove and black crows look like) and connecting that knowledge to something we don't know (just how deep Romeo's love for Juliet is), Shakespeare uses metaphor to push the reader to reach a new level of understanding. Much more vivid than literal description, the use of these metaphors strengthens the play's central conceit: that overpowering, uncontrollable love at first sight is possible. Shakespeare's use of metaphorical language adds a depth to Romeo's feelings that resonates in the hearts and minds of the readers. That is the power metaphor has compared to literal description.

Bringing metaphorical thinking into the teaching of literature provides two benefits: (1) students are more readily able to reach deeper levels of comprehension when they understand metaphor in challenging text (as in the *Romeo and Juliet* example above); and (2) repeated practice recognizing and analyzing metaphor enables students to generate their own metaphorical connections to the text and to the world, thus sharpening their higher-level thinking skills.

When teaching students to appreciate the richness of metaphor, it might help to begin by looking at the different types of metaphor, as shown below:

Term	Definition	Example
Standard metaphor	A figure of speech that makes a connection between two unlike things.	My heart is a rose.
Extended metaphor	A metaphor extended over several lines, verses, or chapters.	Writing this research paper is a grind. My brain is not operating. I am running out of steam. (Each sentence extends the metaphor that the mind is a machine.)
Implied metaphor	A less direct metaphor.	The boxer pecked away at his opponent.
Dead metaphor	A metaphor that has become so common that we no longer notice it as a figure of speech.	My sister drives me out of my mind.
Simile	A figure of speech that makes a connection between two unlike things by using words such as *like, as, than,* or *resembles.*	My heart is like a rose.
Personification	A metaphor in which a nonhuman thing or quality is talked about in human terms.	The casino cheated him.
Metonymy	A figure of speech in which something closely related to a thing is substituted for the thing itself.	This history department needs new blood (instead of needing new teachers).
Synecdoche	The substitution of a part for the whole (or vice versa).	Five hundred hands were needed to build the bridge.

In *Metaphors We Live By,* George Lakoff and Mark Johnson contend that by teaching students to think in metaphorical terms we are helping them cultivate an "imaginative rationality." When we ask a student to think metaphorically, they note, we "permit an understanding of one kind of experience in terms of another, creating coherences by virtue of imposing gestalts that are structured by natural dimensions of experience. New metaphors are capable of creating new understandings, and, therefore, new realities" (p. 235). It is these new understandings—these new realities—that I hope students discover by thinking metaphorically while interacting with text.

Airplanes Good! Helicopters Bad!

The OWL (Online Writing Lab) at Purdue University recommends that students be taught the value of metaphorical thinking for a number of reasons. Here are three:

1. Metaphors enliven ordinary language.

2. Metaphors require interpretation (higher-level thinking).
3. Metaphors create new meanings.

Let's take a closer look at each of these reasons and consider why each is relevant in our classrooms.

Metaphors Enliven Ordinary Language

One of my favorite contemporary authors is Barbara Kingsolver. Here are the first two paragraphs of her novel *The Bean Trees*, a favorite of mine:

> I have been afraid of putting air in a tire since I saw a tractor tire blow up and throw Newt Hardbine's father over the top of the Standard Oil sign. I'm not lying. He got stuck up there. About nineteen people congregated during the time it took for Norman Strick to walk up to the Courthouse and blow the whistle for the volunteer fire department. They eventually did come with the ladder and haul him down, and he wasn't dead but lost his hearing and in many other ways was never the same afterward. They said he overfilled the tire.
>
> Newt Hardbine was not my friend, he was just one of the big boys who had failed every grade at least once and so was practically going on twenty in the sixth grade, sitting in the back, flicking little wads of chewed paper into my hair. But the day I saw his daddy up there like some old overalls slung over a fence, I had this feeling about what Newt's whole life was going to amount to, and I felt sorry for him. Before that exact moment I don't believe I had given much thought to the future.

That is great writing. In fact, that first sentence may be my favorite opening sentence of any novel I've ever taught. But the image that stays with me, the image that resonates with me every time I read that passage, is the picture of poor old Mr. Hardbine hanging off that Standard Oil sign "like some old overalls slung over a fence." That metaphor enlivens the passage—so much so that I still remember it ten years after having read the novel for the first time.

Strong metaphors bring writing alive. To illustrate this, I present students with two versions of a Gary Soto poem, "Oranges" (see Figure 7.1). Version A, on the left, has been altered to remove all metaphors. Version B is the poem as Soto wrote it.

I ask students to read both versions of the poem with a highlighter in hand, indicating the exact places where the poems differ. This serves to make them aware of the three instances of metaphor in the poem (the candies "tiered like bleachers"; fog hanging "like old coats between the

Figure 7.1

With and Without Metaphor: Gary Soto's "Oranges"

Version A	Version B
The first time I walked	The first time I walked
With a girl, I was twelve,	With a girl, I was twelve,
Cold, and weighted down	Cold, and weighted down
With two oranges in my jacket.	With two oranges in my jacket.
December. Frost cracking	December. Frost cracking
Beneath my steps, my breath	Beneath my steps, my breath
Before me, then gone,	Before me, then gone,
As I walked toward	As I walked toward
Her house, the one whose	Her house, the one whose
Porch light burned yellow	Porch light burned yellow
Night and day, in any weather.	Night and day, in any weather.
A dog barked at me, until	A dog barked at me, until
She came out pulling	She came out pulling
At her gloves, face bright	At her gloves, face bright
with rouge. I smiled,	with rouge. I smiled,
Touched her shoulder, and led	Touched her shoulder, and led
Her down the street, across	Her down the street, across
A used car lot and a line	A used car lot and a line
Of newly planted trees,	Of newly planted trees,
Until we are breathing	Until we are breathing
Before a drugstore. We	Before a drugstore. We
Entered, the tiny bell	Entered, the tiny bell
Bringing a saleslady	Bringing a saleslady
Down a narrow aisle of goods.	Down a narrow aisle of goods.
I turned to the candies	I turned to the candies
Lined up in one aisle,	Tiered like bleachers,
And asked what she wanted—	And asked what she wanted—
Light in her eyes, a smile	Light in her eyes, a smile
Starting at the corners	Starting at the corners
Of her mouth. I fingered	Of her mouth. I fingered
A nickel in my pocket,	A nickel in my pocket,
And when she lifted a chocolate	And when she lifted a chocolate
That cost a dime,	That cost a dime,
I didn't say anything.	I didn't say anything.
I took the nickel from	I took the nickel from
My pocket, then an orange,	My pocket, then an orange,
And set them quietly on	And set them quietly on
The counter. When I looked up,	The counter. When I looked up,
The lady's eyes met mine,	The lady's eyes met mine,
And held them, knowing	And held them, knowing
Very well what it was all	Very well what it was all
About.	About.
Outside,	Outside,
A few cars hissing past,	A few cars hissing past,
And it was very foggy.	Fog hanging like old
I took my girl's hand	Coats between the trees.
In mine for two blocks,	I took my girl's hand
Then released it to let	In mine for two blocks,
Her unwrap the chocolate.	Then released it to let
I peeled my orange	Her unwrap the chocolate.
That was so bright against	I peeled my orange
The gray of December	That was so bright against
That, from some distance	The gray of December
Someone might have seen	That, from some distance
It was really bright.	Someone might have thought
	I was making a fire in my hands.

trees"; the orange looking like a fire). Students are then asked to decide which version of the poem they think is better. Without exception, they always pick Version B—the one containing the metaphors. I then ask the students some questions:

- Why is the second version better?
- Why, for example, is it better to describe the fog as "hanging like old coats between the trees"? Why not just say it was really foggy?
- How does the use of metaphor add to the poem?

For homework, students are asked to bring one example of written metaphor to class the next day. They can take their example from literature, music, newspapers, magazines, the Internet—anywhere they want. These examples are then shared in class, and we discuss how the metaphors found in these examples enliven ordinary language.

Metaphors Require Interpretation

Imagine a world in which there are only literal statements. This is the premise of Peggy Parish's children's book series featuring Amelia Bedelia, a hapless maid who goes to work for an affluent family. Amelia's inability to think beyond the literal gets her into repeated trouble. When she is told to draw the drapes, she gets out a sketchpad and begins drawing. She is reluctant to dust the furniture, because it strikes her as odd: she'd rather *un*dust the furniture. When her exasperated employer tells her to hit the road, she grabs a stick and does just that. Driving away, Amelia misses her turnoff when she is preoccupied trying to find a fork—an eating utensil—in the road.

My students, sad to say, have a little too much Amelia Bedelia in them. They often take what they read at face value and have a difficult time interpreting the underlying meaning. They are competent at answering literal "What does it say?" questions, but when the reading requires interpretation, they begin to struggle. Interpretation is hard work, particularly when rich metaphor is involved. The only way to help students develop this higher level of thinking is to provide them with opportunities to practice interpretive thinking.

Interpreting rich metaphor usually requires second-draft reading. To illustrate this with teachers, I have them read one of my favorite poems, Walker Gibson's "Billiards":

Late of the jungle, wild and dim,
Sliced from the elephant's ivory limb,
Painted, polished, here these spheres
Rehearse their civilized careers—
Trapped in geometric toil,
Exhibit impact and recoil
Politely, in a farce of force,
And let's have no absurd remorse,
But praise the complicated plan
That organizes beast and man
In patterns so superbly styled
Late of the jungle, dim and wild.

"Billiards" is a difficult poem to interpret after a single read. When I use this with adults in workshops I tell them that although this poem is entitled "Billiards," it really is not about billiards. I challenge them to read it a number of times in order to deepen their understanding, to discuss the poem in small groups, and to share what they think the poem is really about.

After a few minutes of struggle and some give and take, most participants begin to see Walker's poem as an extended metaphor: he is comparing billiard balls with the human condition. Once this metaphor is identified, we chart the comparisons:

Billiard Balls	Humans
Because they come from the elephant's ivory limb, billiard balls are "late of the jungle."	Humans are "late of the jungle."
Billiard balls are painted and polished. They no longer resemble where they came from. They are far removed from the wild.	Human beings are "painted and polished." They no longer resemble where they came from. They are far removed from the wild.
Billiard balls are "trapped in geometric toil."	Human beings toil in the geometric patterns of modern society.
Billiard balls "exhibit impact and recoil."	Human beings "exhibit impact and recoil."
There are patterns to be recognized in billiards.	There are patterns to be recognized in life.
By harnessing the tusk from elephants, the wild has been tamed and civilized.	By creating rules and regulations, humans' wild past has been tamed and civilized.
A "complicated plan" is involved in organizing beasts into billiard balls.	A "complicated plan" is involved in organizing people into an orderly society.

Walker uses metaphor to give his poem a much richer meaning than it would have had he chosen to express his thoughts literally. There is a complexity here in the use of billiards, a complexity that offers depth and intellectual reward to the reader.

To help students discover the rewards of metaphor, I use easier passages, like the following poem by Edgar Lee Masters:

George Gray

I have studied many times
The marble which was chiseled for me—
A boat with a furled sail at rest in the harbor.
In truth it pictures not my destination
But my life.
For love was offered me and I shrank from its disillusionment;
Sorrow knocked on my door but I was afraid;
Ambition called to me, but I dreaded the chances.
Yet all the while I hungered for meaning in my life.
And now I know that we must lift the sail
And catch the winds of destiny
Wherever they drive the boat.
To put meaning in one's life may end in madness,
But life without meaning is the torture
Of restlessness and vague desire—
It is a boat longing for the sea and yet afraid

The extended metaphor in this passage—comparing your life to a sailboat—is one that students can easily identify, and it serves as a springboard to discussing metaphor generally. It enables me to extend students' thinking by asking:

- Why do you think the author used a sailboat as the central metaphor?
- Why a sailboat? Why not a rowboat? Or a motorboat?
- Is it an effective metaphor? Why? Why not?
- Instead of a sailboat, could the author have used a different metaphor to effectively make his same point?

After students get their feet wet (sorry!), I give them something a bit more challenging, like Sylvia Plath's poem "Metaphors":

I am a riddle in nine syllables.
An elephant, a ponderous house
A melon strolling on two tendrils.
O red fruit, ivory, fine timbers!
This loaf's big with its yeasty rising.
Money's new minted in this fat purse.
I'm a means, a stage, a cow in calf.
I've eaten a bag of green apples,
Boarded the train there's no getting off.

In this poem Plath strings a number of metaphors together to describe pregnancy. This is an excellent poem to use with students to discuss the power and richness of metaphor. After all, which resonates more with the reader: to write simply that the narrator felt morning sickness or to write that the narrator's morning sickness felt like she has eaten a bag of green apples? Students have fun trying to interpret each metaphor in the poem.

Having such discussions about metaphor helps adolescents to move beyond an "Amelia Bedelia" reading mentality and enables them to sharpen their interpretive skills.

Metaphors Create New Meanings

Not long ago I coached my daughter's softball team—a team made up of eight-year-old girls. It is a fun age to coach because the players, many of them new to the game, often arrive at the beginning of the season unskilled. It is a joy watching them develop as the season progresses.

Early in the season it became apparent we needed much practice on the skill of fielding ground balls. How did I come to this conclusion? Because half the ground balls hit in practice went through our infielders' legs. There is perhaps no cuter sight in this world than an eight-year-old who gets her glove down on the ground a fraction of a second too late only to track the ball with her head as it rolls between her legs. She ends up seeing the outfielders upside down.

Though this was cute in practice, I wasn't sure it would be as endearing in a game, so I set aside time to practice fielding grounders. I assembled the girls and told them the reason they were having so many balls roll between their legs was because they were a little bit late getting their gloves down to the ball. The problem, I explained, was that they were placing their gloves down on the ground at the same moment the ball arrived; instead, they needed to have their gloves touching the dirt *before* the ball arrived so that their gloves would be awaiting the ball. This would prevent the ball from rolling between their legs. From now on, I told them, everybody needs to get their gloves down sooner. I asked them if they understood. They solemnly nodded and practice resumed.

You might guess what happened next: the first two ground balls hit after my talk went right through the fielders' legs. Beyond the realization at that moment that I'd never be given the opportunity to manage the Los Angeles Dodgers, I also realized the players had not taken my instruction to heart. They were still making the same errors they were before my pep talk. I reassembled them for another attempt, knowing this time I would have to take a different angle. Our next exchange went something like this:

Coach Kelly: O.K., girls, who can tell me how a helicopter lands?

Ashley: Huh?

Coach Kelly: Who can tell me how a helicopter lands?

Ashley: It lands straight.

Coach Kelly: What do you mean, "It lands straight"?

Ashley: It lowers itself straight down to the ground.

Coach Kelly: Right! Now who can tell me how an airplane lands?

J.B.: It swooshes down (*she flattens out her hand and simulates an airplane approaching a runway*).

Coach Kelly: Right again! So what's the difference between how a helicopter lands and how an airplane lands?

Arianna: Helicopters land straight down. Airplanes swoosh in.

Coach Kelly: Exactly! Now, I want you to remember this when you are fielding ground balls. Some of you are fielding grounders like helicopters—you are lowering your gloves straight down to meet the ball. This is not good. When we field ground balls we do not want to be helicopters. What do we want to be like?

Melinda (*hesitantly*): Airplanes?

Coach Kelly: Yes! We want to be like airplanes. We want to approach the ball like an airplane that is landing. We want to swoosh low to the ground, moving our gloves along the ground toward the ball. (*I demonstrate the difference to them as another dad hits me a few ground balls*). From now on, I want to see airplanes only out there—no helicopters!

Before resuming practice, I briefly considered instituting a new team chant based on the rantings of the animals in *Animal Farm* ("Four legs good! Two legs bad!" In our case, it would be "Airplanes good! Helicopters bad!"), but I decided that my eight-year-old members of the Big Blue Wrecking Crew weren't quite ready for that.

What happened next, however, was a pleasant surprise. The girls immediately began to grasp the concept, and though I can't say we did not have any more ground balls go through the legs of our infielders, I can say the number of times they committed this error diminished drastically. Framing the instruction in the airplane-helicopter metaphor (instead of using literal language) made the instruction more understandable. The airplane metaphor clicked in their minds, and as a result, their fielding improved. (Now if only I could have thought of a metaphor that would have helped them to stop swinging at pitches out of the strike zone!)

Just as using helicopters and airplanes helped my players better understand how to play softball, metaphor can be used to help students better

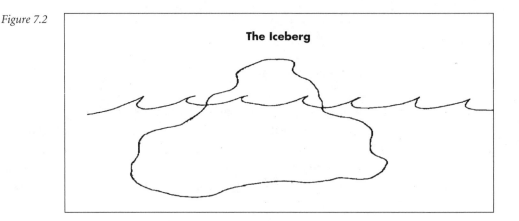

Figure 7.2

The Iceberg

understand how to read challenging text. I have learned much of the value metaphor plays in reading comprehension from John Powers, a friend and mentor of mine. Currently a professor of English at California State University, Fullerton, John has taught both junior high school and high school English, and in his years of teaching adolescents he created and implemented metaphorical graphic organizers to help them build interpretative skills. For example, he uses one called the "iceberg" to help students get a deeper understanding of a specific character. The iceberg is simply drawn on the board as shown in Figure 7.2.

Sometimes, as the captain of the *Titanic* learned, there is more to an iceberg than meets the eye. In many cases, what you see above the water may only be a small piece of the entire iceberg. Often, most of the iceberg—the dangerous part—remains under water, out of sight.

An iceberg is a good metaphor to use when studying a specific character. Like an iceberg, part of a character is easily visible; but at the same time there might be a part, sometimes a large part, of the character that remains unseen. Consider the following examples:

Character	Visible Characteristics	Characteristics Below the Surface
Holden Caufield	Angry, disillusioned, indifferent	Sensitive, susceptible, wounded
Arthur Dimmsdale	Moral, sincere, a leader	Immoral, insincere, devious
Ultima	Mystical, threatening, unapproachable	Nurturing, wise, mentoring
Piggy	Annoying, whining, nerdy	Reasoned, intelligent, insightful
Jay Gatsby	Wealthy, worldly, upstanding	Scandalous, unethical, secretive
Boo Radley	Odd, isolated, reclusive	Brave, caring, protective

All characters reveal something about themselves to others, but sometimes it's more interesting to have students analyze what a character *doesn't* reveal to others. Using the iceberg as an analytical tool produced deeper thinking in my students when I asked them to analyze the seen and unseen

Figure 7.3

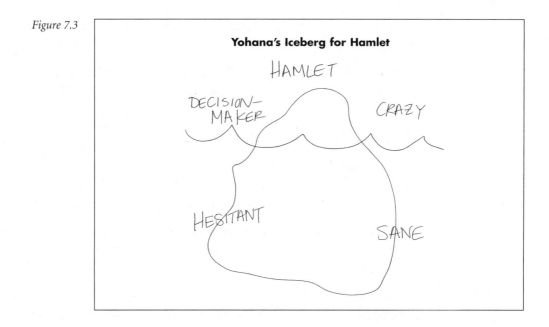

Yohana's Iceberg for Hamlet

characteristics of a character. Figure 7.3, for example, is an iceberg annotated by Yohana, age seventeen, for the character of Hamlet. Above the surface Hamlet is seen as both decisive and crazy. But below the surface Yohana sees him as both sane (he is pretending to be crazy) and hesitant (he delays taking revenge after learning of his father's murder).

In addition to the iceberg, Powers has developed other metaphorical graphic organizers to help students analyze character, plot, and structure, and setting. In this chapter I describe several, providing brief explanations of how each one works, ways to apply each one, and variations worth considering.

Metaphorical Graphic Organizers That Help Students Analyze Character

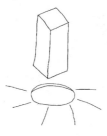

Square Peg, Round Hole

Explanation: A square peg does not fit in a round hole. Sometimes, when a character does not "fit in," he or she feels like a square peg in a round hole. In this organizer, students are asked to consider both society's expectations on a character (the round hole) and the character's needs (square peg).

Application: Square Peg, Round Hole works well in any novel where a character is going against the grain of his or her time or place.

Variation: This organizer can also be used to analyze the conflict between what a character wants to do and what the character "should" do.

Brake Pedal, Accelerator Pedal

Explanation: In the Brake Pedal, Accelerator Pedal organizer, students are asked to consider the forces (people, places, things) that slow a character down as well as the forces that accelerate a character's thinking or behavior.

Application: Brake Pedal, Accelerator Pedal works well in any novel where a character tries to resist others or where a character gets swept up in the action of others.

Variation: Sometimes "braking" a character turns out to be a positive development. Discuss why "slowing down" a character precipitated a positive turn of events.

Ingredients
Sugar, wheat, corn syrup, partially hydrated soybean oil, honey, caramel, color, salt, reduced iron, zinc oxide, vitamin B6.

Ingredients Listing

Explanation: When you purchase food in the market, there are ingredient labels on the packaging. These labels not only list the ingredients found in the product, they also list the ingredients in the order of amount (from most to least). In this organizer, students are asked to list the character's "ingredients" (traits), with the most important first and the least important last.

Application: Ingredients Listing works well with any novel that depicts complex characters.

Variation: If you could add one ingredient to this character, what would you add? Why? If you could remove one ingredient from this character, what would you remove? Why? How would have the story turned out differently had that ingredient been added/dropped?

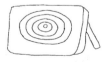

Archery Target

Explanation: The goal in archery is to hit the center circle. Characters may have specific goals as well. In this organizer, students are asked to determine how close a character came to reaching his or her goal (hitting his or her target).

Application: Archery Target works well with any novel that depicts a character working toward a goal.

Variation: Students could identify the main goal in the center of the target and list minor goals in the outer circles, or students could identify a character's long-term and short-term goals. Either way, students could analyze what prevents the character from hitting a bull's-eye.

Wallet/Purse

Explanation: You would learn a great deal about a person if you were permitted to examine the contents of her purse or the contents of his wallet. Of course, some characters—for example, Frankenstein's monster—do not have a purse or wallet. But assuming they did, what would be in it? And what could we learn about a given character from the items found in that character's wallet or purse?

Application: Wallet/Purse works well with any novel.

Variation: What would we find in this character's locker? Room? Backpack?

Metaphorical Graphic Organizers That Help Students Analyze Plot and Structure

Pencil, Eraser

Explanation: A pencil has two ends, one for writing and the other for erasing. Students take a copy of the image and write a character's name on the shaft of the pencil. On the writing end of the pencil, students note the actions that character wishes he or she had done. On the eraser end, students consider what actions the character wishes he or she could erase.

Application: Pencil, Eraser works well with any novel.

Variation: On the writing end of the pencil, students could note what a character actually did in the book. On the eraser end, students try to determine if any of these actions could be completely erased. What steps would the character have to do to erase his or her actions? Is total erasure even possible?

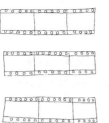

Proof Sheets

Explanation: On a trip to the Grand Canyon, you might shoot a roll of film chronicling your journey. When the film is developed you would have a proof sheet containing twenty-four exposures. These twenty-four pictures do not capture every moment of your vacation; rather, they capture the highlights of your trip. When having students analyze key plot points, they can be given dummy proof sheets and asked to identify the twenty-four key plot points. Students must identify exactly twenty-four points, not twenty-two or twenty-five. This requirement will spur deep discussions about what is important, and what isn't, in terms of the plot.

Application: Proof Sheet works well with any novel that has a complex plot.

Variation: When students have completed their proof sheets, ask them which four "photographs" from their roll they would print and display. Which four pictures are the highlights of the "trip"? Have them explain their selections.

Billiards Table

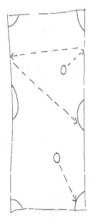

Explanation: For a billiard ball to drop into a side pocket, a chain reaction must occur. A player must strike a cue against a cue ball. The cue ball must travel and hit the target ball. The target ball is struck and then propelled toward the pocket. Sometimes, when the cue ball is not struck properly, balls ricochet off one another or off bumpers, causing unexpected turns of events. When having students analyze plot events, have students identify which character(s) represent the pool cue, the cue ball, the target ball, the other balls on the table, and the bumpers.

Application: Billiards Table works well with any novel containing a chain of events that leads to the climax of the story.

Variation: In billiards, a player who accidentally knocks the eight ball into a pocket is said to have "scratched" and is declared the loser. Describe a character who has "scratched" and analyze the chain of events that led to this character being eliminated from "the game."

Metaphorical Graphic Organizers That Help Students Analyze Setting

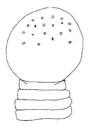

Snow Globe

Explanation: I have a snow globe of New York City that is five inches across. Because of the vastness of New York, representing the city in a five-inch sphere presents a challenge. To capture the essence of the Big Apple, my globe has miniature representations of the Empire State Building, the Statue of Liberty, The Chrysler Building, and the Brooklyn Bridge. If students were to make a snow globe for the novel they are reading, what would they include to help capture the essence of the novel?

Application: Snow Globe works well with any novel where setting plays a key role.

Variation: Have your students rank the settings found in the novel from most important to least important. Which single setting is most critical to the development of the novel? Have them defend their rankings. Or have students create snow globes to represent the lives of specific characters.

Time Capsule

Explanation: In the year 2000, my school buried a time capsule with artifacts to help future generations to understand what life was like as we entered the new millennium. If we were to fill a time capsule to give readers a sense of time and place for a specific novel, what would we put in it? Which artifacts would we choose to give a prospective reader an accurate sense of the setting?

Application: Time Capsule works well with any novel where setting plays a key role.

Variation: Have your students rank the artifacts found in their time capsule from most important to least important. Have them defend their rankings.

Backdrop, Props

Explanation: Putting on a play requires the art director to carefully consider what he or she will use as backdrops for the staging of scenes. Because it is not practical to have more than three or four sets for a single play, both backdrops and props have to be versatile. If we were to stage the novel we are reading, which three or four backdrops would you use to give the audience a true sense of the setting? What props would you use?

Application: Backdrops, Props works well with any novel where setting plays a key role.

Variation: If you had a budget of $300, what would you purchase to be used as props in the performance of this novel? Could any of these props be used for more than one purpose?

Five Considerations

All of these metaphorical graphic organizers are designed to stretch students' knowledge by starting them off with what they are familiar with and having them apply what they know to create new meaning. Like any classroom activity, metaphorical graphic organizers need to be used with careful consideration. To achieve maximum effectiveness, consider the following.

Use Metaphor to Interpret Metaphor

When asking students to complete a metaphorical graphic organizer, make sure they do so in metaphorical terms. Remember Yohana's iceberg for Hamlet (Figure 7.3)? Her responses, while good, are literal. Yohana's thinking could be ratcheted up a notch by requiring all of her responses to be metaphorical in nature. When I asked Yohana to do another draft, with the new draft depicting her ideas metaphorically, she produced what's shown in Figure 7.4. Then I asked her to explain the rationale behind each of her metaphors, which she did, as shown in Figure 7.5.

I especially like Yohana's comparing Hamlet to a calculator because he "calculates how to solve the murder by staging a play and by faking his insanity. The problem with a calculator, however," she continues, "is that its battery may eventually wind down." By introducing the battery idea, she is adding a metaphor to her metaphor. Asking Yohana to interpret Hamlet by responding in metaphorical terms took her thinking to a new level.

Don't Turn Graphic Organizers into Worksheets

In 1987, John Powers invented a wonderful graphic organizer called the Open Mind. It was simply a drawing of an outline of a head with nothing

Figure 7.4

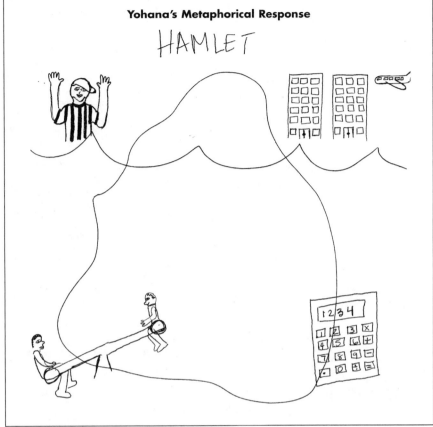

Yohana's Metaphorical Response

HAMLET

in it (in fact, his initial name for it was the Empty Head). In this graphic organizer, students were to fill in the head with the character's thoughts, preferably in metaphorical terms. Using this organizer, a teacher could determine at a glance a student's level of character analysis.

The problem with the Open Mind (like so many good ideas) was that it was misinterpreted and overused. Rather than using it for a specific complex character, teachers started assigning it repeatedly for any and all characters. Some teachers misinterpreted the original idea and had students write down their own thoughts about the character rather than capture the character's thinking. Others required students to record the character's thoughts literally and hence superficially. Because of its overuse, students soon came to see the Open Mind as just another worksheet.

Though the graphic organizers described in this chapter have proven valuable in helping students analyze literature, overusing them will diminish their effectiveness. They should be used sparingly and judi-

Figure 7.5

Yohana's Explanation

"SEEN"

Symbol to Represent __Hamlet__	Explanation of Symbol	How This Symbol Connects to the Character
Hamlet is like a referee because...	A referee understands all the rules and is there to make sure the players follow them. He has to be decisive when he hands out penalties to players who break rules.	Hamlet understands the "rules" of Elsinore, the castle. Hamlet is horrified when his mother and his uncle ignore the rules. As the play unfolds, it is obvious that he is bothered by all the rules violations. To help decide who should be penalized, Hamlet decides to lay a trap by staging a play that re-enacts his father's murder.
Hamlet is like a September 11th terrorist because...	The terrorists who killed many innocent people were insane. They murdered without a second thought.	Like the terrorists, Hamlet appears to lose all reason. He treats his mother irrationally and his erratic behavior drives Ophelia over the edge. He kills Polonius and has Rosencrantz and Guildenstern executed without a second thought.

"UNSEEN"

Symbol to Represent __Hamlet__	Explanation of Symbol	How This Symbol Connects to the Character
Hamlet is like a see-saw because	A see-saw will tilt one way and then the other way.	Hamlet wavers back and forth on his decision to kill Cladius. He says he's going to do it, then he doesn't do it. He waits too long, and as a result, a number of other people end up dying.
Hamlet is like a calculator because...	A calculator figures problems out logically.	Hamlet calculates how to solve the murder by staging a play and by faking his insanity. The problem with a calculator, however, is that its battery may eventually wind down.

ciously, with careful attention to how well they fit with a particular literary work and how well they are apt to prompt deeper meaning of the text. These organizers are not "one size fits all." Another note: I do not simply photocopy them and hand them out; rather, I have students draw their own. Having students take thirty seconds to draw their own metaphorical structure increases their motivation. It seems silly, but having them draw a brake and an accelerator pedal on their paper pulls them into the assignment—even though they theoretically could attempt the same thinking without making the drawing.

Keep the "Newness Factor" in Mind When Assigning Metaphorical Graphic Organizers

To avoid the fate of the Open Mind, keep the "newness factor" in mind when having students think metaphorically. Rather than reusing the same organizers, create new ones as you progress through the school year. For example, last night I finished reading Michael Connelly's *The Poet,* one of his novels featuring LAPD detective Harry Bosch. In this novel, Bosch is tracking a serial killer who leaves poetry in his wake as clues. During his investigation, Bosch interrogates many potential suspects. Some of these interrogations are done brutally, others with finesse.

Maybe it's because I am currently writing a chapter on metaphor, but as I read the novel I couldn't help thinking that Bosch was like a hammer: sometimes he used force to "pound" information from suspects; other times he gently wheedled critical information from witnesses (much like using the claw end of a hammer to carefully remove a tight nail from a wall). If I were teaching *The Poet,* I would draw a hammer and ask students to identify where the detective used force and where he used finesse (both ends of the hammer). This could lead to more analytical thinking, prompting the following questions: Which technique seemed to be more effective, brute force or finesse? Can you identify a time when the detective should have switched tactics (used finesse instead of force, or vice versa)? How would the story have turned out differently had the detective not used force (or finesse) in this scene?

It is unlikely that I'll teach a Michael Connelly novel in a high school class, but that is not the point. Thinking in metaphorical terms has helped me develop the ability to improvise different metaphorical graphic organizers on the fly. This ability comes in handy when I teach my core works. By generating new metaphors for my students to use when they consider their reading, I hope to inspire deeper analytical thinking.

Have Students Create and Draw Their Own Metaphorical Graphic Organizers

Instead of always providing students with a metaphorical graphic organizer, have students begin developing their own. To start them thinking metaphorically, I place students in small groups and have them complete the exercise first described in Chapter 2:

(Character name) is like a _____ because _____.

Depending on what you want your students to analyze, this sentence starter could be worded as follows:

The chain of events in this novel is like a _____ **because** _____ .

The mood in this novel is like a _____ **because** _____ .

The writing style in this novel is like a _____ **because** _____ .

The novel is built (put together) like a _____ **because** _____ .

An endless number of sentence starters can be thought of to move students toward metaphorical thinking. Once they have completed the sentence, students can be asked to represent these metaphors graphically (as in the Hamlet iceberg example). Sharing thoughts in class enables all the students to hear good ideas, thus priming the pump to help them generate new ideas of their own. It's fun to hear a student explain why Jay Gatsby is like an hourglass or why Dr. Jekyll is like a candle.

When students have been given the kind of metaphorical practice outlined in this chapter, they can begin developing their own metaphors to analyze character, plot, setting, and other literary elements.

Use Metaphorical Graphic Organizers as a Springboard to Writing

As a former English coordinator for a large, urban secondary school district (eighteen schools, 34,000 students) and a consultant to other school districts, I visited many English classrooms over several years. One of the perks of my job was that I was witness to a lot of great teaching, particularly in the area of writing. It is heartening to know that outstanding writing instruction is taking place in many of our schools under some rather adverse conditions.

That said, however, I must add that in some schools, students are not writing enough. As noted in a recent study cited in *Because Writing Matters,* a book written by teacher-leaders in the National Writing Project, "children don't get too many opportunities to write. In grades one, three, and five, only 15 percent of the school day was spent in any kind of writing activity. Two-thirds of the writing that did occur was word-for-word copying in workbooks. Compositions of a paragraph or more in length are infrequent even at the high school level" (p. 6). Additionally, other "national studies and assessments of writing over the past three decades have repeatedly shown that students spend too little time writing in and out of school" (p. 13). In short, in many classrooms, writing has become the "forgotten 'R.'"

In this age of high stakes tests and accountability, the amount of writing a student does is critical. The 1998 NAEP reading assessment asked students how frequently they wrote long answers to test questions or reading assignments. The researchers found a clear correlation between how much writing students did and how well they scored on reading assessments. Students who wrote frequently read better and scored higher; students who wrote infrequently did not read as well and scored lower.

The metaphorical graphic organizers presented in this chapter not only offer an opportunity for our students to think metaphorically, but, more important, they also generate thinking that translates well into analytical writing. This raises the last and most important consideration: *above all else, metaphorical graphic organizers should be used as springboards to writing.* One of the problems with the Open Mind, the organizer mentioned earlier, is that students often completed it by itself, without using it to inspire their own writing. Any metaphorical graphic organizer is an effective tool that can help students sort out their thoughts before writing essays.

To illustrate how these organizers can help inspire analytical writing, let's return to Yohana's Hamlet iceberg. Before she wrote her essay on Hamlet, I asked Yohana to add a fourth column to her chart in Figure 7.5 where she could site specific passages to support her assertions for both the "seen" and "unseen" sides of Hamlet. Figure 7.6 shows how Yohana supported her ideas about the "seen" and "unseen" Hamlet. With this organizer now containing specific textual references, Yohana has generated an outline for an essay analyzing the two sides of Hamlet. She is ready to write. This strategy, of course, can be applied beyond *Hamlet* to any major work.

Teaching students to think metaphorically helps them to appreciate the richness and liveliness of language. Thinking this way sharpens their interpretative skills and helps them reach deeper understanding. When we teach students to think in metaphorical terms, we are not only helping them to gain a better appreciation of a particular piece of literature; we are also providing them with cognitive underpinnings they can use to make sense of the world. Being able to interpret metaphors in a novel means that students will be able to interpret metaphors in a politician's speech, or in an advertisement, or in a favorite song. In this way students are taught critical thinking skills that stay with them long after they have read the last book of the school year.

Yohana's Support for the Seen and Unseen Hamlet

The "Seen" Hamlet

Symbol to Represent Hamlet	Explanation of Symbol	How This Symbol Connects to the Character	Passages Cited to Support This Connection
Hamlet is like a referee because . . . (decisive)	A referee understands all the rules and is there to make sure the players follow them. He has to be decisive when he hands out penalties to players who break rules.	Hamlet understands the "rules" of Elsinore, the castle. Hamlet is horrified when his mother and his uncle ignore the rules. As the play unfolds, it is obvious that he is bothered by all the rules violations. To help decide who should be penalized, Hamlet decides to lay a trap by staging a play that re-enacts his father's murder.	Hamlet to himself: "'tis an unweeded garden that grows to seed; things rank and gross in nature possess it merely. That it should come to this!" (I.ii) Hamlet talking about his mother: "Frailty, thy name is woman! . . . she married. O' most wicked speed, to post with such dexterity to incestuous sheets!" (I.ii) Hamlet sets up the trap: "The play's the thing wherein I'll catch the conscience of the king" (Hamlet to himself). (I.iii)
Hamlet is like a September 11th terrorist because . . . (insane)	The terrorists who killed many innocent people were insane. They murdered without a second thought.	Like the terrorists, Hamlet appears to lose all reason. He treats his mother irrationally and his erratic behavior drives Ophelia over the edge. He kills Polonius and has Rosencrantz and Guildenstern executed without a second thought.	Hamlet to Ophelia: "You should not have loved me . . . I loved you not." (III.i) Hamlet to Ophelia: "Get thee to a nunnery: why wouldst thou be a breeder of sinners?" (I.iii) Hamlet to his mother: "Lady, shall I lie in your lap? . . . I mean my head upon your lap? . . . That's a fair thought to lie between a maid's legs." (III.ii)

Figure 7.6

Yohana's Support for the Seen and Unseen Hamlet *(continued)*

The "Unseen" Hamlet

Symbol to Represent Hamlet	Explanation of Symbol	How This Symbol Connects to the Character	Passages Cited to Support This Connection
Hamlet is like a see-saw because . . . (hesitant)	A see-saw will tilt one way and then the other way.	Hamlet wavers back and forth on his decision to kill Claudius. He says he's going to do it, then he doesn't do it. He waits too long, and as a result, a number of other people end up dying.	Hamlet to his father's ghost: "Haste me to know't, that I, with wings as swift as meditation or the thoughts of love, may sweep to my revenge." (I.iv) Hamlet to the ghost: "Time is out of spite, that ever I was born to set it right!" (I.iv) Hamlet to himself: "now he is praying; and now I'll do it: and so he goes to heaven . . . No, up, sword." (III.iii)
Hamlet is like a calculator because . . . (sane)	A calculator figures problems out logically.	Hamlet calculates how to solve the murder by staging a play and by faking his insanity. The problem with a calculator, however, is that its battery may eventually wind down, thus disabling the reason of the calculator. Hamlet's "battery" (his reason) eventually runs down and all his "reasoned" plans lead to disaster.	Hamlet to Rosencrantz and Guildenstern: "my uncle-father and aunt-mother are deceived . . . I am but mad north-northwest; when the mind is southerly I know a hawk from a handsaw." (I.iii) Hamlet to himself: "The play's the thing wherein I'll catch the conscience of the King." (I.iii)

Figure 7.6
(continued)

CHAPTER EIGHT

Leading Students to Meaningful Reflection

Last week in class, Sandy, a student of mine, raised her hand and asked, "Why do we have to start our year by reading *All Quiet on the Western Front*? This book is depressing! Why do we have to read it?" Thirty-four heads swiveled to me expectantly. A fair question, but how should I respond?

From experience, I know how *not* to answer the question. When a teacher is asked, "Why are we reading this?" the following responses are guaranteed to produce in students a reluctance to read that will translate into three or four weeks of reading hell:

- "We're reading this book because it is a classic."
- "You want a good grade, don't you?"
- "We have always read this book at this school."
- "Reading this book will make you more culturally literate."
- "This book is required in the curriculum."
- "This book is number nine on the hundred greatest books list."
- "We're reading this book because (<u>author's name</u>) is an important writer."
- "Because I am the teacher and I said so."

Though all of these responses may be valid answers to the question, not one of them will resonate with adolescents. Not one of them will motivate students to accept the challenge of tackling deeper reading. In fact, just the opposite may occur: when students hear one of these stock responses—responses they have heard repeatedly over the years—alarms are likely to go off in their heads telling them, "Warning! Another boring book is on the way!"

When students ask, "Why are we reading this?" they are really asking, "What's in it for us? Why should we care about this book? Why is it relevant? What will we get out of reading it?" The success of our students' reading experience may hinge on just how effective we are in providing meaningful answers to these questions.

Moving Students Toward Meaningful Reflection

In my earlier book, *Reading Reasons: Motivational Mini-Lessons for Middle and High School*, I outline a number of answers to the question "Why should I read?" I focus on reasons that demonstrate the benefits students get from reading. Students should read because:

- Reading is rewarding.
- Reading builds a mature vocabulary.
- Reading makes you a better writer.
- Reading is hard, and "hard" is necessary.
- Reading prepares you for the world of work.
- Reading well is financially rewarding.
- Reading opens the door to college and beyond.
- Reading arms you against oppression.
- Reading makes you smarter.
- Reading develops a moral compass.

Once a week I give my students a mini-lesson that delves into one of these ten reading reasons. I have found these mini-lessons useful in motivating my students toward our classroom goal of every student's reading two million words a year.

Making students aware of all the reasons they should be readers helps them develop recreational reading habits, but a more targeted approach is needed to help them see why they are about to spend a few weeks reading the same novel together. In many ways, "Why should I be a reader?" is an easier question to answer than "Why should I read *All Quiet on the Western Front* in the next three weeks?" Students readily understand the overall importance of reading in helping them land a good job or get accepted to a university; they have a much more difficult time understanding what specific and immediate benefits they will reap from reading *The Scarlet Letter* or *Things Fall Apart*.

When students ask, "Why are we reading this book?" teachers often rely on one of two stock answers, or both. These answers are legitimate; but alone they do not go far enough when it comes to motivating adolescent readers.

Stock Answer 1: "We're reading this book because it's a great story."

Whether it's fiction or nonfiction, I want my students to appreciate great stories. This probably sounds absurd to people who like to read because they—we—take this for granted; but many of our students have never discovered the pleasure of reading great books. They haven't found the beauty and power the stories have to offer. They haven't experienced unforgettable reading moments. I can still remember the exact moments in my reading life when . . .

Anne Frank's hiding place was discovered.
Boo Radley appeared out of the shadows to rescue Scout and Jem.
Harry Potter defeated Lord Voldermort.
Sethe's daughter was murdered.
Sophie made her terrible choice.
George killed Lenny.
Winston and Julia were discovered in their love nest.

My list of memorable reading moments goes on and on, as undoubtedly does yours. Unfortunately, many of my students look at me oddly when I describe the powerful feelings that can arise from reading memorable books. Some of them have never found themselves in a reading flow—that trance we get into where we become so engrossed with what we are reading that we lose track of time and place. Many have never had the experience of having a book linger in their minds long after they have finished it. They have trouble seeing the greatness of literature.

During the first week of this school year, I asked my senior students to share some reflections they had about themselves as readers. Here are some of their responses:

- "I only read when teachers make me."
- "I never read on my own. It's boring."
- "I have never read a single book on my own."
- "Why should I read when there are so many interesting things to do instead?"

Their aversion to reading is appalling, and I want to change the way they perceive reading. I want to help them discover the greatness of the books we will read over the course of the school year. Though I am not naïve enough to believe that every one of my students is going to love every book I assign, I start with that as a goal. I know that what I do as a teacher will greatly influence the level of my students' involvement. Though not every student will like every book, I want every student to see the *value* in what they are reading.

Have you ever read a great book with your class only to have many of them tell you they found the book boring? When this happens to me, I have to think that maybe it's not the book that is the problem; maybe it's me. When my students are having a hard time connecting with a great book, I am forced to reconsider my approach. Have I provided enough framing? Have I addressed my students' lack of prior knowledge? Have I supported them to make sense of the difficult vocabulary? Have I helped them embrace their confusion? What is getting in the way of their discovering the greatness of this book, and what can I do to remove these obstacles?

As I have emphasized throughout this book, if we want students to fully appreciate great works, we must design lessons that lead students to discover this greatness. If we're asking our students to read a great book, it's our job to nudge students past their reluctance and allow the book's greatness to emerge.

Stock Answer 2: "We're reading this book because it affords us the opportunity to recognize and appreciate the writer's craft."

If my lessons are successful in drawing students into literary works, I then have the opportunity to make the author's craft visible to the students.

Once they understand the story, they can be taught to analyze one or more of the following:

- *Characterization:* How does the author develop the characters? What is the difference between "flat" and "round" characters? Which minor characters play important roles? How do the characters advance the plot and the conflicts?
- *Time and sequence:* How does the author develop time and sequence? Is foreshadowing used? Flashbacks? How does the author craft these time shifts? How do these time shifts advance the telling of the story?
- *Themes:* Which themes emerge from the book? Is there an overriding theme? Do minor themes emerge? How are these themes developed?
- *Author's purpose:* Why do you think the author wrote this book? What did he or she *really* want to say? What was the historical context in which this book was written, and how did this influence the author? Who is/was the author's intended audience?
- *Diction:* How does the author's choice of words advance the story? Is dialogue used effectively? Does the diction ring true? Does the author effectively use figurative language—metaphor, simile, and allegory?
- *Symbolism:* How does the author effectively use symbolism to advance the story? How do these symbols enrich the novel?
- *Voice:* Who is telling the story? Which point of view has the author used? How are the other literary elements revealed through the use of narration, dialogue, dramatic monologue, or soliloquy?
- *Setting:* Where is the story set? How does this setting affect the story's development?
- *Conflict:* What are the central conflicts in the work? How does the author develop these conflicts? Are the conflicts primarily internal or external?
- *Irony:* How is irony used in the story? What kinds of irony (verbal, situational, dramatic) are used? How does the use of irony advance our understanding of the characters?
- *Tone:* What is the author's attitude in this work? How and where is it revealed?

As English teachers, we are already aware of these literary elements, but year in and year out I am surprised by how little my incoming students are acquainted with them. They are accustomed to simply reading books without any awareness of the level of craft employed by the author. Knowing the story is one thing; appreciating the level of craft under the surface of the story is another thing.

Making these techniques visible to students boosts their appreciation of the work. When students examine the time and sequence elements found in Amy Tan's *The Joy Luck Club*, for example, they begin to understand the level of craft that went into the writing of that novel. When students are asked to write a sonnet in iambic pentameter, their appreciation of the Shakespeare play they are reading instantly deepens. If there is real craft involved in the writing of the work and this craft can be made visible to the students, their commitment to reading the work intensifies. Students revel when they discover the craft used in the work.

Making the writer's craft visible has an added benefit: it can help improve our students' writing. If I want my students to write an effective persuasive essay, it helps immensely to provide them with models of persuasive pieces (the "My Turn" essay featured in *Newsweek* is one source of excellent models). When my students learn to spot arguments and counterarguments in an essay they read, they are more likely to make use of arguments and counterarguments in their own essays. Students who are taught how to study the techniques, the structure, and the craft of other writers often find these techniques seeping into their own writing. Models help students write better.

Both of these approaches—appreciating the greatness of books and developing an understanding of the literary techniques employed by the authors—are valuable, so much so that they have become foundational in secondary schools. Indeed, I emphasize both of them strongly in my own classroom. But when it comes time for students to find the relevance a book plays in their lives, they must be encouraged to move outside and beyond the text to consider the following questions: What does this book mean to us today? Why did we read it?

We Read the Book . . . So What?

Soon my senior classes will begin reading George Orwell's dystopian classic, *1984*. (Though you may not teach *1984*, the principles discussed in this section apply to any book you might teach.) Why am I having my students read this book? I can generate a number of reasons:

- It is a great story (stock answer 1).
- It is a uniquely structured text that provides an opportunity to learn specific literary techniques, such as the development of tone through the author's use of diction (stock answer 2).

- It provides students with a chance to read futuristic text—a genre most students are inexperienced in reading.
- Orwell is an important writer.
- I, their teacher, love this novel.
- It is challenging, and I think my students need practice with challenging text.
- The terms "Big Brother" and "Orwellian" have become part of our cultural literacy, and I want my students to understand their origins.

Though all of these reasons are legitimate, none of them is likely to lead students to meaningful reflection. None addresses the "So what?" question. None hints at the real reason I insist my students read this book every year: *1984* serves as a wake-up call to adolescents poised on the threshold of adulthood. Reading *1984* provides students with imaginative rehearsals for critical issues they will confront in their adulthood. Figure 8.1 outlines the many issues in *1984* and gives just a few examples of real-life parallels that students can ponder, discuss, read, and write about.

As they read *1984,* I want my students to appreciate what a great story Orwell has written. Additionally, I want them to recognize Orwell's craft in his construction of this complex novel. But my goals in teaching *1984,* or any book for that matter, must extend beyond an appreciation of the story and the author's craft. *1984* presents students with the opportunity to think about propaganda, censorship, and the role government plays in their lives. If taught properly, it demands that students consider their obligations as adults in a democratic society.

I am not referring here simply to *1984.* The end goal of our teaching any novel should be to help students move through the craft and beauty of the story to areas of deeper, personal reflection. When I began teaching almost twenty years ago, I started each book I was to teach by asking myself the question "Why am I teaching this book?" I have since changed that question to "What do I hope my students will take from this book?" The change is subtle, but important. Asking "What do I want my students to take from this book?" keeps the focus of my instruction on their needs, not mine. Asking myself this question before I begin helps me to tease out the real issues—those universal concerns found in any great book that mean a great deal to teenagers. Issues that lead adolescents to reflection. Issues that illuminate the book's relevance in their world. Issues that answer Sandy's question, "Why are we reading this book?"

	Issues in *1984*	
Issues	*Example(s) in the Novel*	*Examples in Today's World*
Language is used to manipulate people.	The Ministry of Love tortures people; the Ministry of Peace wages war; the Ministry of Truth publishes lies.	The current administration is promoting the "Healthy Forests" program, which allows increased logging of protected wilderness; the "Clear Skies Initiative" permits greater industrial pollution (*San Francisco Chronicle,* July 14, 2003).
The government needs a villain to distract its citizens from more important issues.	Goldstein is the "enemy of the people" and is the centerpiece of the "two-minute hate" (even though there is no real evidence he exists). He is used to whip the citizenry into a frenzy.	The United States focuses on Osama Bin Laden. When it appears he has escaped, the focus shifts to Saddam Hussein. Before Bin Laden, there was Kim Jong Il, Manuel Noriega, Muamar Kaddafi . . .
The government closely monitors its citizens.	Telescreens and hidden microphones are used to spy on citizens.	The Pentagon is developing satellite technology to track any person twenty-four hours a day (*New York Times,* July 4, 2003). The Patriot Act allows the FBI to • search and seize medical records and personal papers without a warrant. • tap phone lines and e-mail accounts. • obtain a record of what books you have checked out of the public library and what books you have purchased from booksellers. (*Portsmouth [NH] Herald,* July 2, 2003) Attorney General John Ashcroft has drafted a measure to expand the Patriot Act's powers. If enacted, it will permit: • authorities to make unannounced searches of homes and businesses. • lawmakers to hold suspects without bail. • police to spy on dissidents. • DNA databases of suspects to be set up. (*Los Angeles Times,* July 29, 2003)

Figure 8.1

	Issues in *1984 (continued)*	
Issues	Example(s) in the Novel	Examples in Today's World
Propaganda is used to influence the thinking of the citizenry.	Big Brother uses music, slogans, rituals, films, and other methods to shape citizens' thinking.	Political advertisements are carefully orchestrated productions. Lighting, camera angles, music, imagery, narration, and pace are all used to influence the viewers' thinking.
		Politicians use imagery in the course of their activities deliberately to influence voters (e.g., Michael Dukakis driving a tank; George W. Bush landing on an aircraft carrier).
		Advertisers manipulate language to pull money from our wallets. "Used cars" are called "previously owned vehicles." A store advertising "up to 75% off" may mean only a 5% discount on the item you're interested in.
The citizenry cannot focus on what's really important.	The "proles" cannot see the real issues—they are distracted with drinking, pornography, gambling, and are not given real news by the media.	Local newscasts are often filled with fluff pieces that have very little news value.
		An over-the-top media focus on O.J., Scott Peterson, Kobe Bryant, Janet Jackson, and Michael Jackson—sensationalism that interferes with our ability to focus on serious issues of national and global importance.

Figure 8.1
(continued)

Mining the Levels of Reflection

When leading students to reflect on the important issues found in and beyond their texts, it can help to think of reflection in terms of layers. John Powers, whose work with metaphor was introduced in Chapter 7, created a model that depicts various levels of reflection (see Figure 8.2).

Reflection begins with the self, and this is the level of reflection adolescents are most comfortable with. When students are reading a great book, they naturally ask themselves, "What does this text mean to me?" But we want them to move beyond the self and into deeper levels of reflection. We want them to consider the other circles of reflection shown in Figure 8.2:

Figure 8.2

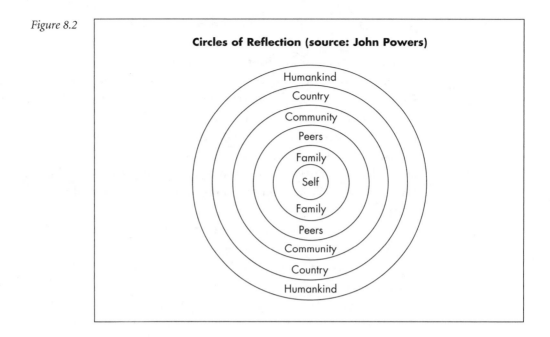

In asking our students to reflect, we want to push them beyond the self
and encourage them to think in terms of the outer circles of reflection.
When I teach *All Quiet on the Western Front,* for example, I want students
to understand the novel but, more important, I want them to consider the
role war plays in their lives. As I write this, the United States is occupying
Iraq. I want my students to understand our rationale for being there. But
beyond that, I want them to consider the implications this war has on
their loved ones, their peers, our community, our nation, and our world.
I want them to understand the costs, both in human lives and in expendi-

Bullet points:

- What does this book mean in terms of my family? ("Family" can extend
beyond bloodlines to include close friends and loved ones.)
- What does this book mean in terms of my peers? Why should people my
age be concerned with the issues presented in this book?
- What does this book mean in terms of my community? How do the
ideas in this book affect both my community and others'?
- What does this book mean in terms of thinking about my country?
What relevance does it play in relation to our national well-being?
- What does this book mean about the human condition? What can I
learn about humanity from reading this text? What are the universal
truths it contains?

tures, and the benefits of this war and to carefully consider the issues involved. They have read editorials supporting the war and editorials denouncing the war. It is not my intention to argue that the U.S. occupation is necessary or unnecessary, right or wrong. I want them to hear the reasons why our decision-makers believe this war is worth the price, and I want them to hear the dissenters and their reasons for opposing the war. My students need to hear these issues, examine these issues, discuss these issues, write about these issues. Having students delve deeply into these areas of reflection is a much more important purpose of their reading than making sure they can graph the plot line or analyze the author's use of irony.

This is where the real value of teaching literature is to be found. Whether my students are reading *All Quiet on the Western Front* or *1984*, *The Scarlet Letter* or *Their Eyes Were Watching God,* it is always my goal to push their thinking beyond personal implications and toward larger connections. Making connections between the literature and their loved ones, their families, their community, their nation, and their world is important because it is these connections that make up the

> central component of problem solving, one of the critical aspects of thinking. In reflection, [students] are challenged to abandon trite ideas that they cannot validate against their own experiences. Reflection leads beyond such superficial understanding as "We will all die sometime"; beyond wishful understandings, "I hope everyone will want peace"; and beyond moralistic imprints, "We should be kind to one another." It asks for understandings that delve into and explore what we have in common—the universal truth of what it means to be human beings. (California Department of Education 1993, p. 1)

It is this quest to recognize our commonalities, to move beyond "trite" thinking, to develop a deeper understanding of what it means to be a human being that we seek to develop in our students. In doing so, we are preparing them for the critical issues of adulthood. We are providing them with important imaginative rehearsals for the real world—a world they are soon to inherit.

How can our lessons be structured to encourage students to move beyond the book and into deeper levels of reflective thinking? How do we encourage them to think beyond simple personal reflection and toward the other layers of reflection? The remainder of this chapter outlines seven strategies effective in moving students into deeper levels of reflection.

Strategies to Encourage Reflection

Three Degrees of . . .

All forms of murder are horrible, but the law makes a distinction between degrees of murder (with first-degree murder the most severe). Upon completing a novel, have students consider the central theme and how it is found in degrees in the contemporary world. After reading *To Kill a Mockingbird*, for example, they might identify racism as a central idea and search for three degrees of racism in our modern world. Paul, a sophomore, brought in the following newspaper examples culled from the Internet:

- *First-degree racism:* The Ku Klux Klan held a rally this weekend in Kentucky to promote a white-only state.
- *Second-degree racism:* Recent racial-profiling statistics have shown that blacks and other people of color are more likely to be pulled over by the police.
- *Third-degree racism:* Though there are many black players, there are very few black coaches in college football,

The racism in all of these examples is abhorrent, but ranking them requires Paul to consider that racism found in the novel still exists in today's world and it comes in different forms and degrees.

Depending on the novel being read, students could search for three degrees of evil, compassion, oppression, sacrifice, greed, love, or any central idea found in the book. Having students think and write about these issues in terms of degrees found in contemporary life requires them to be reflective as they argue why one example is more or less severe than another.

The Most Valuable Idea

After finishing any major work, students can be asked "What is the most valuable idea that can be taken from this book?" Have students complete a "Most Valuable Idea" chart (see Figure 8.3). The directions are as follows:

- At the top of the paper, students write what they think is the single most important idea found in the book. This idea must be written in a complete sentence.

Figure 8.3

"Most Valuable Idea" Form

In a complete sentence, write the most valuable idea found in the book:

_____

_____

Affix an article here that illustrates the Most Valuable Idea	*This idea is still valuable today because . . .*

- In the left-hand column, students find an example in the real world that illustrates this idea.
- In the right-hand column, students explain the connection between the idea found in the book and the real-world example.

For example, Brenda, a ninth-grade student, identified the Most Valuable Idea in *Romeo and Juliet* as the following: "Sometimes secrets should be told." In Figure 8.4 you can see how she connected this idea to the modern world.

The Most Valuable Idea assignment reinforces the notion that the big ideas found in literature are still important today.

Theme Notebooks

Another way to help students see that issues and conflicts found in novels and other forms of fiction still exist in contemporary life is the Theme Notebook project. Students begin this project with a whole-class discussion, identifying themes in the book they have read and writing these themes in complete sentences. In *To Kill a Mockingbird*, for example, through classroom discussion, students generated the following list of themes:

Figure 8.4

Most Valuable Idea

Sometimes secrets should be told.

Mahony Comes Up Short

Explanation of Connection

Cardinal Roger M. Mahony has insisted throughout the allegations of priestly abuse of minors in the Los Angeles Archdiocese that his top priority was the protection of victims. Unfortunately for all involved in this heartbreaking affair, the available evidence finds him still dragging out the process.

Even in Mahony's welcome and heralded "Report to the People of God," issued this week, there's little that's new. For instance, although the report states that 244 priests, deacons and others associated with the Catholic Church have been accused of abuse, only the 211 names already made public by the press or in court proceedings are given in the report. Providing authorities with the names of the other 33 people accused of misdeeds, no matter what the archdiocese deems the quality of the accusations, would have been new and worthy. Instead, through litigation the archdiocese continues to block the release of personnel files that would move all such cases forward.

Handing over needed information to authorities would not dismiss a presumption of innocence. It would, however, show a commitment to protecting children from possible continued abuse by allowing civil authorities to decide on the allegations' worth. For more than 20 months the district attorney's office has sought archdiocese records regarding allegations of child sex abuse. Through its legal resistance, the archdiocese, under the umbrella of protecting the possibly innocent, sends a message that its clergy carry more weight than protecting and providing justice to children.

Mahony should release to authorities the files of accused church employees as well as ensure that all those facing credible accusations who are still employed by the archdiocese are suspended from the ministry or from other church-related employment until their cases are cleared.

Mahony no doubt sees himself as torn between two responsibilities, to his priests and to the faithful, but this is a case in which the cardinal must place his faith in civil authority. The innocence of priests accused of pedophilia is not for Mahony or church lawyers to decide.

Cardinal Roger M. Mahony's report, "Report to the People of God," have included the names of 211 priests of the 244 priests that are allegated for child abuse. This leaves the authorities with 33 blank priests. It would be more helpful to the authorities to have the 33 names.

In Romeo and Juliet the Friar also holds information that would have been in everyone's benefit to tell Capulet + Montague.

Mahony's resistance of giving helpful information would prove protection and justice to children who could be abused. In Romeo and Juliet the Friar holds information that could have saved their lives.

- Real courage is not always readily seen.
- Courage often comes from unexpected sources.
- Extraordinary efforts are needed to fight injustice.
- Role models are crucial to the development of children.
- Ignorance breeds ignorance.
- Ignorance is often at the root of trouble.
- One dedicated person can make a difference.

- Hardship is necessary to the development of one's character.
- Education is vital to a society's well-being.
- School often gets in the way of education.
- People should not be judged by first appearances.
- People often have an unseen inner strength (or beauty).
- Someone of extraordinary strength is often needed to step forward when others hesitate.

Students are then asked to choose one theme to serve as the focus of their Theme Notebooks (from here on, each student works independently). They are to search for evidence of this theme in today's world. In doing so, I ask students to find evidence of their chosen theme in at least ten separate sources. Sources may include:

Movies
Newspapers
Magazines
Advertisements
Political cartoons
Song lyrics
Poems
Drama
Short stories
Children's stories
Television programs
Novels
Stories students have written
Quotations
Photographs
Art (e.g., drawing, painting, sculpture)
Comic strips
Jokes
Internet articles
Video games

This project is an excellent way to help students make connections between the text and their world. Additionally, it gives the teacher an opportunity to introduce them to some resources they might not be familiar with. One day I might bring in a number of books containing interesting quotations (*Bartlett's Familiar Quotations, Toastmaster*

Guides); another day I'll spread out poetry books and give my class the opportunity to peruse them.

The Theme Notebook project culminates by having students write an analytical essay, discussing the importance of the theme to the book and why this theme is still relevant today.

Casting Call

Students may be asked to cast real people to play the roles of the characters in the novel. They need to carefully consider who would be qualified to play each part. The people they cast can be famous (George Bush, Eminem) or relatively unknown (an uncle, Coach Mike). However, they shouldn't pick famous people just because of their fame. When students are asked to cast the roles, they have to consider the real connections their cast selections have to the characters in the book. They need to be able to explain why a particular person is qualified to play a particular role. What qualifies this person to play the role of this character? What are the parallels between the character and the real-life person? In other words, they shouldn't pick Ben Affleck because he's handsome or because he is their favorite actor. They have to explain his connection to the character. I am not interested in their casting decisions nearly as much as I am interested in the students' explanations of their casting.

A variation of this assignment is to have students create a baseball card set, but instead of baseball players, the cards depict characters from the novel. Like the casting assignment, the baseball cards must depict real people who would play the roles of the characters. Each card can explain the connection on the back.

Asking students to make connections between characters in a novel and living human beings again underscores the idea that characters in novels reflect the people in the real world.

Theme Layers

In the activity I call Theme Layers, each student identifies a central theme and then demonstrates various layers of real-world connections to that theme. For example, after reading *Romeo and Juliet*, Ramon, a freshman, also worked with the central theme: "There are times when secrets should be told." With this theme in mind, he then charted how this theme connected with himself, his family, his community, and his nation (see Figure 8.5).

Figure 8.5

Ramon's Theme Layers for *Romeo and Juliet*

Myself

Last year when I attended junior high school I had a lot of friends. We would say, "Friends never tell on friends." On the last day of school my friend told me he wanted to get in a fight. I knew he was serious because my friend never fights. I had a chance to stop it, but I didn't act quickly enough. My friend ended up expelled and wasn't able to walk for graduation I felt as if I was the reason.

My Family

About four years ago my sister and I were home alone. She told me she wanted to call her boyfriend so they could watch a quick movie. About 15 minutes before he arrived my parents told me to make sure my sister let no one in. I didn't tell, and about a week later my sister announced she was pregnant. I thought to myself, "If only I would have said something."

↓   ↓

Romeo and Juliet *Theme: There are times when secrets should be told.*

↑   ↑

My Community

I know there are a lot of people who either buy or sell drugs in the neighborhood. If someone would say a word to the police maybe they could get these guys off the streets. Many deaths and crimes could be prevented but some people don't know when to tell a secret.

My Nation

9/11 could have been prevented if someone who knew about the attack had told a secret. These acts are planned, which means more than one person knows something. In situations like this secrets must be told. One person saying something could save hundreds of lives.

Anchor Questions

One way to encourage student reflection throughout a literary unit is to provide an anchor question for students to consider while they read the book. Jeff Wilhelm, Tanya Baker, and Julie Dube, in *Strategic Reading*, explain how they frame many of their units with a central question. When teaching a unit on irony, for example, they might ask students: Can irony make us better people? The students then start the unit by examining irony in comic books before moving on to more sophisticated vignettes, poems, and short stories. Wilhelm notes that while "my students read these short selections, they discussed whether the irony helped them understand things in a new way, and whether that understanding might change their behavior. They examined whether there was a difference between sarcasm and irony . . . as they worked, they wrote out their own rules for recognizing clues that a text was ironic" (p. 43). By giving the students the central question *before* they begin the unit, Wilhelm not only provides a focus for his students' learning, he does so in a way that encourages his students to think in reflective terms.

I tie many of my core work units to anchor questions. Here are some examples of questions that have made the study of literature more interesting in my classroom:

Core Work	Anchor Question
1984	What does it mean to be a responsible adult in a democratic society?
All Quiet on the Western Front	Are wars avoidable?
Animal Farm	What are the real threats to a true democracy?
Dr. Jekyll and Mr. Hyde	Can evil be kept in check?
Hamlet	Does absolute power corrupt absolutely?
Night	Who shares responsibility for the Holocaust?
Romeo and Juliet	Can long-term feuds be buried?
The Bean Trees	Is there equal opportunity in America?
The Great Gatsby	Can class status be changed?
To Kill a Mockingbird	If Martin Luther King, Jr., were alive today, would he feel his dream has been fulfilled?

One variation of tying a book to an anchor question is to tie an entire year of study to a single, overarching question. Recently, for example, every senior at our high school began the year by studying T. S. Eliot's "The Wasteland." For the remainder of the school year, all the literature centered on two questions: How was a "wasteland" created in this work? From our readings, what lessons can we learn that will help us overcome a modern wasteland? These questions arose from the students' comment that everything they were reading was depressing (a comment that I must say was not without foundation). Instead of focusing on the tragedies of the core works, our discussions focused on how the "wastelands" found in each work could have been avoided (for example, How did Hamlet's actions lead to a wasteland? If you were in his shoes, what would you have done differently?).

The Hunt for the Author's Purpose

This last idea may be the simplest, but it is very effective in prompting reflection from adolescents. I assign the following final exam question to students *before* we begin reading the book:

> What was the author's purpose in writing this book? In an essay, explain the purpose the author may have had in mind. Cite specific passages to reinforce your thesis. Discuss why this purpose is still relevant to the modern reader.

By asking this question prior to reading the novel, I prompt students to take note of the big ideas found in the work as they read. Because I already know the final exam question, I can design lessons that help students "discover" and chart the author's purpose as they read. And because *they* already know the final exam question, they can read the book with the author's purpose in mind, thus reading with a focus that helps them make sense of the text.

These seven activities have proven effective in getting students to see why literature matters. They allow students to see the importance and relevance of great books, and they help us teachers to provide a meaningful answer to the ever-asked question "Why are we reading this book?"

CHAPTER NINE

Reading
the World

I write this chapter in the shadow of testing mania. In an effort to leave no child behind, students must now take schoolwide quarterly benchmark assessments, district-mandated essays and multiple-choice exams, yearly state-required tests, nationally normed assessments, midterms, final exams, and high school exit exams. In addition, many students will also take the SAT I's, SAT II's, advanced placement exams, and college entrance exams (in California, they might take both the English Placement Test and the Golden State Exam—I'm sure your state has equivalent assessments). All of these tests are in addition to the many assessments classroom teachers regularly give. With all this emphasis on testing, it often seems we are one or two exams away from not teaching at all—students will be busy taking tests for the entire school year.

Perhaps that may be a bit of an exaggeration, but all these exams have put pressure on teachers and administrators—pressure that has caused normally reasonable educators to (for lack of a better phrase) lose their marbles. A case in point: I once sat in a staff meeting and heard a worried high school principal make an interesting proposal to her staff. Here is a rough paraphrase of her address to the faculty: "As you all know, the state exams are now a month away. It is imperative that we meet our school's goals, so I am proposing that for the three weeks prior to the exam we suspend the normal curriculum and focus on critical thinking skills. These skills will help our students raise their scores. I know giving up three weeks of your time is difficult, but if we don't raise our scores, the consequences will be worse for all of us. Three weeks is a small price to pay, and when the test is over, you can return to your normal curriculum." Later, privately, the principal told me that reading novels was important, but that we really needed to step back momentarily from the literature and emphasize critical thinking skills. At this point I began to suspect that "critical thinking skills" was the superintendent's new mantra.

Funny, but I thought I *was* teaching critical thinking skills. Aren't students thinking critically when they

> move beyond a surface–level understanding of the text?
> reread to look for deeper meaning?
> tap prior knowledge to assist their comprehension?
> consciously monitor their comprehension?
> employ fix-it strategies to comprehend difficult text?
> reach deeper understanding through meaningful collaboration?
> interpret text metaphorically?
> make connections between the text and other people, books, films, and real-life incidents?
> challenge the text while reading?
> judge what the author's purpose might be?
> consider not only what was said but what was left unsaid?
> understand what relevance the book holds for the modern reader?

Rather than "suspend" the curriculum so that critical thinking skills can be taught, we should be looking for ways to give students *more* exposure to a curriculum that, when taught with rigor, provides them with richer opportunities to think critically. When we teach students to read more deeply, we are not only helping them to understand the book in front of them, we are also sharpening their critical thinking skills. Developing the ability to read and pass a test is desirable; developing the ability to read the world is even more important.

A number of years ago I began to see myself less as a literature teacher and more of a *literacy* teacher. What good is it, I asked myself, if a student of mine can analyze a novel while sitting in my class but is later unable to apply these same interpretive skills to the real world? Frankly, ten years from now I would rather my students be able to critically "read" their local school board candidates than to be able to discuss Golding's use of symbolism in *Lord of the Flies.* Sure, I want them to be able to analyze literature in my class, but the bigger goal is that they develop these cognitive skills to a level where they may be transferred beyond the classroom. As Paulo Freire has said, the world is a difficult text. I want my students to leave my class at the end of the year with an increased capacity to read it critically. Students who are unable to do so, who graduate still reading the world at a surface level, are in for hardship.

So how do we, as teachers, take the deeper reading principles described in this book and use them to teach our students to read the world? In the remainder of this chapter, I share a number of lessons that have helped my students sharpen their real-world reading lenses.

"Loaded" Language

To introduce the idea that language is used to manipulate our thinking, I bring up euphemism with my students. I begin by sharing the definition of the term (euphemism: the use of a mild or indirect expression instead of one that is harsh or unpleasantly direct—from the *World Book Dictionary*) before turning to my favorite language cynic, George Carlin. In *Brain Droppings,* Carlin lists favorite euphemisms he has encountered in his travels (two examples: a truck stop advertises itself as a "Travel Plaza"; a loan shark offers "interim financing"). Using Carlin as a source, I have students read the euphemisms below and predict the actual words these euphemisms are trying to cover up. Try the list yourself (keep in mind that these are all terms that George Carlin has found actually being used):

Real-World Euphemism	Prediction of Actual Word(s)
Custodial interference	
Sleep system	
Nail technician	
Remains pouches	
A meaningful downturn in aggregate output	
Previously owned vehicle	
Pipe frame exercise unit	
Collateral damage	
Direct marketing	
Beauty mark	

How'd you do? Here is the answer key:

Real-World Euphemism	Actual Word(s)
Custodial interference	Kidnapping
Sleep system	Bed
Nail technician	Manicurist
Remains pouches	Body bags
A meaningful downturn in aggregate output	Recession
Previously owned vehicle	Used car
Pipe frame exercise unit	Monkey bars
Collateral damage	Civilian casualties
Direct marketing	Junk mail
Beauty mark	Mole

(*Note:* Carlin's complete list of euphemisms contains examples that are inappropriate for classroom use.)

Having students play with these euphemisms gives me the opportunity to ask some pointed questions about the use of language: Why would a car dealer selling a used car rather call it a "previously owned vehicle"? Why would a military spokesperson use the term "remains pouches" instead of "body bags"? Why do people who are trying to persuade us choose their words carefully? How can carefully chosen language influence us?

After reflecting on the purpose of euphemisms, we continue to examine language manipulation by examining personal want ads. All students have dating concerns, so it is fun to discuss ads from singles who are seeking dates. I ask students if they think people are always honest when they describe themselves in chat rooms or dating ads. After they laugh at that idea, I ask them how prospective daters might manipulate language in their ads to make them seem more attractive than they might really be. I then share with them the Personal Want Ad "Code Word" Dictionary (from personal.riverusers.com):

Code Word(s)	What It *Really* Means
Affectionate	Needy
Appreciates quality	Expects someone else to pay for it
Beautiful	Spends a lot of time in front of the mirror
Educated	Will always treat you as intellectually inferior
Enjoys long walks	Car has been repossessed
Excited about life's journey	No concept of reality
Gentle	Near-comatose
High standards	Blind to own flaws, unforgiving of others'
Life of the party	Poor impulse control
Outgoing	Loud
Perfect	Self-delusional

Though this is a bit of humor, the "dictionary" helps students see that people can and do use language as a means of manipulating others.

If you want to study the use of manipulative language in other places, you need not look any further than your mailbox. Imagine opening an envelope sent to you from the one of the magazine clearing houses and finding the following statement in large type:

> Department of Automobile Prize Distribution
> WINNER'S WARRANTY
> . . . This winner's warranty confirms in a few days you will receive a Ford Taurus Guarantee of Delivery Form as part of an Express Bulletin from Publishers' Clearing House. Contingent upon selection of your Guarantee of Delivery Form as the winner, this warranty verifies that your choice of Ford Taurus or $35,000 cash will be delivered to the following address.

You look and, lo and behold, your address is listed! You're a winner! You have to make an enviable choice: should you have a new car delivered to your house or should you accept a check for $35,000? What a delightful dilemma! You look out your window, halfway expecting to see Ed McMahon already walking up your drive! Unfortunately, there is one small catch: you haven't won anything. Read the message again, paying close attention to the dependent clause beginning with the word "contingent." Though it sure sounds like you were a winner, this letter was actually a carefully crafted ruse to lure you into purchasing magazines. What's worse, you were not alone. Thousands of nonwinners received these "WINNER'S WARRANTIES" in the mail.

Lest you think this one example is unusual, mailings containing manipulative language arrive at my home on a daily basis. In the past week alone, I have received a number of envelopes, each containing a misleading statement on the outside tempting me to open it. A closer reading of them revealed a number of deceptions. Here are just a few examples:

The Tease	What It *Really* Meant
"Signature required. Open Immediately."	Inside the envelope was a credit card pitch.
"Renewal Statement Enclosed"	Inside the envelope was a "renewal" form for a magazine for which I have never subscribed.
"Urgent Documents—Your Membership Has Lapsed."	A plea for me to send money to a political party—a party to which I have no membership.
"Rush Priority Express Letter: Rush to Addressee. Extremely Important"	A pitch for mortgage refinancing.
"Insurance Overpayment Advisory"	A request for me to change my automobile insurance carrier.

Sharing these deceptions with students opens their eyes to what Kenneth Wilson calls "weasel words." In *The Columbia Guide to Standard American English,* Wilson defines weasel words as "sly, cunning, and sneaky; they lack integrity, and they conceal the truth. In the end they say one thing and mean something quite different." My students have a tendency to take everything they read at face value; introducing them to the concept of weasel words using my daily mail as examples helps them begin to develop their critical reading lenses. Of course, after they are introduced to the concept of weasel words, students need practice finding them. What better place to practice uncovering weasel words than the world of advertising?

Cradle-to-Grave Consumerism

McDonald's Corporation is the largest advertiser and marketer in the world, spending millions of dollars annually to foster brand loyalty. Why do they spend this kind of money? Because it works. According to Eric Schlosser, author of *Fast Food Nation,* 96 percent of American schoolchildren can identify Ronald McDonald, and the Golden Arches now have a higher degree of recognition than the Christian cross. In fact, McDonald's advertising campaigns aimed at children work so effectively, many companies have adopted similar "cradle-to-grave" advertising strategies. They share a common goal: to get you to identify with their brand from an early age so that you develop a sense of nostalgia for the brand—nostalgia that will keep you coming back as a lifelong customer. It is not a coincidence that McDonald's is the nation's largest owner of private playgrounds and one of the largest toy distributors in the world. They want your loyalty, and they want to get it as early in your life as possible.

This, of course, raises many concerns. Consider the following information and what effect it may have had on the students sitting in your classroom (from Focusonyourchild.com):

- Children begin distinguishing brands during their preschool years. Six-month-old babies can recognize corporate logos and mascots.
- Brand loyalty begins as early as age two.
- The average three-year-old recognizes 100 different brand logos.
- Toddlers cannot distinguish a commercial from a television show.
- It isn't until age eight that kids begin to realize that advertising can be untruthful and misleading.

Elizabeth Moore, assistant professor of marketing at the University of Notre Dame's Mendoza College of Business, estimates that children in the

United States watch an average of twenty-eight hours of television a week, and in doing so, see 25,000 commercials each year. Advertisers spend $15 billion annually to market their wares to children; and, though it is true that older students develop a healthy skepticism, they are still likely to be adversely affected by commercials. (Look at your students and ask yourself if advertising influences them.) In their lifetimes, our students will "read" many thousands more commercials than books. They will be better equipped to handle this onslaught if they can interpret these ads with the same critical reading skills they have been taught in their approach to books.

How can we arm our young people against those advertisers who at this very moment are sitting in rooms on Madison Avenue plotting how best to take their money? How can we teach students to read these advertisers as critically as we are teaching them to read *To Kill a Mockingbird*? The answers may lie in sharing real-world examples—examples centered around three things teenagers like to do: eat, talk, and use the computer.

Let's Eat!

Students are interested in food, but they are often unaware of the deceptions used to manipulate them into purchasing what they are eating. My favorite claim of all time is often found on boxes of junk cereal: "This cereal is part of a complete nutritional breakfast." *Anything* can be part of a complete nutritional breakfast if you eat a complete nutritional breakfast with it.

I introduce the idea of deceptive food claims by sharing some specific examples with my students. One interesting claim, according to the magazine *Consumer Reports,* is made by the makers of Nature's Path Optimum cereal, which comes in either "regular" or "slim" versions. When you read the labels of each box you will find that there are fewer calories in the "slim" version, *but only because the serving size is smaller.* If you were to eat one cup of each version, you would find that the "slim" version (200 calories) actually contains *more* calories than the "regular" version (190 calories). How many of our students would be savvy enough to read these cereal labels and figure out this sleight of hand?

Here are some other recent deceptive food claims that have come to the attention of both the Federal Trade Commission and the Center for Science in the Public Interest, a consumer advocacy group:

Claim	Reality
Tropicana Twisters is made with "real fruit juice."	The product contains only 10 to 15 percent real fruit juice.
Sunsweet Prune Juice is good for the eyes.	This claim is oversold.
Total cereal helps you lose weight.	You'll lose weight only if you reduce your intake of other high-calorie foods.
Ocean Spray Cranberry Juice is good for your urinary tract.	It's only partly juice and its claims are questionable.
Klondike ice cream bars are "99% fat free."	The ad only describes the bar's ice cream content. When the chocolate coating is figured in, a Klondike bar actually consists of 40 percent fat.
The ad depicts a glass of milk being poured into a slice of Kraft cheese, implying that the consumer would get the same amount of calcium from eating the slice of cheese as he or she would from drinking a glass of milk.	Some of the cheese's calcium content is lost when it is processed.
People are shown eating what appears to be ice cream, but the consumer is told that it is "O.K." because it's Dannon Pure Indulgence frozen yogurt. The implication is that this product is not nearly as fattening as ice cream.	The yogurt is as laden with fat and calories as ice cream.
Taking one-half of a Bayer baby aspirin a day could reduce the risk of a heart attack.	The ad forgot to mention that this advice might not be appropriate for patients with certain medical conditions.

Introducing these examples to students helps them become aware of the levels of manipulation to which advertisers resort. When we teach students to carefully consider what is said, and what is not said, in these ads, they become better-educated and savvier consumers.

Another benefit of discussing food ad deceptions is that it helps students understand why 25 percent of American children and adolescents nowadays are obese—double the proportion from thirty years ago (Childrennow.org). Each year, the obesity rate among kids increases by 1 percent. Could it be that our students' rising levels of obesity are partially due to their inability to critically read and understand deceptive food advertising and labels?

Talk Is Not Cheap

You may have noticed that adolescents like to talk. One way to help them recognize and understand manipulative language is by showing them that talk may not be as cheap as they think. With the growing number of confusing long distance and cell phone calling plans being dangled in front of them, our students need to be able to sort through the various claims.

To start them thinking in this direction I begin by showing them misleading long distance ads. One example, noted in *Consumer Reports,* is an ad for the PennyTalk Calling Card, which entices readers with the question "Where can a penny take you?" Their answer? One penny can take you to any of the fifty states via their one-cent-a-minute phone card. That's a long way on a single penny, but it's actually not as long as it appears once one reads the fine print and learns that there is a "low 49 cent connection charge" when each call is answered. Additionally, there is a monthly 99 cent service charge. On an initial reading you might think that making ten five-minute calls will only set you back 50 cents, but in reality you'll be paying $6.39.

Clearly, one way to avoid being taken to the cleaners is to ask the right kind of questions before making any purchase. Which questions should consumers ask before deciding on a phone service? Ask your students to generate a list, and then compare it with questions generated by the National Consumers League, a nonprofit organization, which recommends the following on its Web site, nclnet.org:

- Does the advertised rate only apply to calls made at certain times of the day or days of the week? If so, does that fit your calling patterns?
- Does the advertised rate only apply to calls to certain geographic areas (out-of-state versus in-state, specific countries, or within a specific number of miles)? Are those the calls you typically make? If not, what are the charges for the places you do call?
- Is there a monthly fee in addition to the costs for the calls? How does that affect the total cost based on your typical calling habits?
- Is there a minimum charge even if you talk for less time?
- If the advertised rate is for calls up to a certain number of minutes, what is the charge if you talk for more minutes?

I then ask my students to bring advertisements for three different cellular calling plans to class. For each plan, they compare the benefits (large print) with the drawbacks (small print); then they write a piece stating which plan offers the best value, and why.

"Spam" Is a Four-Letter Word

According to the U.S. Department of Education, 88 percent of children use computers and 53 percent have Internet access. One can only surmise that these numbers will continue to rise. With the growing popularity of the Internet comes a burgeoning new form of advertising: computer spam.

The Federal Trade Commission, in an attempt to measure how quickly spam grows, "seeded" 175 different locations on the Internet with 250 undercover e-mail addresses and monitored these addresses for six weeks. The sites included chat rooms, newsgroups, Web pages, free personal Web-page services, message boards, and e-mail service directories. Here is what they found: 100 percent of the e-mail addresses posted in the chat rooms received spam, with the first receiving spam just eight minutes after the address was posted. Of the addresses posted at newsgroups and Web pages, 86 percent received spam, as did 50 percent of addresses at free personal Web page services, 27 percent from message board postings, and 9 percent of e-mail service directories (Federal Trade Commission 2002, p. 2). It is becoming increasingly clear that spam on the Internet has become the great new advertising frontier. This raises a key question: can our students read this new medium critically?

When you receive an e-mail message, it usually carries a subject line. By now, we all know that we should not open unfamiliar e-mail, so advertisers are becoming more savvy (or, to paraphrase Kenneth Wilson, more "weaselly") in prompting you to "bite" on their advertisements. Here are some recent examples of e-mail subject lines of messages sent to me from people or firms trying to get me to open their advertisement:

Payment Past Due
Check Unclaimed
Urgent—account update
From your friend, John
Haven't heard from you lately
Where have you been?
Did you hear the news?
Hey! You were right!
Your order has shipped
Honest mistake
Long time no see!

FrontBridge Securities, an e-mail security firm, analyzed hundreds of millions of e-mail messages and concluded that deceptive tactics increased more than 50 percent in the first half of 2003 alone. They have generated a list of the top ten deceptive spam headers (found on the Web site mail-archive.com):

Re: the information you asked for
Hey

Check this out!
Is this your e-mail?
Please resend the e-mail
Re: your order
Past due account
Please verify your information
Version update
Re: Fourth of July

I share these with students and ask them which ones would be most effective in prompting them to open the message. We discuss what may happen when you respond to unsolicited e-mail. Among the risks is an increased chance of:

- acquiring a computer virus.
- being barraged with pop-up advertisements.
- having your e-mail address sold to other advertisers.
- being "spoofed." (Spoofing occurs when false "from" information is used in the e-mail message, making it appear that an innocent third party was the sender. Your e-mail address, for example, might be cut and pasted so that it can be used as a heading to entice others to open unsolicited spam.)

Once a computer ad is opened, students are confronted with the same weasel words found in television and print ads. Students should know that, although the medium might vary, all forms of advertising share one common characteristic: they contain propaganda techniques to influence us—techniques our students should be taught. Here are some specific propaganda techniques advertisers use to gain our trust—and our cash (adapted from U.S. Army 1979):

- *Appeal to authority.* Appeals to an authority to support a position, idea, argument, or course of action. Example: *LeBron James trusts his feet to only one shoe when he is playing ball: Nike.*
- *Bandwagon.* This promotes an "everyone else is doing it, you should too" appeal. *Four out of five Americans use this toothpaste. Shouldn't you?*
- *Glittering generalities.* Use of intensely emotionally appealing words so closely associated with highly valued concepts and beliefs that they carry conviction without supporting information or reason. *If you love our country, you will buy this product.*

- *Time crunch.* Creating the impression that your action is required immediately or your opportunity will be lost forever. *This offer is only good for the first one hundred callers!*
- *Plain folks.* Using people just like you and me to state a case. *If you have dandruff like I do, you'll want to use this shampoo. It worked for me!*
- *Red herring.* Highlighting a minor detail as a way to draw attention away from more important details or issues. *Order this oven now and we'll throw in a free cutlery set.*
- *Transfer.* Linking a known personal goal or ideal with a product or cause in order to transfer the audience's positive feelings to the product or cause. *For every dollar spent on our product we will donate 5 percent to the American Cancer Society.*
- *Snob appeal.* Associating the product with successful and admired people to give the audience the idea if they buy or support the same things, they may also have "what it takes." *Buy a BMW: the Ultimate Driving Machine.*
- *Testimonial.* Using the testimony or statement of someone to persuade you to think or act as he or she does. *Bob Dole uses Viagra. You should too.*
- *Prestige identification.* Showing a well-known person with the object, person, or cause in order to increase the audience's impression of the importance or prestige of the object, person, or cause. *Cindy Crawford only wears Rolex watches.*
- *Flag waving.* Connecting the person, product, or cause with patriotism. *Chevrolet—as American as apple pie!*
- *Card stacking.* Telling one side of the story as though there is no opposing view. *There is simply no better vacuum cleaner on the market!*
- *Generating disapproval.* Getting the audience to disapprove of an action or idea by suggesting that the idea is popular with groups hated, feared, or held in contempt by the target audience. *Why would you vote for this candidate? He has accepted donations from the tobacco industry.*
- *Vagueness.* Statements that are intentionally vague so that the audience may supply its own interpretations. *Everything in the store is marked off up to 70%.*
- *Fear.* Appealing to a person's desire to fit in with the crowd. *Are you sure your deodorant is providing you with enough protection?*

If we want our students to be critical readers of the world, they must learn to recognize propaganda. To help them internalize the techniques described above, I assign a project that requires them to find real-world examples of propaganda. Specifically, they are asked to find one example of each of the techniques listed above. They may look in the following four media to find their examples:

newspapers
magazines
the Internet
traditional television commercials

This project can be done individually or in groups. As a final exam, I show the class a thirty-minute infomercial and have each student identify as many of the propaganda techniques used in the television spot as they can.

The critical examination of advertising helps students internalize how manipulative language is used, and also prepares them to apply critical reading skills to other real-world applications. There is a much broader world out there beyond advertising. Once we complete our unit on advertising, it is time for my students to branch out and apply their newly honed critical thinking skills to other areas. The newspaper is a good place to start.

Read All About It

One recent study on newspaper readership has found what I have suspected for some time: the younger you are, the less likely you are to read the newspaper (Sweep 2002). For example, while 76 percent of polled readers between the ages of 60 and 64 said that they read the paper the day before, only 36 percent in the 18-to-24 age group said they did. Based on an informal survey of my adolescent students, I suspect the percentage of teenage newspaper readers to be much lower.

As a teacher, I am responsible for preparing adolescents for adulthood, and it concerns me that they are not reading the newspaper. Again, I'll paraphrase what I said earlier in this chapter: if a student graduates with the ability to analyze *The Scarlet Letter* but is unable to apply these same critical reading skills to real-world texts, I have come up short in making this student a literate person. I want all my students to become informed members of society, and reading the daily newspaper plays a part in having them become—and remain—informed.

When it comes to developing students into newspaper readers, two questions arise: How do I familiarize them with the newspaper in the first place? And once they are comfortable with reading the newspaper, how do I get them to read it with a critical eye?

To get my students' feet wet, I have found the following three activities effective in introducing adolescents to the benefits of newspaper reading.

It's a Wacky World

This first idea may fall under the "get a life" category, but I admit, I have been collecting odd newspaper articles for a number of years; and I have found it useful to share them with my students. Here are some of my favorites:

- Padlocks kept getting lost at a dog kennel in Illinois. The employees were stumped until they x-rayed Rascal, a year-old Labrador. There on the x-ray were seven locks—the dog had swallowed them all. Both dog and locks (removed after surgery) are now fine.
- A Montana motorist's anger over a $5 speeding ticket has cost him more than $200,000 after his years of legal appeals ended.
- A twenty-three-year-old woman in Mansfield, England, was surprised when doctors solved her lifelong breathing problems. During surgery, they removed a tiddlywink that she had apparently pushed up her nose when she was a toddler.
- A man in Anthon, Iowa, has been hiccupping nonstop for sixty-three years.
- A man in California tied weather balloons to his lawn chair and went for a little ride. He didn't get nervous until he was at 16,000 feet and staring airline pilots in the eye. He descended by shooting one balloon at a time with a pellet gun.
- A man was arrested in a bank after arousing the suspicion of the tellers. What drew their attention to him? He was standing in line reading a newspaper. That, in itself, may not create suspicion, but the man was holding the newspaper upside down. It turns out he could not read and was pretending to do so while building up the courage to hand the teller a stick-up note.
- A man was elected to the city council. There was only one problem: he had died months earlier.
- Jay Luo, age twelve, became the youngest university graduate in U.S. history, receiving a degree in mathematics from Boise State University.

- A New York man couldn't afford the airfare to visit his parents in Texas. His solution? He mailed himself. Upon delivery, he was noticed peering from the crate and was subsequently arrested.
- A photographer was killed while filming a documentary on the danger of low highway bridges. He was struck by a low highway bridge while filming as he stood in the back of a truck.

I know what you're thinking—some of these examples are on the morbid side. You're right; they are. And my students love them. Reading these articles makes my students interested in reading the newspaper and opens the door for me to talk about the more important benefits of reading the paper.

Scavenger Hunt

Students often come to me unaware of the components of a newspaper. Many of them, for example, do not know the difference between an editorial and a straight news story—they are unaware that these are two different genres of writing, that they are found in two different sections of the paper, and that they are separated from each other for a reason. To help them get a better idea of the elements of a newspaper, I have students go on a newspaper scavenger hunt (see Figure 9.1). The scavenger hunt is designed to enable students to familiarize themselves with all the components of the newspaper, from op-ed pieces to obituaries, from the stock market to Dear Abby.

Newspaper Reading Minute

To underscore the idea that the newspaper is a rich source of information, I designate a specific month to be Newspaper Reading Minute Month. I pass out a calendar and have each student sign up for a given day. Every day we spend the first minute of class sharing one interesting newspaper article, brought in by the student who signed up for that day. I challenge each student to bring in the most interesting article possible—to consider articles that are serious, humorous, bizarre, informative—whatever they find interesting. I have everyone in the class record a one-sentence reaction to each one-minute presentation. After every presentation, I pin the article to a bulletin board entitled "Why We Should Read the Newspaper." In this way we create a collage of interesting newspaper articles. At the end of the month, I have students vote on the best articles, and those who have brought in the winning articles are treated to lunch in my room.

Figure 9.1

Newspaper Scavenger Hunt

Name _____ Date _____ Period _____

Newspaper: _____
Date of newspaper: _____

Search the newspaper for the following information. When you find the answers, cut them out and paste them next to the questions.

Questions   *Cut and Paste Answers Here*

---

1. Bruce Springsteen was the top concert moneymaker in 2003. Who were the other performers in the top 10?
2. What are the five levels of terrorism alert outlined by the Department of Homeland Security?
3. List three tips for traveling during high alert.
4. This year's flu vaccine might not prove effective. Why not?
5. How can you tell the difference between a cold and the flu?
6. Name one fitness trend that will shape 2004.
7. What is today's weather forecast?
8. When and where is this year's Auto Show?
9. What time is the Macy's four-hour sale?
10. Who was named *Time* magazine's Person of the Year?
11. Find two letters to the editor: one criticizing the governor and one praising the governor.
12. Hope Lange died. Who was she?
13. How did AOL stock perform yesterday?

Because I want my students to handle a real newspaper, articles from the Internet are not initially accepted. After students complete a month of newspaper sharing, we begin a new month of newspaper sharing, but this time the articles must come from out-of-state newspapers. This requires students to find and read newspapers online. I want them to realize that daily access to the *New York Times,* the *Washington Post,* the *Denver Post,* or any other newspaper in the country is only a few clicks away.

Sharing wacky articles, creating top ten lists, designing scavenger hunts, and having students share newspaper reading minutes are all effective ways to familiarize students with the newspaper. Once this foundation is set, I turn my attention to the important task of ensuring that my students can dig below the surface and read the paper critically.

Deeper Newspaper Reading

Once students are familiar with the newspaper, it is time to push them to begin reading it with the same critical eye they use to read literature. Here are some ways to move them in that direction.

Just the Facts?

There is supposed to be a clear distinction between a straight news story and an editorial, but that line, as we know, is often blurred. To help students understand that news stories contain bias, I show them how different newspapers present the same news story. For example, as I write this, a judge in the city of San Francisco has decided to allow gay couples to marry despite state law that defines marriage as a union "between a man and a woman." To date, 2,464 same-sex couples have been married. Not surprisingly, this has received a lot of media play, and biases in the articles are often so apparent they can be seen even before the articles are read. Just look at these two headlines:

Gay Marriage Ban Flouted in California
San Francisco Opens Marriage to Gay Couples

Where does the bias show? Through the verbs in each headline. "Flouted" has a strong negative connotation, bringing to mind a sense of contempt, a sense of disobedience. "Open," on the other hand, conjures an image of removing obstacles, a sense of allowance, a kind of freedom.

Beyond the headlines, bias can be found in the newspaper articles themselves. Read the introductory paragraphs from two newspaper stories about the gay marriage issue in Figure 9.2, taking note of the biases involved.

Let's look at some of the "loaded" language used in the two articles. The piece headed "Judge Says Gay Marriages in San Francisco Appear Illegal but Doesn't Stop Them" used the following words and phrases:

- "violating the law"
- "stop"

Two Articles on Gay Marriage

Judge Says Gay Marriages in San Francisco Appear Illegal but Doesn't Stop Them

A judge said San Francisco appears to be violating the law by issuing marriage licenses to gay and lesbian couples, but he declined Tuesday to order an immediate halt to the weddings.

A conservative group had asked Judge James Warren to immediately stop the weddings and void the 2,464 same-sex marriages performed in the city since Thursday. Instead, Warren issued a nonbinding order urging the city to halt the weddings, and told city lawyers to return March 29 to explain their legal position.

"We are extremely happy and gratified that a stay was not issued," City Attorney Dennis Herrera said.

Mayor Gavin Newsom said through a spokeswoman that the city would keep performing the marriages despite the judge's urging.

"We will continue to issue marriage licenses until the court rules we can no longer do so," spokeswoman Darlene Chiu said.

The Proposition 22 Legal Defense and Education Fund had asked the Superior Court judge to issue an order commanding the city to stop issuing the licenses, or show cause explaining why it would not.

Warren did just that—after arguing for a while about the punctuation in the group's proposed order. But he made his order nonbinding, frustrating conservatives who also failed earlier in the day to persuade another judge to halt the weddings as part of a separate challenge.

Judge Ronald Quidachay said he was not prepared to rule until at least Friday in the challenge filed by the Campaign for California Families.

"This is municipal anarchy," said Robert Tyler, a lawyer for the Alliance Defense Fund, which argued the case before Warren on behalf of the Proposition 22 group.

Gay couples from as far as Europe have been lining up outside City Hall since Thursday, when city officials decided to begin marrying same-sex couples in a collective act of official civil disobedience.

Newsom said the city will pursue a constitutional challenge through the courts. Newsom says the equal protection clause of the California Constitution makes denying marriage licenses to gay couples illegal.

Associated Press, Feb. 18, 2004

San Francisco Opens Marriage to Gay Couples

The ceremony, arranged in great haste, was brief and held behind closed doors of a dreary municipal office. Del Martin and Phyllis Lyon, a lesbian couple together for 50 years, stood facing each other and beamed when a city official pronounced them not husband and wife but "spouses for life."

They had not become domestic partners, or joined in a civil union. The couple, both pioneering activists in the gay rights movement, had signed full-fledged marriage licenses and been wed with San Francisco's official blessing, a momentous step that city leaders said has no precedent.

Word of the wedding—which took place after San Francisco's new mayor, Gavin Newsom, defied state law earlier this week and asked city clerks to remove all references to gender on local marriage forms—spread fast. By Thursday evening, San Francisco's ornate City Hall had begun to resemble a one-of-a-kind wedding chapel as city officials married about 80 gay couples who had rushed to exchange vows.

Newsom's sudden move to sanction same-sex marriage, a decision that some politically conservative groups are denouncing as illegal and vowing to stop through the courts, comes as a national debate over the issue is rippling through statehouses, the White House, and the Democratic presidential primary races.

In Massachusetts, opponents of gay marriage were attempting to enact a constitutional amendment that would define marriage solely as a union between a man and a woman. On Thursday, the Virginia House of Delegates gave preliminary approval to legislation that would ban the recognition of same-sex civil unions and domestic partnerships.

California, and particularly liberal San Francisco, has some of the world's broadest protection of gay couples, but it does not sanction gay marriage. In 2000, voters backed an initiative that in effect banned the practice.

But Newsom, a 36-year-old Democrat who was inaugurated last month, said he decided to change San Francisco's marriage regulations because he was convinced they violated the state Constitution, which he said "leaves no room for any form of discrimination." He said he began thinking about making the changes after listening to Bush disparage gay marriage in his State of the Union address last month.

By Joe Dignan and Rene Sanchez, *Washington Post*, Feb. 14, 2004

Figure 9.2

- "void"
- "halt"
- "frustrating"
- "municipal anarchy"
- "constitutional challenge"

By contrast, the piece "San Francisco Opens Marriage to Gay Couples" used these words and phrases:

- "beamed"
- "spouses for life"
- "pioneering activists"
- "San Francisco's official blessing"
- "broadest protections for gay couples"
- "no room for any form of discrimination"

Giving students articles with contrasting biases and having them highlight the loaded language helps them understand that bias may be found even in the "straight" news section of any newspaper.

Weekly Reflection

To encourage deeper newspaper reading, I ask each student to clip and bring one newspaper article to class every Friday. For every article they bring, they are to write a reflection. These reflections are assigned the previous Monday, and they vary. Here are some examples of the types of reflections students are asked to submit with their articles:

- Create a t-chart. On the left side, in a bulleted list, summarize the points in the article. On the right side, list what the article doesn't say. What is being left out?
- Write one question and one comment about the article.
- Find a trouble spot (an area you do not understand) and generate questions around it.
- Complete the following: This article reminds me of _____ because _____.
- Create a t-chart. On the left side write down one thing you learned from reading the article. On the right side write a reflection on why learning that piece of information might be of value to you in your life.
- List the reading strategies you employed to make sense of this article.

- Write three unfamiliar words found in the article. Copy the sentences in which they are found. Predict their meanings before looking them up in the dictionary.

At first, students can choose freely from the entire newspaper, but later I assign specific sections. One week I might ask them to submit a national news story. The next week they may be asked to reflect on a business or feature story. This requires them to read the entire paper and prevents them from reading only their favorite sections.

Reading Political Cartoons

Another area of the newspaper that students are woefully underprepared for is political cartoons. Like challenging text, political cartoons need second and even third-draft readings. To introduce this idea to students, I place a cartoon like the one shown in Figure 9.3 on the overhead projector.

Figure 9.3

A Political Cartoon

Before students can clear up cognitive space to analyze the cartoon, they must first complete a careful first reading. I ask them to examine the cartoon carefully, listing everything they see. For the cartoon in Figure 9.3, for example, the following list was generated:

- A man.
- He is wearing a vest with the stars and stripes on it.
- He is holding a bandage box.
- The box is labeled "U.S. Terror Readiness."
- He has a bandage on his wounded finger.

Listing everything they see in the cartoon may seem simplistic, but it has been my experience that students often look at political cartoons without seeing all the literal details in the cartoon. Having them list all the elements ensures that they will look at the cartoon closely.

Once they have noticed the literal elements of the cartoon, I start asking some of the deeper reading questions:

- What is the subject of this cartoon?
- What is the context of this cartoon?
- What is the cartoon's purpose?
- Who is the intended audience? Why are they the intended audience?
- What is the thesis of the cartoon? What point is the cartoonist trying to make?
- What is left unsaid in the cartoon? What opposing views are left out?

Once students have gained experience reading political cartoons, show them opposing cartoons on the same subject. For example, the two cartoons in Figure 9.4 were published shortly after Saddam Hussein was captured. Read them closely and see if you can express how these cartoons can be seen as opposing one another.

Cartoon A depicts George Bush and Donald Rumsfeld delivering the "mother of all rats" (Saddam in a cage) "to the Iraqi people and the rest of the civilized world." The implication is that the United States, through delivery of Saddam Hussein, should be praised for removing a tyrant from power.

Cartoon B depicts Saddam Hussein on trial. As his first character witness, Saddam is requesting Ronald Reagan, who, according to the newspaper he holds, had earlier supplied arms to Saddam. The implication is that the United States should be criticized for having a foreign policy that helped Saddam Hussein solidify his power in the first place.

Figure 9.4

Opposing Views in Two Cartoons

A

By permission of Chuck Asay and Creators Syndicate, Inc.

B

Copyright © Mike Keefe. Reprinted with permission.

After having students analyze a pair of opposing cartoons, they are then asked to search in newspapers and online for additional opposing examples, adding analysis of their own. Two of my favorite Web sites for political cartoons are Daryl Cagle's cartoon index at Cagle.slate.msn. com/, which has cartoons categorized by subject, and the *New York Times* Web site (NYTimes.com), which has daily postings from the following cartoonists: Jeff Danzinger, Bill Deore, Doonesbury, Glenn McCoy, Pat Oliphant, Rudy Park, Ted Rall, Ben Sargent, and Tom Toles.

After students demonstrate they can read the newspaper at a deeper level, it's time to give them practice in another reading area they will encounter throughout their lives: interpreting statistics.

The Untruth About Statistics

Benjamin Disraeli said that there are three kinds of lies: lies, damned lies, and statistics. Living in a world where complex information is often conveyed in simple statistical form, our students need to develop a healthy dose of skepticism when encountering such data. To help students understand that statistics, too, should be read at deeper levels, I begin by writing the following statement on the board:

> Your final exam is worth fifty points. Therefore, you should spend a lot of time studying.

I then ask my students, "What might be untrue about this statement?" Their first response is that maybe the exam is not worth fifty points. I assure them that that part of the statement is accurate. I then ask them why the second sentence ("Therefore, you should spend a lot of time studying") might be misleading. After some brainstorming, they begin asking the right questions:

- Is fifty points a lot in the scope of the entire term?
- How many total points will be possible for us to have at the end of the semester?
- Will this test make or break my grade?
- What if I have a strong "A" already? Do I need to spend a lot of time studying? Or can I focus on my other final exams?

If I were a student, I would be very concerned if fifty points constituted 25 percent of my final grade; but I would be considerably less concerned if fifty points only amounted to 5 percent of my final grade. Many of my students do not know how to ask these critical questions. They read "fifty points" and automatically assume it must mean a lot.

From there, I move on to real-world examples of statistical manipulation. For example, why might the following statement be misleading?

Four out of five dentists recommend this toothpaste.

According to the Internet article "Math Talk," this kind of claim falls under the "If at first you don't succeed, try, try again" category:

> You ask five dentists, but only one of them recommends your brand. So, forget you ever asked them! Ask another five dentists. This time, two of them recommend the brand. Forget them! Ask another five. Keep trying, until by random fluctuation, you get lucky and four out of five recommend the brand. Then, show your television commercial. Whatever you do, do not talk about the 13,925 dentists you had to survey before you got lucky, and don't mention that only 8% of them recommended your brand.

"Surveys" like these are often used to manipulate statistics. Suppose two politicians are debating a school bond issue. One of the politicians "proves" that her constituency overwhelmingly supports the bond by releasing the results of a survey showing that a majority of the citizenry approves the bond measure. The other candidate, however, has polled the same population and found that a majority *opposes* the bond measure. Both candidates are telling the "truth." How can this be? The answer lies in the way each politician has worded the question:

- Candidate A: "Should we invest more in our children's future by passing the school bond?"
- Candidate B: "Should we raise taxes to fund more and bigger government bureaucracy by passing the school bond?"

The questions are each crafted in a way that manipulates those asked into giving the desired response, thus allowing both candidates to claim the support of the public.

Now let's say you live in a town that has two major hospitals, Mercy Hospital and County Hospital. Though you are healthy now, your employer requires you to fill out a form stating which hospital you'd prefer to be taken to in an emergency. You remember reading in the newspaper the following statistics regarding the two hospitals:

	Mercy Hospital	County Hospital
Patients admitted who lived	790	900
Patients admitted who died	210	100
Percentage of patients who survived	79%	90%

If you made your decision based on a surface-level reading of the previous chart, you would choose County Hospital because it appears that your chances for survival are better there. But are they? Suppose you asked a few questions and found that the previous statistics could be broken down into more specific data, as follows:

	Mercy Hospital	County Hospital
Number of patients admitted in fair or better condition who lived	580	860
Number of patients admitted in fair or better condition who died	10	30
Percentage of patients admitted in fair or better condition who survived	98%	97%
Number of patients admitted in poor condition or worse who lived	210	40
Number of patients admitted in poor condition or worse who died	200	70
Percentage of patients admitted in poor condition or worse who survived	51%	36%

When you look at the aggregate numbers, as was done originally, the decision seems straightforward—County Hospital is the better choice. But when you break the information down, an entirely different picture emerges. After examining the table above, does your decision change?

The seemingly contradictory picture that emerges when you break larger figures down into more specific categories is a phenomenon known to statisticians as "Simpson's Paradox." Teaching this paradox to my students helps bring home to them the dangers involved in accepting data on a surface level and reminds them to be cautious when drawing overly hasty or simplistic conclusions from numbers.

Having played with the ideas that statistics can be manipulated, you are now ready for the three-question quiz I give to my students. The answers follow, but don't peek. Good luck.

- Problem 1. A small town's newspaper reports that violent crime has risen 100 percent in town in the last year. If you were a resident there, should you consider moving?
- Problem 2. Macy's is selling a raincoat for $100. They advertise 20 percent off the regular price, and then an additional 30 percent off the reduced price. Bloomingdale's also sells the raincoat for $100. They are advertising half off the regular price. At which store should you purchase the raincoat?
- Problem 3. A poll conducted by the school newspaper asked students who their favorite musicians were. Eminem led the voting with 29 percent of the vote, followed by Good Charlotte (24 percent) and Christina Aguilera (19 percent). Your friend reads the survey and says most of the students at your school like Eminem the best. Is your friend correct?

How did you do? Here are the answers:

- Problem 1: Probably not. When you are working with small numbers, any slight change can alter the percentages greatly. An increase of 100 percent in violent crime might simply mean that last year there were two robberies instead of one. The small town, even with this increase, might still be far safer than the neighboring communities.
- Problem 2: The raincoat will cost $56 at Macy's and $50 at Bloomingdale's.
- Problem 3: Most of the students do not like Eminem the best: 71 percent prefer a musician other than Eminem.

After they have a little practice identifying misleading statistics, students are asked to look around and bring one example of a misleading statistic to class. I ask them to create a t-graph on which they are to note what the statistic says and what the statistic does not say. Misleading statistics can be found in almost any daily newspaper. For example, the following was found in my newspaper, the *Los Angeles Times*, just this morning:

What the Statistic Says	What the Statistic Does Not Say
The nation's official jobless rate is 5.9 percent, a relatively benign level by historical standards.	The figure does not include the "underemployed"— people who are working part-time and would rather be working full-time. The figure also does not include people who want to work but have grown so discouraged they have given up looking for employment. When these groups are added to the jobless rate, it climbs to 9.7 percent, an *increase* over last year.

On the assigned day, students break into groups and share their examples of misleading statistics. Each group then selects and shares its best example with the class.

Statistics are used daily to manipulate our thinking. Training students to read them with a healthy degree of skepticism will allow them to reap lifelong benefits.

Garnering Appreciation Through Deeper Reading

In this chapter I have argued that the deeper reading skills we teach adolescents to help them make sense of challenging literature are the same skills they need to apply beyond the classroom. To help them make the connection, I give my students real-world practice, having them identify euphemisms and weasel words and getting them to critically read advertisements (including spam and "snail" mail), newspaper articles, political cartoons, and statistics. These skills might be considered "defensive" in nature—they help protect our students from advertisers who are scurrilous, politicians who are devious, and statistics made to mislead. But gaining the ability to read more deeply gives our students benefits far beyond defensive reading—it gives them a deeper sense of appreciation as well.

To show how deeper reading can lead to deeper appreciation, I share a painting with my students and ask them to "read" it. I often use Pieter Brueghel's *The Fall of Icarus* (search this title on Google to view the painting). Just as they were asked to list what they see in a political cartoon, students are asked to generate a list of everything they see in the painting. This is what one class saw during their first-draft reading:

- A man plowing a field.
- A large sailing ship and some smaller ships.
- A sheepherder with his sheep.
- A man in the lower right-hand corner with his arm out. Is he pointing?
- Trees.
- Rocks.
- An island—is that a castle?
- Two legs sticking out of the water to the rear of the large ship.

Once their initial reading is charted, students are asked to reread the painting, looking for things they may have missed the first time through. Figure 9.5 shows the questions I use to prompt a second, deeper reading, along with some responses I've received to those questions.

Because my students were unfamiliar with Icarus, I told them the story of how Icarus used wax to attach wings to his arms and learned to fly. His father warned him not to fly too close to the sun. Icarus did not heed his father's warning. He flew too close to the sun, which melted the wax holding his wings together, causing him to plummet into the sea.

My questions and the story prompted students to reconsider the painting at a deeper level. Moving them deeper into the discussion, I asked the students what they thought the painting might *really* be about. To help them, I shared two poems with them: W. H. Auden's "Musee des Beaux-Arts" and William Carlos Williams's "Landscape with the Fall of Icarus":

Musee des Beaux-Arts

About suffering they were never wrong,
The Old Masters: how well they understood
Its human position: how it takes place
While someone else is eating or opening a
    window or just walking dully along;
How, when the aged are reverently, passionately
    waiting
For the miraculous birth, there always must be
Children who did not specially want it to happen,
    skating
On a pond at the edge of the wood:
They never forgot
That even the dreadful martyrdom must run its
    course
Anyhow in a corner, some untidy spot
Where the dogs go on with their doggy life and
    the torturer's horse
Scratches its innocent behind on a tree.

In Brueghel's Icarus, for instance: how everything
    turns away
Quite leisurely from the disaster; the ploughman
    may
Have heard the splash, the forsaken cry,
But for him it was not an important failure; the
    sun shone
As it had to on the white legs disappearing into
    the green
Water, and the expensive delicate ship that must
    have seen
Something amazing, a boy falling out of the sky,
Had somewhere to get to and sailed calmly on.
    W. H. Auden

Landscape with the Fall of Icarus

According to Brueghel
when Icarus fell
it was spring

a farmer was plowing
his field
the whole pageantry

of the year was
awake tingling
near

the edge of the sea
concerned
with itself

sweating in the sun
that melted
the wings' wax

unsignificantly
off the coast
there was

a splash quite unnoticed
this was
Icarus drowning
    William Carlos Williams

By asking probing questions and sharing these poems with the students, they were pushed to uncover a deeper level of meaning in Brueghel's painting. Moving far beyond their initial reading, the students began to understand that the painting serves as a commentary on humankind's indifference to suffering. This understanding did not

Figure 9.5

Questions for a Deeper Reading of Brueghel's *The Fall of Icarus*

My Questions	*My Students' Responses*
What do you notice about the colors in the painting?	The painting is dark around the edges. The sky is clearing and is bright where there is a break in the sky. The ship seems to be sailing towards the light.
What else do you notice about the colors?	The bright red shirt worn by the plowman stands out.
Why is the bright red in the forefront of the painting?	The painter wants you to notice this person immediately.
What can you say about movement in the painting? Is there a direction?	Everything seems to be moving towards the left of the painting. The farmer, the sheepherder, the boats are all moving in this direction.
Who does not seem to be heading in the same direction as the rest of the painting?	The man in the lower right-hand corner who seems to be pointing at the legs in the water.
Those legs in the water seem interesting. Whose legs are they?	It's possible someone fell off the ship. No, they seem too far away from the ship for that to be the case.
Do the legs seem to belong to someone out for a swim?	No, they look like they are thrashing or struggling. The person could be drowning.
Why do you think the painter has all the direction of the painting moving away from the person struggling in the water?	So you don't notice it right away? To draw your attention away from him or her?
Let me tell you the title of this painting. It is called *The Fall of Icarus*. Does anyone know the story of Icarus?	(No one knew the story.)

instantly emerge; it came gradually after they did what good readers do: they reread the "text," considered what the painting "said," considered what the painting did not say, made connections outside the text, and shared their thinking.

This lesson teaches students that learning to read at deeper levels has implications far broader than simple self-defense; it enables them to appreciate art, by which I mean to include film, music, and theater along with painting and sculpture.

If We Don't, Who Will?

Those of us who treasure the traditional English curriculum may be troubled by what I advocate in this chapter. I hear your concerns: How will we find the time to teach these skills? Won't we have to sacrifice other units in our curriculum? Is it now my job to teach students to read advertisements, newspapers, and political cartoons? Don't I have enough to do already? I hear these concerns, and I share them. But I have another concern as well: that students are leaving our schools unprepared to meet the growing literacy demands they will find in college, in work, in life. So for those teachers who are struggling with what I am saying in this chapter, I ask you this:

- Do you believe our students are graduating adequately prepared to read the world at a deeper level?
- What will happen to students who leave school unprepared for the literacy challenges that lie outside our curriculum?
- What is more important ten years from now: our students' remembering the key literary elements in *The Great Gatsby,* or our students' being able to make sense of a ballot initiative?

This chapter is not a call to abandon difficult literature in favor of reading real-world materials with our students. On the contrary: what I am arguing is that students use the skills they learn in reading challenging literature and be taught how to apply these skills to a much broader text—the world. If this means we teach a bit less literature, then so be it. The loss of a bit of the traditional curriculum is outweighed by the lifelong benefits our students will receive while learning how to apply reading skills in the real world.

If you still are not sold on the call to break out of the traditional curriculum, consider this: I conducted a poll, and four out of five teachers agree with me.

CHAPTER TEN

The Art of Teaching Deep Reading

Many students come to me at the beginning of each school year knowing exactly two "strategies" for coping with a challenging reading assignment:

- Student "strategy" 1: They begin reading, struggle briefly, and give up.
- Student "strategy" 2: They begin reading, become lost and, out of duty, continue reading—even when they don't understand most of what they are reading.

Sound familiar? If your students are like mine, their reliance on these two "strategies" makes it painfully obvious that they need help from their teachers. It is clear that they need to be taught how to make meaning from challenging text. That makes us, their teachers, the single most important factor in the classroom.

In *Reading Reasons,* I cited some studies on the impact a good teacher can make. I think they are worth repeating here:

- A 1998 Boston study on the effect public school teachers have on learning found that "in just one academic year, the top third of teachers produced as much as six times the learning growth as the bottom third of teachers. In fact, tenth graders taught by the least effective teachers made nearly no gains in reading" (Haycock 2002, p. 28).

- "Research in Tennessee and Texas shows that these effects are cumulative and hold up regardless of race, class, or prior achievement levels. Some of the classrooms showing the greatest gains are filled with low-income students, some with well-to-do students . . . It's not the kids after all: Something very different is going on with the teaching" (Haycock 2002, p. 28).

Clearly, what the classroom teacher does, or doesn't do, matters a great deal. Knowing that our students struggle when it comes to reading difficult text and knowing that we teachers are the critical factors in their learning to become better readers lead to one central question: How can we design classroom lessons that help our students reach deeper meaning when they read?

Planning Deeper Reading Lessons

Which single book in your curriculum is the hardest to teach? Imagine you will begin teaching this book Monday morning. You know that this book will be extraordinarily difficult for your students to read. Where will you begin? How will you structure your lessons so that your students can read and understand this text at the deepest and richest levels possible? Which strategies will you use? When and where will you use them? How long should the unit be? Monday morning is approaching—where do you start?

In Chapters 2 through 8, I discussed the many stages of deeper reading comprehension. As teachers, we can focus the reader, facilitate first-draft reading, design lessons to maximize second-draft reading, encourage student collaboration, prompt students to think metaphorically, and require deeper reflection from our students. When planning a reading lesson I keep each of these stages in mind. But to help me decide which instructional approaches I should take in moving students through these various stages, I center my lesson planning on four key questions:

1. Without my assistance, what will my students take from this reading?
2. With my assistance, what do I want my students to take from this reading?
3. What can I do to bridge the gap between what my students would learn on their own and what I want them to learn?

4. How will I know if my students "got it"?

To give you a sense of how these four questions can guide effective lesson planning, let's apply them to a one-page "My Turn" essay from *Newsweek,* entitled "Africans Need More Than Our Sympathy" (see Figure 10.1). Pretend that you will be teaching this article to a seventh-grade class. (Though this essay might not typically be taught in an English classroom, I have chosen it to demonstrate that the planning principles described are applicable to text in any content area, not just an English curriculum—though, as I argue in Chapter 9, I believe students in English classes need practice reading real-world selections.) Read the article, and then we'll explore how the four questions can work in concert with each of the reading stages to help you design an effective unit.

Question 1: Without My Assistance, What Will My Students Take from This Reading?

If my students were to read this article on their own, I would expect them to understand its main points:

- The author, a doctor, began working in Zambia in 1994; he and his family moved there two years later.
- They witnessed firsthand the devastation AIDS has caused in Africa.
- The author adopted a Zambian boy, Cletus, who now lives in America.
- Africans do not have enough access to the drugs that combat AIDS.
- The disease is so rampant that people sell coffins on street corners.
- Many in Africa are still dying needlessly from AIDS.
- The author believes that the United States should provide more funding to fight AIDS in Africa.

Most of my students would be able to cull this information from the article without my assistance. But as their teacher, I know they will have a deeper reading experience if I step in and provide some assistance.

Question 2: With My Assistance, What Do I Want My Students to Take from This Reading?

In addition to the information from the piece in Figure 10.1 that they'd be able to get on their own, I want my students also to be able to:

My Turn

Africans Need More Than Our Sympathy

It's easy to feel overwhelmed by the AIDS crisis, but only real action will help those who are suffering

BY PAUL S. ZEITZ

IT WAS A BEAUTIFUL FALL AFTERnoon when I arrived at the soccer game in which my 16-year-old son Cletus was playing. This was his first opportunity to play on the varsity team of Churchill High School. As the sun glittered and the leaves fell from the trees, I watched proudly as Cletus led an offensive push toward the goal. I was amazed at his strength and determination.

My mind flashed back—as it frequently does—to the days when my family and I were living and working in Lusaka, Zambia, where we made a life-changing decision to adopt Cletus. I started working in Zambia in 1994, and then moved there with my family two years later, because my wife, Mindi, and I share a deep love of Africa. We are both doctors, and we wanted to ensure that the poor received basic health services. The Zambians welcomed us warmly and impressed us with their faith, as well as their love for community and family.

In our first months there, we saw death and suffering from poverty and AIDS everywhere we turned. As I drove my three sons to school each morning, we would pass a city cemetery that was full of mourners. We would hear the wailing cries of parents and loved ones as the long funeral processions reached the seemingly endless rows of graves.

One image that is burned into my memory is that of a small child's coffin resting on the floor of our family van. We had used our van for many family outings, but now it was pressed into service as a makeshift hearse, carrying the coffin of one of the children who had lived in our town, a baby named David. He had died of AIDS after only three months of life.

Nor can I forget my many friends and co-workers who succumbed to the disease.

They didn't have access to the lifesaving AIDS medications that I knew would have kept them alive for less than a dollar a day. During our four years in Zambia I went to so many of their funerals it brought me to despair. I could not stop thinking that what

NEW HOME: We fell in love with a bright-eyed boy who told us—and everyone who'd listen—that he wanted a family

I was seeing was just a fraction of a crisis that would destroy many more lives. I felt angry because I knew that the most effective programs—those that educate young people about prevention and provide patients with lifesaving medications—were so small and underfunded, as they still are.

One day, as I was driving through Lusaka, I came upon a minivan parked near a busy intersection. I was shocked to see a young man selling coffins to passersby. I couldn't believe I was living in a world that would let this epidemic take so many lives.

To renew our faith and conquer our

grief, Mindi and I worked with the wife of Zambia's vice president to help start an orphanage in our community. We organized a volunteer program in which Americans living there joined together with Zambians to build a safe place for these vulnerable children. Mindi and I fell in love with a bright-eyed, healthy boy (only about 25 percent of children born to HIV-infected parents have HIV themselves) who had recently lost his mother. He stood out from the other children by boldly telling us—and everyone who would listen—that he wanted to find a family. When we returned to the United States, we brought Cletus with us as our adopted son.

My wife and I now have five sons, and we teach them that America is greatest when it opens its heart to others' suffering. My sons frequently accompany me to demonstrations for more funding, and last summer Cletus returned to Zambia to volunteer at the orphanage.

Every day I remind myself that there are 42 million people in the world living with AIDS, and that 8,000 of them will needlessly die that day. I reflect on the fact that there are 14 million children who, like Cletus, lost their parents to the disease.

We can do more. United Nations experts estimate that it will cost at least $15 billion a year to respond to AIDS. Considering the United States' relative wealth (it controls 30.8 percent of global GNP), it should pay one third of that amount, yet our legislators have approved just $2.4 billion.

In my house, we frequently discuss how we can—as a family and as individuals—help end this scourge. We often pray together for those who are suffering, and as Cletus enters adulthood, my wife and I have made sure he understands the choices he must make in order to stay healthy. But we also know how important it is for all Americans to mobilize their communities, their schools and their religious groups to raise money and take political action. If we do, people who are living with AIDS may get to see their children grow up, full of hope for the future. Mindi and I are fortunate beyond measure because we can do just that, and because we have Cletus to inspire us with his accomplishments and his life.

ZEITZ lives in Potomac, Md.

Figure 10.1

- identify the author's thesis.
- recognize the techniques the author uses to communicate his thesis.
- understand the author's use of diction and key vocabulary: wailing, makeshift, succumbed, epidemic, GNP.
- learn some background knowledge to help deepen their understanding, including:
  —Zambia's location in Africa.
  —why the AIDS epidemic is so rampant there.
  —how Africa's AIDS epidemic compares with AIDS in the United States.
  —why, as Americans, we should be concerned about the African AIDS epidemic.

Having my students read this article at the deepest level possible is my goal, and what I do as their teacher will determine their level of involvement and understanding. As I consider what I want them to take from this article, I realize that some of the prior knowledge they probably need in order to read it at a deeper level is not contained within the article itself. I will have to teach outside and around the article so that when my students do sit down to read it, they will have the necessary context to appreciate it on a deeper level.

Let's revisit these two questions—and the answers—this time presented in a two-column format (see Figure 10.2). As is evident from Figure 10.2, there is a gap between what the students would understand if left to read the article on their own (the column on the left) and what I think the students can learn with the help of their teacher (the column on the right).

Question 3: What Can I Do to Bridge the Gap Between What My Students Would Learn on Their Own and What I Want Them to Learn?

To bridge the gap between what students can do on their own and what they can learn with teacher assistance, I must design lessons that will move students to read more deeply. In drawing up these lessons, I keep one question uppermost in my mind: What is it that I want my students to take away from this piece? There are a number of possible results I might have in mind from my students' reading this article (for example, having a better understanding of AIDS or being aware of what we can do to combat the crisis), but I have decided I want my students to be able to write an essay in which they address the following questions:

Figure 10.2

What My Students Can Learn from the Article	
Without my assistance, what will my students take from this reading?	*With my assistance, what do I want my students to take from this reading?*
	To identify the author's thesis.
	To recognize the techniques the author uses to communicate his thesis.
	To understand the author's use of diction and key vocabulary: wailing, makeshift, succumbed, epidemic, GNP
	To learn some background knowledge to help deepen their understanding, including:
	—Zambia's location in Africa.
	—why the AIDS epidemic is so rampant there.
	—how Africa's AIDS epidemic compares with AIDS in the United States.
	—why, as Americans, we should be concerned about the African AIDS epidemic.
The author, a doctor, began working in Zambia in 1994; he and his family moved there two years later.	The author, a doctor, began working in Zambia in 1994; he and his family moved there two years later.
They witnessed firsthand the devastation AIDS has caused in Africa.	They witnessed firsthand the devastation AIDS has caused in Africa.
The author adopted a Zambian boy, Cletus, who now lives in America.	The author adopted a Zambian boy, Cletus, who now lives in America.
Africans do not have enough access to the drugs that combat AIDS.	Africans do not have enough access to the drugs that combat AIDS.
The disease is so rampant that people sell coffins on street corners.	The disease is so rampant that people sell coffins on street corners.
Many in Africa are still dying needlessly from AIDS.	Many in Africa are still dying needlessly from AIDS.
The author believes that the United States should provide more funding to fight AIDS in Africa.	The author believes that the United States should provide more funding to fight AIDS in Africa.

In your estimation, is "Africans Need More Than Our Sympathy" an effective essay? In answering, consider the following: Why did the author write this article (purpose)? What techniques did he use to drive home his point?

This essay will be the finish line of the unit. Knowing where I want my students to end *before they begin reading* allows me to create a much more effective unit. Everything I now plan will be with the idea of enabling the students to answer these questions as best they can.

Figure 10.3

AIDS Fact Sheet

AIDS will cause early death in as many as half of the teenagers living in the hardest hit countries of southern Africa.

Two-thirds of the fifteen-year-olds living in Botswana will die of AIDS.

Of all the people in the world with AIDS, 90 percent live in Africa. In 2002, 58 percent of those infected in the region were women.

Up to 1,000 adults and children are dying of AIDS every day in some African countries.

Worldwide, 42 million people are infected with HIV/AIDS.

Of those infected, 1.3 million are children under the age of fifteen.

In 2003, 5.4 million people were infected with HIV/AIDS.

Source: UNAIDS/UNICEF/WHO, *British Medical Journal*, July 10, 2003

Using the steps outlined in the previous chapters, one lesson outline for teaching "Africans Need More Than Our Sympathy" might look like this.

Focusing the Reader

To generate interest before reading, I ask students to predict which continent has the worst AIDS crisis. We share our predictions and the reasons for them. Students are then given an "AIDS Fact Sheet" (Figure 10.3) and asked to read it quietly. After that, I ask them to write a three-minute reflection on the back of the sheet. These reflections lead to small-group and whole-class discussions, thus warming up the students for the reading.

Students are then told that they are about to read an essay that discusses the AIDS epidemic. Before having them read, I give students the following questions and tell them that they will be answering these questions upon the completion of the unit:

In your estimation, is "Africans Need More Than Our Sympathy" an effective essay? In answering, consider the following: Why did the author write this article (purpose)? What techniques did he use to drive home his point?

Also before they read, I show the students a map of Africa so as to orient them to Zambia's location.

Figure 10.4

Vocabulary Predictions			
Word	Prediction Before Reading the Article	Prediction After Reading the Article	Prediction After Group Discussion
Wailing			
Makeshift			
Succumbed			
Epidemic			
GNP			

First-Draft Reading

Before reading the article, the students are given five words and are asked to predict their definitions (see Figure 10.4). I tell them that as they read the text, they should keep a lookout for the five words and see if the context for each word seems to confirm or counter their initial predictions of what the words mean. This activity provides them with a purpose as they read.

I then read the first three paragraphs aloud and ask the students to complete the reading silently.

Second-Draft Reading

Upon completing an initial reading, students revisit their vocabulary predictions. Now they have the advantage of having seen the words in context. With this context in mind, they may choose to revise some or all of their five predictions.

Next, I ask each student to take out a sheet of paper and write the following across the top:

The author's purpose in writing this essay is _____.

After filling in the blank, students are given two highlighters, each a different color. With the darker color, they highlight the single sentence in the essay they think best captures the author's thesis statement. With the lighter one, they highlight key areas that support this thesis.

Collaboration

I ask students to share their revised vocabulary predictions with others in small groups so that they can see how close their predictions are to one

Figure 10.5

Map for "Africans Need More Than Our Sympathy"

Paragraph	What the Author Did
1	Starts with a personal anecdote about his son, Cletus, playing soccer. This anecdote is set in the present day.
2	Flashes back in time—to the days where he and his family lived in Africa. Introduces wife and occupations. Explains love of Africa.
3	Introduces AIDS problem through series of general images.
4	Gives a specific story. The person who died has a name.
5	Explains the root of the problem—underfunding.
6	Tells another personal story—selling coffins on a corner.
7	Discusses actions he has taken. Describes meeting and adopting Cletus.
8	Returns to present tense. Teaches his sons to help through volunteering.
9	Introduces epidemic statistics.
10	Discusses funding problems. Makes plea that the United States should pay more to help solve the problem.
11	Returns to discussing how his own family can help end this scourge.

another's. Findings and thoughts are then shared in a whole-class discussion. This gives me the opportunity to discuss the importance context plays in figuring out the meaning of unfamiliar words.

Students remain in their groups and are given time to share their highlighted thesis statements and supporting text. Each group is asked to reach consensus on the author's purpose, and one person from each group is picked at random to share his or her group's findings with the rest of the class.

I tell students that a good persuasive essay usually includes a call to action. In other words, authors of this kind of writing not only want you to agree with them; they also want you to *do* something. This call to action can be either stated directly or implied. I then ask students to return to the article and circle any evidence of the author's call to action. Responses are then shared.

Next, I ask students to consider the structure of the essay. They are to number every paragraph, and on a separate sheet of paper make a "map" of what the author did in each paragraph. (Figure 10.5 is an example of what a map for this piece might look like.) Students are encouraged to create their maps in small groups; they gain insight from the give-and-take.

Looking at these maps can prompt students to see some of the techniques used by the author in this essay, specifically:

- He starts the essay by writing "small"—with a simple, personal story about his son, Cletus.
- He employs a shift in time. The author starts in the present, flashes back to his experiences in Africa, and returns to the present again.
- He gives specific examples, which add power to the essay (e.g., a man selling coffins on a street corner).
- He augments his ideas with powerful statistics, both to outline the severity of the problem and to appeal to readers to get involved.
- He gives the essay a circular feeling by ending it where it started—with Cletus.

Later in the school year, I will have students write their own persuasive essays. Having them create essay maps to see how other authors structure their essays and asking them to notice the techniques authors use provide students with models for writing essays of their own.

Metaphorical Response to the Text

I ask students to think about the African AIDS epidemic in symbolic terms. This I do in the context of the reflective part of the lesson.

Reflective Response to the Text

Sixty million Africans have been touched by AIDS, according to Dr. Peter Piot, Executive Director of the Joint United Nations Programme on HIV/AIDS (UNAIDS). These people are either living with the HIV infection, have died of AIDS, or have lost their parents to AIDS.

To our students, "sixty million" is just a number. To help them get a sense of the enormity of the problem, I ask them to think about this number in terms they can understand. For example, the school where I teach has approximately 1,600 students. One would have to fill our school 375,000 times to reach sixty million people. In other words, one would have to replace the current student population with a completely new population every day for nearly 103 years (including weekends and holidays) to reach the number of Africans who have been directly affected by the AIDS crisis. A new student population every single day until the year 2107!

Once students see the number in these more personal terms, I ask them to illustrate that number in terms of their own. For example, Boston's Fenway Park would have to be filled every day for nearly four years; Madison Square Garden in New York would have to be filled every day for nearly seven years. Students pick their own venue, do the math, illustrate it in symbolic form (metaphorically), and share in groups.

After students have grasped the enormity of the problem, I might ask the following questions: What is left unsaid? Why is Africa so severely affected? What factors do you think most contribute to the depth of this epidemic in that region of the world? What can be inferred from the article? Students meet in small groups to theorize the factors that drive the epidemic. According to UNAIDS, these contributing factors are as follows:

- high poverty rate
- low levels of literacy
- high levels of migration both within and between countries
- internal wars in some countries
- low status of women
- poor health care systems

Question 4: How Will I Know If My Students "Got It"?

When hundreds of thousands of people are suffering and dying I hope it is not too difficult for my students to understand why they should care, but just in case they need another reason I finish the framing of this article by explaining that Africa, though most severely affected, is not alone in facing this problem. To illustrate this, I share some of the recent statistics about AIDS in the United States (see Figure 10.6). I then have the students write short reflections on the information and share their thoughts.

Students are now ready for their essay. I reintroduce them to the questions we started the unit with:

> In your estimation, is "Africans Need More Than Our Sympathy" an effective essay? In answering, consider the following: Why did the author write this article (purpose)? What techniques did he use to drive home his point?

To answer these questions thoroughly, students must demonstrate a knowledge of the AIDS epidemic as well as an understanding of the writing techniques employed by the author. I will know whether they "got it" when I read their essays.

Figure 10.6

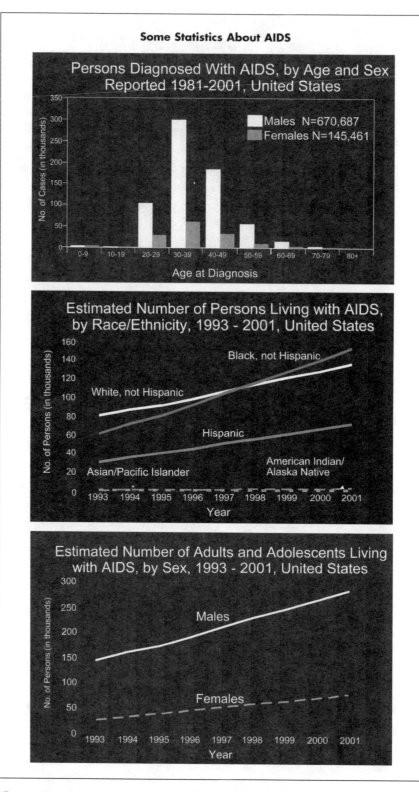

The Importance of Backwards Planning

Picture this: Your students have just finished reading a novel. Tomorrow they will be assessed in class. You sit up the night before, creating a test you think will fairly measure their level of understanding. You consider both what your students might have learned and what they may have overlooked while reading the book. You put the finishing touches on the exam before going to bed, knowing you have created a challenging assessment for your students to tackle.

I must confess I have done this many times in my career; but, despite my best intentions, I have come to believe that this was poor teaching on my part. Writing tests after the reading is completed creates a guessing game: students take the novel home to study, trying to guess what the teacher is going to ask on the exam; the teacher takes the novel home, guessing which areas of knowledge the students might be most (or least) prepared to answer.

This method of designing assessments is not conducive to fostering deeper reading. The problem with this approach is that the teaching drives the assessment, and when this occurs, "fuzzy" teaching and learning are the result. Instead, the assessment should drive the teaching. When teacher and students know the assessment beforehand, more focused teaching and learning result. We should start every unit with a "backwards design" approach in mind (Wiggins and McTighe 1998).

Note, for example, that the "Africans Need More Than Our Sympathy" unit began with students reading the final questions before they read the article. This helped students focus while they read (they would pay attention to the author's techniques and whether they resulted in an effective essay); it also established a "finish line" for the teacher to teach toward (the teacher would focus on what has to be taught in order to prepare students for the final assessment).

I also use this backwards-planning approach in the secondary reading course I teach at a local university. These students are working toward obtaining their teaching credentials, and I hand out the final exam question on the first night of class:

Final Exam Question

You are being interviewed for a teaching position. The principal asks you the following: "We are very focused on raising our reading abilities across the curriculum. What specific steps will you take in the teaching of (fill in your content area) to make sure your students are successful readers?"

As the semester progresses, we pull the question out periodically and reread it. Knowing what the final exam question will be, students are very focused in their note taking as they read the textbooks, listen to lectures, and work in collaborative groups.

Now let's consider once again the hardest book your students must read in your curriculum. Isn't it true that upon completing this work, you could design a test that blows your class out of the water? I have confessed to reading *Hamlet* over fifty times, and I know I still do not understand the work completely. Considering this, are my students going to understand *Hamlet* deeply on every possible level four weeks from now? An assessment that truly measures whether a reader understands *Hamlet* at the deepest levels possible would probably take many days to administer. The play is so rich, so complex, so layered—to truly assess whether someone completely understood it would be next to impossible.

Instead of trying to assess whether our students understand every layer of a complex work, we would better serve them if we consider the one or two areas within the text we think to be the most important and target those areas for our students' consideration. Before reading a novel, for example, students might be provided with one or more of the following final exam essay questions, each of which provides a certain focus:

- Why did the author write this book? What is his or her big idea (theme)? How is this theme advanced?
- Which character undergoes the most change from the beginning of the story until the end? What causes this change? What does this change reveal about the character?
- Which minor character has the most influence on the outcome of the book? Trace this character's influence.
- How does the author's use of setting (or diction, or symbolism) help tell the story?
- Which character in the story do you consider to be the most heroic? The most cowardly?
- How does the author use humor in the story? What purpose does this humor have in such a serious work?
- Choose a character caught between conflicting desires, ambitions, obligations, or influences. What does this conflict reveal about the character?

Any of these questions could serve as a final assessment of a literary work, and knowing them beforehand would accomplish two things: it would drive the teacher to better instruction, and it would generate deeper reading from the students. If, for example, I begin a novel knowing that my final exam will be an essay question requiring my students to identify and analyze the author's use of symbolism, then my lessons will be designed to help students identify and analyze symbolism as they work their way through the book. Students would also be reading the book with a purpose: to focus on the symbolism. Thus, the final exam question helps focus both my instruction and my students' reading. Now that I know this, I never again will be up the night before the final exam writing the test. It will have been written weeks ago.

What You Test Is What You Get

When considering a reading assessment, it helps to remember an acronym coined by Jim Cox, formerly the director of assessment in my school district: WYTIWYG (pronounced "witty-wig"), which stands for "What you test is what you get." The acronym reminds me to consider the importance that my assessment plays in drawing deeper thinking from my students. In other words, if I measure my students' thinking through shallow assessments, I will receive shallow thinking from them; if I measure their thinking through assessments that require deeper thinking, I will receive deeper thinking from them.

Judi Conroy, who teaches in the Education Department at the University of California at Irvine, underscores the importance WYTIWYG plays in drawing deeper thinking from students by having her teaching candidates consider the value of various reading assessments. For example, in Figure 10.7 you will see two different types of assessment for *The Great Gatsby*. The assessment on the left is a five-question sample from a traditional multiple-choice test; the example on the right consists of five sample essay questions. Consider these two forms of assessment (multiple-choice and essay) with Conroy's central question in mind: What kind of thinking is valued in each of these assessments?

What kind of thinking is valued by the multiple-choice questions?	What kind of thinking is valued by the essay questions?
Recalling facts	Recalling facts
Identifying names	Identifying names
Surface-level comprehension	Applying (e.g., constructing new meaning)
Test-taking strategies (e.g., eliminating answers, educated guessing)	Analyzing (e.g., inferring)
	Synthesizing (weaving ideas together)
	Evaluating (e.g., judging, supporting, comparing and contrasting, defending, critiquing, interpreting)
	Organizing thoughts into written form

Figure 10.7

Assessments for *The Great Gatsby*

Multiple-Choice Questions for The Great Gatsby

Essay Questions for The Great Gatsby

Jay Gatsby's real name is _____.
a. James Gatz
b. Jay Gass
c. James Gas

Dan Cody was important to Gatsby because _____.
a. When he died he left Gatsby the money necessary to succeed in his transformation.
b. He took Gatsby under his wing and helped him solidify his change from James Gatz to Jay Gatsby.
c. He paid for Gatz's college education.

Gatsby is killed by _____.
a. Tom Buchannan
b. George Wilson
c. Meyer Wolfshiem

Jordan Baker works as a _____ for a living.
a. model
b. magazine writer
c. professional golfer

Gatsby made his money by _____.
a. bootlegging and organized crime
b. a brilliant and savvy law career
c. a massive inheritance

Compare and contrast the characters of Tom and Gatsby. How are they similar? How are they different? How does Fitzgerald create these similarities and differences?

What value does reading *The Great Gatsby* hold for the modern teenager?

Analyze Fitzgerald's use of symbolism in *The Great Gatsby*. How does his use of symbolism advance the central themes?

Choose a minor character in *The Great Gatsby* and explain why this character is important to the development of the novel.

What is the central theme of *The Great Gatsby*? Discuss how this theme is developed through Fitzgerald's use of setting and characters.

Source: cliffsnotes.com

The multiple-choice questions value shallow thinking, and so they inspire surface-level thinking. The essay questions value deeper thinking, and when they are used in assessment, they move students to a deeper level of comprehension. Jim Cox is right when he says that what you test is what you get. In my classroom, the assessment drives the level of thinking in my classroom; knowing the assessment ahead of time elicits better teaching from me and deeper learning from my students. In short, if I really want to know whether my students "got it," I must start with an assessment that will get them there.

Danger Lurks!

Using the four key questions given earlier in this chapter to plan lessons has proven enormously beneficial to me as I plan. Having said that, however, I must mention two possible dangers associated with them.

Danger 1: Overteaching the Book

A teacher could theoretically spend an entire year teaching a single literary work. When teaching *Hamlet,* for example, I could spend weeks preparing the students by focusing on the background of Shakespeare, the origin and historical context of the play, the literary allusions we will encounter in the play, the techniques Shakespeare uses to play with the language (iambic pentameter, couplets, sonnets, puns), and the unfamiliar vocabulary that lies ahead. All of this before the students even begin reading! I could continue the unit by giving the same level of attention to the students' first-draft reading, multiple second-draft readings, collaborative assignments, projects that require metaphorical thinking, reflective essays, and other assessments. Thus, I could easily take an entire year to teach one complex work. If I were to do so, two results are guaranteed:

1. My students would know the work inside out.
2. My students would hate the work and would probably hatch a plot to tar and feather me.

When it comes to helping students make sense of challenging works, there is a fine line between teaching and overteaching. When we overteach, we risk two things:

- The literature may get lost. When we break down everything in the novel for the students to consider, their reading experience gets too choppy, too fragmented. The flow of reading the book is interrupted so often that the great story drowns.
- The students may lose interest. Offering enough scaffolding so that students gain a deeper appreciation of the literature is one thing; overwhelming them with strategies and activities is another. Overdoing it is a recipe for turning students off to a great book. The strategies advocated in this book should be used judiciously.

Danger 2: The Student Becomes Overreliant on the Teacher

In the beginning of the year, I do a lot more scaffolding of the text in order to build up my students' courage to embrace difficult text. As the year progresses, and I try to increase my students' capacity to read through ambiguity, I may not offer as much teaching support. My goal, of course, is that by the end of the year my students will be much better equipped to read difficult text without much, if any, help from a teacher. They will have begun to internalize strategies good readers employ when reading challenging text. When my students begin to understand what good readers do, it is time for me to begin reducing my role in this process. If I don't do so, students may leave my class at the end of the year still relying on their teacher to make meaning from challenging works.

The Teacher as Artist

When designing deeper reading lessons, it might help to think of yourself as a painter. When creating a painting, the artist is faced with a blank easel and palette. In most cases, he or she probably has a finished product in mind (a seascape, for example, or a vase of roses), but before deciding what colors to place on the palette, the artist has to give careful consideration to a series of questions:

- What do I want my finished product to be?
- What colors would be most effective?
- How should I use these colors?
- Where should I start?
- How should I start?
- What techniques should I employ?

The artist thinks about all these things before beginning to paint.

Literature teachers are like painters. We know what we want our finished product to be (our students' deeper reading of the text) but we also begin with a blank palette. Before a teacher can decide what "colors" (strategies) to place on his or her teaching palette, a similar series of questions must be asked:

- What do I want my students' finished "product" to be?
- Which strategies should I use?

- How and where should I use these strategies?
- Where should I start?
- How should I start?
- How do I support my students' reading of the text without simply handing it to them?
- Where do I let them struggle with the reading?
- How much support is too much?

Like the painter, the literature teacher asks all of these questions *before* any reading occurs.

Teaching Versus Assigning

Let us return to the scenario posed earlier in this chapter: You are starting a challenging book with your students on Monday morning. You are staring at a blank easel—your lesson plan book. Where do you start?

When faced with the task of teaching a complex book, it helps me to refer to a "cheat sheet" I have devised to shape my thinking. This sheet combines the four key questions discussed earlier in this chapter with the various stages to consider as students work their way through challenging text (discussed in Chapter 1). I tape the sheet (shown in Figure 10.8) at eye level above the desk where I plan my lessons.

Deciding how to answer these questions varies from text to text. Even within a given text, the instructional approach I take varies year by year, class by class, and sometimes even student by student. Unfortunately,

Figure 10.8

How to Plan an Effective Reading Lesson

1. Without my assistance, what will my students take from this reading?
2. With my assistance, what do I want my students to take from this reading?
3. What can I do to bridge the gap between what my students would learn on their own and what I want them to learn? What support should I offer in the following stages?
   —Focusing the reader
   —First-draft reading
   —Second-draft reading
   —Collaboration
   —Metaphorical response
   —Reflective response
4. How will I know if my students "got it"?

---

there is no one-size-fits-all way to teach a literary work. There isn't a single set of plans that will work for both my students in Anaheim and your students in Alaska (or New Mexico, or Maine, or . . .). Having this planning template prompts me to consider what my students need and when they need it. This is where the art of teaching comes into play.

A Final Note

Comparing the role of a teacher with the role of an artist brings to mind the best definition of reading I have ever read:

> Reading comprehension is a process that involves the orchestrations of the reader's prior experience and knowledge about the world and about language. It involves such interrelated strategies as predicting, questioning, summarizing, determining meanings of vocabulary in context, monitoring one's own comprehension, and reflecting. The process also involves such affective factors as motivation, ownership, purpose, and self-esteem. It takes place in and is governed by a specific context, and it is dependent on social interaction. It is the integration of all these processes that accounts for comprehension. They are not isolable, measurable subfactors. They are wholistic processes for constructing meaning. (Bartoli and Botel 1988)

I have read this definition a hundred times, and every time I read it I am struck by the many complex factors that come into play when one reads difficult text. If my students are to have any chance of becoming deeper readers, I must do more than simply assign questions at the end of each chapter or pull worksheets from a file cabinet. There is a big difference between *assigning* students difficult reading and *teaching* them how to read deeply. This definition reminds me that I am a *teacher*, not merely an information dispenser; and as a teacher, I will enter my classroom tomorrow morning with the goal of helping my students learn what deeper readers do.

"Advertising and Kids." 2004. http://www.focusonyourchild.com/entertain/art1/a0000029.html.

"AIDS Has Become Africa's Biggest Challenge." 2003. *Newsweek,* July 10: 14. http://www.thebody.com/unaids/africaaids.html.

Associated Press. 2004. "Judge Says Gay Marriages in San Francisco Appear Illegal." February 18.

Auden, W. H. 1991. *Collected Poems by W. H. Auden.* New York: Vintage.

Barnes, Douglas, and Frankie Todd. 1995. *Communication and Learning Revisited: Making Meaning Through Talk.* Portsmouth, NH: Heinemann.

Bartoli, Jill, and Morton Botel. 1988. *Reading/Learning Disability: An Ecological Approach.* New York: Teachers College Press.

Beers, Kylene. 2003. *When Kids Can't Read, What Teachers Can Do.* Portsmouth, NH: Heinemann.

Bennett, N., and E. Dunne. 1992. *Managing Classroom Groups.* Hemel Hempstead: Simon and Schuster.

Blau, Sheridan. 2003. *The Literature Workshop.* Portsmouth, NH: Heinemann.

Bransford, J. D., and N. S. McCarrell. 1974. "A Sketch of a Cognitive Approach to Comprehension: Some Thoughts About Understanding What It Means to Comprehend." In W. B. Weimer and D. S. Palermo, eds., *Cognition and the Symbolic Processes.* Hillsdale, NJ: Erlbaum.

Burke, Kenneth. 1968. "Psychology and Form." In *Counter-Statement,* 2nd ed. Berkeley: University of California Press.

California Department of Education. 1993. *Writing Assessment Handbook: High School.* Sacramento: California Department of Education.

Carlin, George. 1997. *Brain Droppings.* New York: Hyperion.

Carnevale, Linda. 2001. *Hot Words for the SAT I.* Hauppauge, NY: Barron's.

Case, John. 1998. *The First Horseman.* New York: Ballantine.

Chesley, Bruce. 2003. "Top 10 Deceptive Spam Headers." http://www.mail-archive.com/accmail@listserv.aol.com/msg01647.html.

CliffsNotes. "Lit Quiz." http://www.cliffsnotes.com/tests/greatgatsby/quiz.asp.

Dale, Edgar. 1956. *Audio-Visual Methods in Teaching.* New York: Dryden Press.

Daniels, Harvey. 2002. *Literature Circles: Voice and Choice in Book Clubs and Reading Groups,* 2nd ed. Portland, ME: Stenhouse.

Dugan, Joe, and Rene Sanchez. 2004. "San Francisco Opens Gay Marriage to Gay Couples." *Washington Post.* Feb. 13.

Educational Research Service. 2001. *Helping Middle and High School Readers.* Arlington, VA: Educational Research Service.

Feathers, Karen. 1993. *Infotext: Reading and Learning.* Scarborough, Ontario: Pippin.

Federal Trade Commission. 2002. "Federal, State, and Local Law Enforcers Tackle Deceptive Spam and Internet Scams." Nov. 13. http://ftc.gov/opa/2002/11/aetforce/htm.

Freire, Paulo. 1987. *Literacy: Reading the Word and the World.* New York: Bergin & Garvey.

Gallagher, Kelly. 2003. *Reading Reasons: Motivational Mini-Lessons for Middle and High School.* Portland, ME: Stenhouse.

Geisel, T. S. 1958. *Yertle the Turtle.* New York: Random House.

———. 1975. *Because a Little Bug Went Ka-choo!* New York: Random House.

Gibson, William. 1954. *The Reckless Spenders.* Bloomington: Indiana University Press.

Gilcrest, Laura. 2003. *Food Chemical News* 45, no. 1 (Feb. 17).

Golding, William. 1954. *Lord of the Flies.* New York: Perigee Books.

Guymon, Ned. 1950. "Conversation Piece." *Ellery Queen's Mystery Magazine.*

"Harper's Index." 2003. *Harper's.* May. http:://www.harpers.org/harpers-index/listing.php3.

Haycock, Kati. 2002. "Closing the Achievement Gap." *Educational Leadership* 58, no. 6: 28–31.

Human Rights Watch. 2000. "Incarceration and Race." http://hrw.org/reports/2000/usa/Rcedrg00-01htm#P16728183.

Ives, Matt. 2004. "A Report on Childhood Obesity." *New York Times.* Feb. 25. www.childrennow.org.

Jago, Carol. 2000. *With Rigor for All.* Portland, ME: Calendar Islands.

———. 2004. *Classics in the Classroom: Designing Accessible Literature Lessons.* Portsmouth, NH: Heinemann.

Johnson, Jerry. 2002. "Misleading Aggregates: Simpson's Paradox." July. http://unr.edu/homepage/jerryj/NNN/Aggregates.pdf.

Kingsolver, Barbara. 1988. *The Bean Trees.* New York: HarperCollins.

Kingston, Maxine Hong. 2000. *The Woman Warrior.* New York: Vintage.

Lakoff, George, and Mark Johnson. 1980. *Metaphors We Live By.* Chicago: University of Chicago Press.

Lamott, Anne. 1994. *Bird by Bird: Some Instructions on Writing and Life.* New York: Anchor.

Lee, Harper. 1960. *To Kill a Mockingbird.* New York: HarperCollins.

Leff, Lisa. 2004. "Gay Marriage Ban Flouted in California." Associated Press. Feb. 13.

Levine, Mel. 1991. *Keeping a Head in School: A Student's Book About Learning Abilities and Learning Disorders.* Arlington, VA: Educational Research Service.

Levy, David H. 2001. "The Search for Other Worlds." *Parade Magazine.* Sept. 30: 4–6.

"Making Cents of PennyTalk." 2003. *Consumer Reports.* February: 63.

Masters, Edgar Lee. 1992. *Spoon River Anthology.* Mineola, NY: Dover.

Matarese, John. 2003. "Deceptive Labels." June 6. http://www.wcpo.com/wcpo/localshows/dontwasteyourmoney/e655b3.html.

"Math Talk: The Untruth About Statistics." 2003. http://www.hoa.aavso.org/mathtal.htm.

Maxwell, William. 1983. "Love." *The New Yorker.*

Michaelis, David. 1998. *N. C. Wyeth: A Biography.* New York: Knopf.

Muhlberger, Richard. 1993. *What Makes a Bruegel a Bruegel?* New York: Viking.

National Writing Project, and Carl Nagin. 2003. *Because Writing Matters: Improving Student Writing in Our Schools.* San Francisco: Jossey-Bass.

Ogle, D. 1986. "K-W-L: A Teaching Model That Develops Active Reading of Expository Text." *Reading Teacher* 39: 563–70.

Olson, Carol Booth. 2003. *The Reading/Writing Connection: Strategies for Teaching and Learning in the Secondary Classroom.* Boston: Allyn and Bacon.

Palincsar, A. S., and A. Brown. 1984. "Reciprocal Teaching of Comprehension: Fostering and Comprehension Monitoring Activities." *Cognition and Instruction* 1, no. 2: 117–75.

Parish, Peggy. 1979. *Amelia Bedelia Helps Out.* New York: Avon.

Pinker, Steven. 2000. *The Language Instinct: How the Mind Creates Language.* New York: Perennial.

Plath, Sylvia. 1981. *Collected Poems.* New York: Perennial.

Preston, Richard. 1995. *The Hot Zone: A Terrifying True Story.* New York: Anchor.

———. 2002. *The Demon in the Freezer.* New York: Random House.

Prine, John. 1993. "It's a Big Old Goofy World." In *Great Days: The John Prine Anthology.* Rhino Records.

Ravitch, Diane. 2003. *The Language Police: How Pressure Groups Restrict What Students Learn.* New York: Random House.

Readence, John E., Thomas W. Bean, and R. Scott Baldwin. 1985. *Content-Area Reading: An Integrated Approach.* 2nd ed. Dubuque, IA: Kendall/Hunt.

"Scaffolding Learning." 2003. Myread.org/scaffolding.htm.

Schlosser, Eric. 2001. *Fast Food Nation: The Dark Side of the American Meal.* New York: HarperCollins.

Short, Kathy, Jerome Harste, and Carolyn Burke. 1996. *Creating Classrooms for Authors and Inquiries.* 2nd ed. Portsmouth, NH: Heinemann.

Smith, K. A., D. W. Johnson, and R. T. Johnson. 1981. "Can Conflict Be Constructive? Controversy Versus Concurrence Seeking in Learning Groups." *Journal of Educational Psychology* 73: 651–53.

Soto, Gary. 1995. *Gary Soto: New and Selected Poems.* San Francisco: Chronicle.

Sousa, David. 2001. *How the Brain Learns.* Thousand Oaks, CA: Corwin Press.

Stallworthy, Jon. 1974. *Wilfred Owen.* New York: Oxford University Press.

Styron, William. 1982. *Sophie's Choice.* New York: Bantam.

Sweep, Duane. 2002. "Newspapers and the Younger Audience." http://www.journalism.berkeley.edu/conf/conference2003/present/sweep.ppt.

Tann, S. 1981. "Grouping and Group Work." In B. Simon and J. Willcocks, eds., *Research and Practice in the Primary Classroom.* London: Routledge and Kegan Paul.

Their, Marlene. 2003. "How Media Literacy Fosters Critical Thinking: Developing a Healthy Skepticism." *ASCD Classroom Leadership* 6, no. 4 (December 2002–January 2003): 1.

Tierney, R. J., and P. D. Pearson. 1983. "Toward a Composing Model of Reading." *Language Arts* 60: 568–80.

U.S. Army. 1979. *Psychological Operations Field Manual No. 33–1.* Appendix I: PSYOP Techniques. Washington, D.C.: Department of the Army.

U.S. Census, Bureau of Justice Statistics. 1996. "Correctional Populations in the United States." U.S. Department of Justice.

Weaver, Constance. 2002. *Reading Process and Practice.* Portsmouth, NH: Heinemann.

Wiggins, Grant, and Jay McTighe. 1998. *Understanding by Design.* Alexandria, VA: Association for Supervision and Curriculum Development.

Wilhelm, Jeffrey, Tanya Baker, and Julie Dube. 2001. *Strategic Reading: Guiding Students to Lifelong Literacy, 6–12.* Portsmouth, NH: Heinemann.

Williams, William Carlos. 1962. *Collected Poems: 1939–1962, Volume 2.* New York: New Directions.

Wilson, Kenneth G. 1993. *The Columbia Guide to Standard American English.* New York: Columbia University Press.

World Book Dictionary. 1984. Chicago: Doubleday.

Zeitz, Paul S. 2003. "Africans Need More Than Our Sympathy." *Newsweek,* December 1: 14.